The 5L's

Live, Love, Laugh, Let go, and Let God!

PART 2

Right Don't Wrong Nobody!

Donquies A Sledge

Published by Book Writing Pioneer

Cover design by Book Writing Pioneer

ISBN: Printed in the United States

Table of Contents

Introduction

I like to start out by saying hello. How are you doing? How is your day going? I hope you are having, or have had, a wonderful day. You are a great person. You are an awesome person. You should **LOVE** every day that way. Always love and be loved. Be happy, always smile, and **LAUGH** with your family and friends. **LET GO** of all the negativity that's in your life. **LIVE** your life to the fullest. **LET GOD** lead you to your success in life. You are in control of your own destiny. You have the power of free will. You have the power of choice. There will always be a good choice and a bad choice. The power is yours to choose. Always remember. You are great. I shouldn't have to tell you that. You should already know that. You have to always believe in yourself when life pushes against you. You always push back harder. Keep hope in your heart and faith in your soul. Sometimes, people lose their way. That's what this book is all about. It boosts the greatness, hope, and faith that you already have inside you. No one is perfect. We all make mistakes. We can't let our mistakes define who we are. We just have to keep breathing and keep moving forward. You are the only one who can stop you from achieving your goals and chasing your dreams in life. Live your life positively, and never forget how great you are; your existence matters.

Page Blank Intentionally

Chapter 1

Live

Right, don't wrong, nobody! You breathin', ain't you?!

Those are the words my grandfather used to say to me. Those words are significant. I'm not ready to talk about those words for the moment. But those words echo in my mind, leaving an indelible mark on my soul. Remember those words. I will come back to those words later.

Are you living, or are you surviving? This is the question that I asked in the first book. Living is doing what you want to do. Living is enjoying your life, being free of misery, and recognizing who you are as a person. Surviving is doing what you must do—doing things you don't want to do. Let me explain! I don't like working at Burger King. That is my preference. If I work at Burger King, I will be setting myself up to do something I don't want to do, but I will have to do it so I can pay bills or buy food or anything along those lines, to survive. I would be unhappy with my life. I would find myself getting angry for no reason. I would find myself lashing out against other people because of how I lived my life. Treating others poorly just because you're dissatisfied with your life is unfair. Don't get me wrong. I'm not saying working at Burger King is a bad thing. I'm just saying it's not for me. If you love working at Burger King and you love what you do. That is what you call living and doing things you want. It doesn't matter what the job is. It could be lawn care if you love cutting grass and trimming hedges. That is great for you, but you will be unhappy if you love working at Burger King and have a lawn maintenance job. You start complaining about coworkers or even talking bad about your boss. All because you don't like that job. The good thing is you have the power of free will. You have the power to change your life for the better. It would help if you did not sit around at a job you don't like because you feel that you have to. I said it before, and I will repeat it: if you don't like your job or the way you live, you can always change it. You're the only person who can stop you from succeeding. You are in control of your own destiny. You are a great person, but I can't tell you that. You have to believe and see that within yourself. You have the power to make yourself better. If you don't like where you work, change it! If you don't like where you live, change it. If you don't like the way you look, change it. If you don't like the way you live, change it! You have the power to make yourself happy. You're the only one who can make you happy. You shouldn't sit around and blame the government, your parents, your siblings, your partner, your kids, or anyone or anything for your unhappiness. You can always transform your life into something that entices you and makes you satisfied with your choices. You are in control. You always have been in control of your life. Some people focus way too much on the negativity in their lives. They focus on negativity so much that it is impossible to be positive. That's when the urge to make excuses or blame others for their lack of success takes over.

There was this guy I once met. Every time I saw him, he was unhappy. Every time I talked to him, he always complained about other people in his life because he was unsuccessful. He told me his dad left when he was young. His mom was on drugs. He said his siblings never helped him with anything. He said that when he got older, he found a wife who didn't help him. He goes on and on, complaining about other people and making them the reason he was unsuccessful. He never once blamed himself. He had a victim mentality. He said he was tired of always struggling.

So I asked him, "What do you do for a living?"

He said he works odd jobs. I asked him what he wanted to do for a living. He said he wants to be an electrician.

Then I asked him, "Did you graduate?"

He said, "No!"

I asked him why not. He said his mom and dad were not there for him. I asked if he had tried to return to school since he's grown.

He said, "No!"

I asked why not. He said that because he has to work a lot to pay the bills. He said he didn't have time to go back to school. I asked what about online school? He said that he doesn't have the money for online school. I said, "Well, there are grants to help people like us go to school." He told me he didn't even have time to file for a grant. I asked him if his wife could help him file for that grant. He said she couldn't. She won't help him do anything. For everything I asked him, he always had an excuse for it.

I looked at him and said, "You're not tired of struggling. If you were tired of struggling, you would stop making excuses and do something about it." I told him that he has the power to change himself for the better. I said you're not tired yet. When you get tired, you are going to do something about it. Tired people don't give up; they keep pushing forward despite exhaustion and challenges.

When people make excuses, they hold themselves back. You are the only one to blame for holding yourself back. Your life is your life. Why blame others for your excuses? Some people may have it harder than others, but there is no excuse for why you're not successful in life. You have to want success. You have to crave it. You don't only need to work hard for it, but work smartly as well—

after all, no pain, no gain. Otherwise, success doesn't fall in your lap. You have to earn it. You have to make it happen.

Making excuses is not going to make it happen. Success is not easy, especially if you are starting from scratch. You have to keep pushing. You have to keep moving forward. To be successful, you're going to make some mistakes. You will fall, but each setback is an opportunity to learn and grow stronger. We are human. That's what we do. We make mistakes. It's not how hard or how many times you fall. Success is how many times you get up. Don't focus on the mistakes. Just sit back, relax, figure out what you did wrong, make amends, and go at it again and again and again until you get it right. You will succeed. The only times you fail at something are if you don't try or you quit when you fail. When I make a mistake or fail at something, my grandfather used to say, "You breathin', ain't you?!" I never knew what that meant until I got older. When I was younger, and every time my grandfather said "You breathin', ain't you?!" in my head, I thought my grandfather had issues. I think everyone has to breathe to live. That's the nature of life.

I remember this one particular day when I was about sixteen years old; we didn't have central air and heat. For us to stay warm in the winter, we had to chop wood for the stove. I was chopping wood on this day. Usually, I would stay focused on what I was doing, but I was upset on this day. I was upset because I went to bed late. After all, I had worked in the yard that whole day through the evening. Then that night I had to chop wood. I wanted to stay in my bed just a little bit longer, but my grandfather wanted me to get out of bed and chop wood so we could have wood for the upcoming night. I was tired. My grandfather was a man who, if he wanted something, would just get up out of bed and get it on his own. There was no lying around all day. I was lying in bed when my grandfather told me to get up. The rule was when my grandfather spoke, you listened. He only wanted to say it once. I did not want him to say it twice, or I would be in big trouble. I got up and out of bed. I went to chop wood, but I was careless. Instead of staying focused and standing the wood up to chop it, I did something I usually don't do. I let it lie on the ground lengthwise to chop it. I thought just randomly swinging the axe would be faster, so I could get back in bed. That wasn't the case. The first two pieces of wood worked out for me, but the third piece of wood wouldn't split. So I put my foot on it to hold it, and everything went wrong. My grandfather sat right there watching me. He never once said, "Don't do that." I think he wanted to see if I was dumb enough to leave my foot right there, and sure enough, I did. I gave it everything I had when I chopped down on that piece of wood. I looked down and saw that the corner part of my shoe was split. Then I felt an excruciating pain, seeing and then realizing that I had chopped off half my toe. A big chunk of my toe was sitting inside the part of the shoe I cut off.

I hollered and ran around the house so fast. My brother and grandfather watched me run and holler after I stopped running. They checked on me. My momma bandaged my toe. After that, my grandfather and brother laughed at me. To this day, my brother still laughs at me. I even laugh at myself when I think about it. I remember my grandfather sat me down and said these words on that day, "You breathin', ain't you?!"

I said, "Yes, sir."

At that time, I knew somewhat what it meant, but I didn't fully understand it. My grandfather said, "Now go finish chopping wood."

I said, "Yes, sir." I hobbled back out there and finished chopping the wood.

Years passed, and my grandfather had passed away by this time. I had a car, a 1981 Oldsmobile 98. I was working on the carburetor. One day, I broke a bolt when I was taking the carburetor out to clean it. Okay, let me put it like this: to the people who don't know about cars, breaking a bolt in the carburetor can cause major problems like air leaks. The air leaks are bad—troubling. I won't get into the logistics of why it's bad for air leaks. Just take my word for it. It's not a good thing.

Now, here I am, just sitting there with a broken-down car. At that time, I stayed way out in the country, where there was no auto part store or anything around, so I could go to get my car fixed. The next morning, I had to be at work, so I had to get that car fixed. At that point, I was frustrated. I was throwing around tools, just mad, didn't want to talk to anybody, and just wanted to be left alone. Then, all of a sudden, I heard my grandfather's voice echoing in my head, "You breathin', ain't you?!" At that moment, I finally understood what he meant. By then, my brother showed up. I asked him if he could take me to the auto parts store to get the tools I needed to remove that bolt I broke while I was trying to take the carburetor out. He took me to the store, and I got the necessary tools to remove the broken bolt. I replaced it and fixed my car, so I was able to go to work. At that moment, I realized what my grandfather was talking about. The same voice followed me, saying, "You breathin', ain't you?!" This means you are still alive. No matter how bad the problem is, no matter how often you mess up or fail at something, there is always time to fix it. So I ask you, "You breathin', ain't you?!" You may not succeed at what you are trying to accomplish today. It may not be tomorrow. It may not even be next week, but you will succeed as long as you keep moving forward and breathing.

No one is perfect. Everyone fails, does something wrong, or makes mistakes, but you control how you want to fix it. I had nothing growing up, but I knew I wanted to be successful. I started at the bottom. A lot of us start at the bottom. Don't let where you start your life predict where you want to go in life. Some people say that you should make lemonade when life gives you lemons. Yes, you can look at it that way. I look at it like this. I don't like lemons like that. So whenever life gives me lemons, I make lemonade, but I plant the seeds from that lemon to make lemon trees. Now, I have enough lemons to trade for watermelon, oranges, apples, or other fruits or vegetables to be successful and comfortable with my life. Metaphorically speaking, take what life throws at you, take that, and use it to your advantage.

Being successful can look different for everyone. Your success might be just working at a fast-food restaurant. There is nothing wrong with that. If you love it, do it! Just that simple. Don't worry about what other people say. Do what you love doing. Other people's success might be becoming a doctor. It could be a lawyer. Your success can be anything you love doing. Most people will tell you that the only way you can be successful is to become an entertainer, such as by getting into music or acting, or to become a lawyer, doctor, lecturer, or even join the military. People will make you feel bad because you haven't become highly paid. That's not success. Success is doing what you love, not earning more. Success is doing what makes you comfortable. Let me be real. Most people believe success comes from becoming an athlete, singer, rapper, actor, or chasing any other dream job. You might be wondering why I call those types of jobs "dream jobs." Here is why. There is a very small chance you will become an athlete, singer, rapper, or actor. Out of those, over 1 million student-athletes graduate from high school each year. Only 6-7% of them make it into college. That's about 70 to 80 thousand students out of those students. Thousands of them try to become professional athletes. It's not only college students who try out. There are those people who are walk-on athletes who try out for the pros. Only about 853 athletes make it a year out of over a million who graduate high school. That's about 0.00075% who are able to go pro. That's not very good; it's odd when I say athletes. I'm including professional wrestling. Sad to say, but it's easier to get into the MLB, NFL, or NBA than into professional wrestling. And in getting into the music business, acting, or any other entertainment industry, the odds aren't any better. Ninety percent of singers, rappers, and musicians fail. Only ten percent make it in the music industry. Only two percent of actors make it to the big screen. I'm not saying all this for you to give up on your dreams. I'm just saying it's difficult and not impossible! Never ever give up on your dreams. Work hard and keep pushing for that dream. I want to tell you to never give up on your dreams and work on your career. What's the career you want? When I say career, I'm referring to things like becoming a doctor, lawyer, judge, dentist, electrician, plumber, law enforcement, engineer, government official, teacher, CDL driver, working in fast food, retail, or any job you would love to do. Always have that secondary plan in case your dreams don't work out for you. I'm not going to tell you what you want to hear. I'm going to be that friend to tell you what you need to hear—the harsh reality. I'm saying yes, you can make it as a professional athlete, make it big in the music industry, or act on the big screen, but the chances are rare. You have to work hard. Never give up, and keep pushing forward. Your success might not be as a professional basketball player. Your success might be in real estate. Your success might not be as a professional soccer player. Your success just might be to become a dentist. You never know. Never give up on life or success because you didn't become that professional. Your success just might be in that career you are working towards. I can't say you will or will not become a professional athlete, actor, singer, or other entertainment person. I am saying that you will become a successful person only if you believe in yourself.

The biggest thing is that when you are becoming successful, you should never forget to enjoy life between the grind of chasing your goals and working day and night to achieve your dreams. Do things you really enjoy doing. It could be riding a bike, going for a jog, cherishing your solitude, or visiting your favorite coffee café to read a book or listen to music.

Walking around and looking at nature can, too, be therapeutic. You can also walk your dog or just hang out with friends. Being successful is nothing if you lose yourself in it. You should never constantly focus on work without resetting your mind. It's indispensable to refuel. Always remember to enjoy your life while becoming successful. Personally, I like to enjoy nature. I like sitting by the water and listening to the birds. That is peace of mind for me. You have to give yourself peace of mind to ensure you do not stress yourself out.

I had this job that I worked a lot. It was a decent job. I got up at 4:00 a.m. Sometimes, I didn't get off until 12:00 a.m. I used to spend the night at the job to get right back up at 4:00 a.m. It was taking a toll on me and my physical and mental well-being. The pay was good, but I was losing myself. I found myself getting angry with people for no reason. I wasn't getting enough rest. After a while, I found myself cranky. My mood was never good. One day, I fell asleep on the tracker I was driving and almost ran into a pole. I found myself not enjoying life like I wanted to. All I did was work and work and work, trying to be successful. I was actually losing my mind working all the time. I was neglecting my family. All I was thinking about was work. I didn't think about having a balance in my life for working and becoming successful, as well as enjoying life. I had to find that balance. I had no time to do what I wanted, so I had to change my job. Don't get me wrong. Some people love that job, and it is good for them. That wasn't my thing.

The job you want isn't that hard to find. You must get out there, apply yourself, and go after what you want. You just have to believe in yourself to get it. The real key to getting the job you want or owning your own business or whatever it is you want to do is to be persistent, confident, self-aware, and courteous. That's it! When I say be confident, I mean knowing what you want. You must stay strong and believe that you will get what you want. When I say persistent, that means you never give up. You keep moving forward. You keep trying and trying until you get what you want. When I say self-awareness, I mean your safety, health, and mindset are very important in the job you want to accomplish. When I say be courteous, that just means be courteous to customers. Be gracious to your boss. Be considerate of coworkers. If your coworker is doing a good job, compliment them and show them support. If your coworker is working hard and trying their best but they are still lacking in their work, offer some help or encourage them to keep trying and don't give up.

No matter if it's your own business or working on a job, know what you want to do and just do it. Get yourself out there and put yourself in place to receive those opportunities to become successful. To get what you want out of life and achieve the goal you're aiming for. I got almost every job I went after because I believed in myself. When I first started in the workforce, I had no idea what to do, but I got the hang of it. If I can do it, you can do it. I am no better than you. None of us is perfect, but we can be great. And I will not leave you hanging without telling you how I did that.

I leveraged on the following gifts that nature has bestowed on ALL OF US: Persistence, Confidence, Self-awareness, Courtesy. Allow me to share some snippets about each.

PERSISTENCE: My very first job was at Winn-Dixie. At first, I was just trying to get a job anywhere. I needed a job. I was eighteen. I looked for a job for a month, and when I didn't find any, I just gave up on looking for a job. I had no high school diploma. One day, I was sitting at home. I was quite upset. My grandfather asked me what was wrong. I told him I couldn't find a job.

He said, "Don't act like that." Then he added, "With that attitude, you will never find a job. You have to keep at it. Be persistent!"

When that didn't move me, he said, "Don, listen." (My grandfather called me Don.) Whenever my grandfather said, "Don, sit down here and listen," he was about to tell me one of his stories, which always had a great meaning behind it.

I guess that's where I get my storytelling. My grandfather told me a story about working at the paper mill. He said he went to work every day. He worked hard, and there was this guy named Mr. Smiley with whom he worked. They did the same job, but Mr. Smiley was getting paid more money. He kept at his supervisor about getting the same pay as Mr. Smiley. He said he asked his supervisor if he was doing the same job as Mr. Smiley. Why can't he get the same pay? He never gave up. He was persistent. Every day, he kept at them. He started doing a better job than Mr. Smiley. He was always on time and never late for work. One day, the boss asked him to do a favor outside of his job description. He said he would. Mr. Smiley said he wouldn't do it. As time went on, my grandfather kept asking for a raise. After a while, my grandfather said he went and told them that he was just going to do what he was paid to do and that there would be no extra. He said they would just have to get Mr. Smiley to do it because he is not getting paid extra. My grandfather said the next day, he was out fishing. He saw somebody coming down the road in a car. He said it was his boss. His boss had been looking for him all day. He said his boss jumped out of the car and said Mr. Underwood, you now get the same pay Mr. Smiley gets. He had finally got equal pay. He didn't want to leave the job, but would not be taken advantage of either. He was persistent about equal pay, and he got it. He told me to keep looking. If you want a job, you have to sell yourself. The next day, I went into Winn-Dixie and talked to the hiring manager. I let him know that I was a great worker. He didn't hire me at that time. I went back for two weeks straight. He said you're not going to give up, are you? I said no, sir. He said you're hired. Come back tomorrow and start work. Persistence got me my first job.

CONFIDENCE: About 20 years ago, I didn't have a high school diploma and was in a job I didn't care for. I was always unhappy. I had to find my confidence. I was a roofer. Working that kind of job is very difficult. Doing that job gave me a lot of respect for people who do roofing. Roofing is really hard work. The weather made it difficult in the summer on top of that roof. The sun gets extra hot, and the wind is extra cold in the winter. So yes! It was a job that I didn't want to do. When I had the job, it wasn't all bad. There were some good things about the job, but they weren't for me. The thing was, I had no benefits. My brother at the time had a county job. He had great benefits. He took extra time off on holidays, and I had to work. He had the weekends off. I had to work. When he got sick, he used sick leave from his job and took extra time to heal. I still have to work when I get sick, or I don't get paid if I miss days off. Then, my bills would get behind, and catching up would be hard for me. When it would rain, my brother went to work and got paid, while I was sitting at home, not getting paid.

My bills started to pile up after about two years of struggling. I had had enough. I started believing in myself. I wanted to go back to school and get my high school diploma. I found the confidence that I could do it. I had gotten a GED book. I downloaded study apps. I started taking practice tests. I was even on YouTube learning. I did what I had to do to go to the next level in my life. I wanted my high school diploma, so I went and got it. I got my high school diploma because I had confidence that I could do it.

SELF-AWARENESS: I had a job working in lawn care. The job was good. It was not a hard job. It was easier than roofing, but it was another job I had gotten without benefits. While I was still searching for the job I wanted, I had to work to keep the bills paid. When I was eating lunch one day, I didn't know what had happened, but I had a toothache. I couldn't afford to go to the dentist. As time went on, it got worse. My oldest brother came over to check on me. He asked me if I wanted to get more out of life.

I asked, "What do you mean?"

He said, "You are sitting here with a toothache. You have to go to work; if you don't, you don't get paid. How will you pay your bills if you don't have money? I love you, and don't want to see you struggling."

By this time, I was in excruciating pain. He looked at me and said, "You need to go to the dentist."

I replied, "I can't afford it."

He looked into my eyes and said, "How are you going to take care of your family if you don't take care of yourself?" Then he added, "You are a very important part of your family. Your bills can't get paid if you're in the hospital or a graveyard. You need to take care of yourself."

Again, he told me he loved me, and I told him I loved him, too. An hour later, the pain got worse. I went to the hospital. The doctor prescribed me some painkillers and antibiotics, but the damage was already done. My throat had swollen by the time I got the medicine. I had to go back to the hospital. The abscess in my tooth had gotten worse. I spent seven days in the hospital. I didn't get paid. I got way behind on my bills, and on top of that, I owed a hefty hospital bill. All because I didn't take care of myself. I needed self-awareness. You have to love yourself enough to take care of yourself.

COURTESY: I had finally gotten a decent job as a county worker, with great benefits and good pay. I was in the public eye and used my excellent customer service skills. I worked with five coworkers. Let's just call them Coworker 1, Coworker 2, Coworker 3, Coworker 4, and Coworker 5. My boss was decent at the beginning. The only thing that went wrong was that I had a coworker who didn't like me. That was Coworker 1. Everyone got along when I first got the job. I was a maintenance worker. I came into that job, and I fixed everything that needed fixing. I did my job well. I was helping everyone who needed help. I congratulated them on doing a good job every time they fixed something. I encouraged them when they thought they couldn't do something. The boss was bragging about me. All my coworkers told me I was doing a great job. All my coworkers loved how I worked, except one. I was about six months into the job. One day, Coworker 1 asked me how I felt about the situation that she was getting into with Coworker 4. I told her that I didn't want to get in the middle of that. She looked at me meanly and said, "Okay, I got you." Well, I didn't think anything of it. I just continued to be myself, working hard and getting my job done. The next day, I was supposed to clean the restrooms. So I did. My boss called me on my two-way. She said I didn't clean the restrooms all the way. She said there was trash behind the toilets. I said I will take care of it. I didn't think anything of it. I just thought that I missed some trash. So the next day, I took a late lunch to finish the electrical job I had started. I didn't want to leave electrical wires hanging down the wall. I finished the job, and then I ate my lunch. After lunch, I got another call from the boss. She told me to come up to the office. I got to the office, and she had written me up for taking a long lunch. I explained to her that I wanted to finish the job. I told her that before I took my lunch, I wanted to make sure it was safe for me to leave. I didn't leave on time for lunch for safety reasons. I told her that I had to take a late lunch. By then, Coworker 2 walked into the office and overheard the conversation. He intervened in the conversation and told her I was telling the truth. So, she didn't write me up.

The next day, I was supposed to clean the restrooms again. I cleaned them perfectly and ensured I didn't leave any trash behind the toilets. I got a call from my boss again, saying I didn't get the trash behind the toilets. I knew for a fact that I cleaned up all the trash. I went into the restroom, and right behind the toilet was a can. At this moment, I started to get suspicious. I never saw my boss come out of the office. I wondered how she knew if I had missed trash or not. I knew who was setting me up but didn't have proof yet. The next day, a water pipe burst. Coworker 1 was trying to fix it. She couldn't figure out how to get it done. I saw her upset, so I went over to give her a helping hand. I ended up fixing it for her. I got a call from the boss when I finished it. Coworker 1 went up there with me. We walked into the office together. As soon as we got into the office, Coworker 1 went straight to the boss before anything was said, and she told the boss that she had fixed the water pipe. I looked at her and said, "You fixed it!" sarcastically. I didn't say anything else about it. I let her take the credit. After all, we were supposed to have been a team. The boss told her, "Good job." Then, the boss turned to me and said that I was on the phone all day instead of working. When she heard my boss's words, Coworker 1 left the office. She didn't say anything about me helping her, and that the accusation of me being on the phone wasn't true. My phone had been in the break room all day. She hadn't seen me that whole day. I knew at that moment that I was being set up. Therefore, I got written up. A week later, I started working on another project. I was working on an electrical outlet. The day after that, someone plugged into the outlet, and the outlet started sparking. I knew I fixed that outlet. I was thinking maybe I didn't fix it right. I got a call from the boss again. I told her I was working on an outlet. I can't come to her at the moment. My boss said I would just come to you. So she came down. She said I heard that outlet almost shocked someone. I thought you fixed it yesterday. I said I did. I don't know what happened. By that time, my Coworker 2 and Coworker 5 walked up, and Coworker 5 said he saw Coworker 1 around the outlet when I finished it. The boss called Coworker 1 over. After I finished, my boss asked her if she had messed with the electrical outlet. She said she came over to look at it to see if I had done it right, but she really didn't have time to look at it. By that time, all the coworkers were there. All the other coworkers didn't believe her. My boss asked Coworker 2 if he could fix it because she didn't trust me to do it. He told her that I was the best person for the job. My boss told me to get it done.

Then she said, "After that, I need you to clean the restrooms."

I said, "Yes, ma'am."

I fixed the electrical outlet to perfection. I went to clean the bathroom, but this time after I was finished. I called Coworker 3 over to inspect the restrooms. She looked at the restrooms and said that they looked very clean. She even looked behind the toilets. She asked me why I called her over to inspect the restrooms. I told her I thought Coworker 1 was setting me up to look bad. I told Coworker

3 everything that Coworker 1 was doing to me. To prove what I was saying. I and Coworker 3 left out the restrooms but hid behind the building this time. All of a sudden, Coworker 1 showed up at the restrooms. We stayed hidden until she came out of the restroom and walked away. When she left, I told Coworker 3 that the boss was about to call. By the time I said that, my two-way beeped. My boss said I had just left the premises, but there was trash behind the toilets. I knew my boss hadn't come to see for herself and that only one person had entered those restrooms. Coworker 3 and I went into the restrooms, and sure enough, there was trash behind the toilets after they were cleaned. Now I had proof that Coworker 1 was sabotaging me. Coworker 3 was mad. Coworker 3 said she would let the boss know what was going on. That was a Friday. My boss would not return until Monday. The next day, we had a horse show at the Equestrian Center. My job was picking up trash and making sure the restrooms were clean. I cleaned the men's restroom, but there was a long line at the women's restroom. While I was waiting to get into the women's restroom to clean it, a lady came up to me and said that her electric outlet at the horse stall wasn't working. I knew it would be a while before I could get into the women's restroom to clean it, so I went to help the lady get her electrical outlet working. When I finished working at the outlet, my boss called and asked where I was. I told her I was helping a lady with her electrical outlet at the horse stall. My boss said okay and that I needed to clean

the women's restroom. My boss wasn't there, so I already knew who told her. Monday morning, my boss called me to the office. When I got there, my boss told me she wanted me to sign a write-up slip. I said for what? She said it was because I left the premises when I was on the clock. I told her that I didn't leave the premises. I said, I talked to you and told you what I was doing. She said I was seen leaving the premises. She said I could have been anywhere when I was talking to her. By then, Coworker 3 had walked in and overheard the conversation. I walked out. I was upset. About twenty minutes later, Coworker 3 came over to me and said that she had overheard what the boss was saying to me. Coworker 3 said she told the boss that I was being sabotaged. She told the boss that I was doing a great job. Coworker 2 came up to me. He said he went to the boss and told her that I wasn't doing anything wrong. He said he told the boss I was doing a great job. I thanked them. The next day, things started turning around. Coworker 1 started getting caught up in her lies. She got caught sabotaging me. Long story short, she quit the job because she felt like everyone turned on her. Being courteous to my coworkers and helping them when they needed it actually helped me in the end because they showed me courtesy back.

Some people don't deserve that boss/supervisor title. I got this job as a sanitation driver. Everyone loved me there. I helped everyone I could. The customers always complimented me. My supervisor was proud of my work. As time went on, I ended up with a new supervisor. That's where everything went wrong. From day one, when he came into that position, he had it out for me the very first day. He knew all the routes that my coworker and I ran, but he still wanted to do it his way. As our new supervisor, we listened to him out of respect. Needless to say, we didn't finish our route that week. So we had to work on the weekend to get the routes finished. The next week, the same thing. So, in the third week, they wanted me to devise a way to run the routes. Out of curiosity, I asked the supervisor if I could run the routes my way. He said yes. We ran the routes and finished in time. We ran the routes my way the second time, too. Again! We finished the routes in time. In that third week, the supervisor wanted to start running it his way again. Some of my coworkers wanted him to let the routes stay the way I mapped them out. The supervisor cursed my name, said I didn't know anything, forgot me, and said I was nothing. Note! I just gave you the clean version of what he said about me. Back to the story.

As time passed, we kept working the routes he wanted us to work out of respect. We had to work many weekends to catch up on our work, and if anyone brought my name up, he cursed again. Time goes on a little more. I remember this happened on a Tuesday. It was a special pickup he wanted me to do. I went as he asked. He wanted me to pick up this big industrial refrigerator. I got there and looked at the refrigerator. I called the supervisor to let him know I didn't think my coworker and I could pick it up and put it in the back of the garbage truck. I asked him if he could send the claw truck out to pick up this heavy refrigerator. He said no. He said if I didn't get it, I couldn't come in, and if I didn't come in with that refrigerator, he would tell the boss that I wasn't doing my job, and they would let me go. Well, I had no choice but to get the refrigerator or leave my job. My coworker and I tilted it so the refrigerator's top would lie on the back of the garbage truck. Then we tried picking it up from the bottom to shove it in the back of the garbage truck. That refrigerator was super heavy. As we were picking it up, my right leg slipped, and the refrigerator landed on my left leg. The way I landed, I tore my labrum in my hip. The next day, my leg swelled up. I told the boss what happened. The boss sent me to the doctor to get it checked. The doctor couldn't find anything at first. They gave me the rest of that week off work to heal. Then, the next week after that, I returned to work. But I was still in pain, and my leg swelled up again. I told the supervisor because I could barely walk. He told me to act like it didn't hurt so I could keep working. I told him no. So, I went to the boss and let him know I was still hurting. He sent me back to the doctor's office. They sent me home until they could find out what was wrong with my leg. A couple of weeks later, I got a letter in the mail saying I was no longer needed at my job. I went to the office to talk to the boss. I found out that the supervisor told them that I wasn't doing my job and that he didn't want me on his crew. I felt like I got fired because I didn't want to work; it hurt. I was hurt and jobless. I kept breathing and kept the faith. The doctor found out my labrum was torn in my hip, and he gave me injections. I got another job and was doing great. I gave respect, but I didn't get it back. Courtesy goes a long way.

My grandfather told me always to do the right thing. He also told me to treat people right, but the biggest thing he told me was, "Right, don't do wrong nobody." That stuck with me. What is right will always be right, and what is wrong will always be wrong. You shouldn't treat people wrong and then expect them to treat you right. If you think positive, you will do positive things. If you think negative, you will do negative things. I had a friend whom I grew up with. As long as it was just me and me hanging out, he treated me great, but when other people were around, he treated me horribly. He talked down on me and picked on me. I was always the poor kid who didn't have anything. His dad bought him everything. Even though he treated me horribly, I never treated him badly, even once. He was always getting into trouble. The older we got, the more I distanced myself from him. You don't have to do wrong to get someone to like you. Lots of people do horrible things to fit into the crowd. I have seen people talk down on other people to be popular. I have seen people rob other people to be popular. I have seen people smoke weed and do other drugs to be popular. I have seen people mentally and physically break down others just to be popular. That's not right. That is wrong. You shouldn't step on someone to lift yourself up. It takes strength to do the right thing. A weak person will always do the wrong thing because they need that attention from others. They need to hurt someone to make themselves feel good. You don't have to do that. Always do the right thing and stay positive.

Doing the right thing doesn't mean you always have to say yes to everyone and everything. It doesn't mean you can't stand up for yourself. You can say no and still be a good person. You should always stand up for yourself. You don't have to be a pushover. I had a big problem with saying no to anyone. If anyone asked me for anything, my answer was always yes. I never stood up for myself. If someone was bossing me around, I just did what they wanted because I always tried to avoid confrontation. I always knew right was right, no matter what. I always backed down from confrontation. You can stand up for yourself without being negative. Some people think you have to be negative to get results. Well, I'm here to tell you. That's not true at all. If you do this negatively, you get a negative response. You positively do things, and most of the time, you get a positive response. You may wonder why he said the same thing most of the time. I'm just going to tell you this: There are people out there who are always going to be negative, no matter how positive you are. You just have to avoid such people. Sometimes, I know it will be hard to avoid these people. These people may include a family member, a neighbor, or it could be a co-worker. Sometimes negativity can't be avoided, but you must find a way to stay positive. I'm not saying you should take what they are doing to you. You should always stand up for yourself, but do it positively. If someone comes at you negatively, accusing you of doing something you know you didn't do. There are ways to handle it positively. Let them know you're sorry for whatever happened to them, but you had nothing to do with it. Ask them if there's anything that you can do to help them. Do it calmly.

Some people will drop it and let it go. Some people will keep being negative towards you until they get a negative response. You have to stay firm, stand strong, and stay positive. Let them see that you're not a pushover and you will not stoop to a negative level. Always be the bigger person. I'm going to be very honest. Even though you do your best to avoid negativity, it still comes your way. Sometimes, people like to bully other people. Sometimes, people bully just to impress other people. Sometimes, they bully because they have a lot of negativity in their life, and that's all they know. Bullying is not cool. I don't tolerate bullying.

When I was in high school, people bullied me all the time. Let's face it. I was a pushover. I was a 230-pound pushover. I'm from the country. Chopping wood and working the field made me strong as an ox, but I never cared to be violent. That's what made me a target; I was also the poorest kid in school. I got picked on all the time. I had to wash my school clothes in a bucket the night before

I went to school. I couldn't get the clothes as clean as they would be if they were cleaned in a washing machine. They had stains. Some of my clothes even had holes in them. My shoes had holes. Every day, I got picked on. They used to say things like, "The only reason he came to school is so he can eat." It hurt my feelings, but I couldn't get mad because it was somewhat true. I even tried to ask a girl out. She told me no. She said I was cute, but I was too poor for her. That really hurt my feelings. Not everyone talked badly about me. A few people stuck up for me, but most of the kids bullied me.

One day, I was walking to class, and the bottom of my shoe fell out. So, I ended up walking on the ground. Before class, I went to the shop and got duct tape to mend my shoes. I couldn't escape the bullying. I never stood up for myself as time went on. There was this poor kid who was a grade junior to me. He was getting picked on. I walked up and saw that. I got upset. That was the only time I stood up and said no more. I got in those bullies' faces and asked them if they wanted to pick on someone. Pick on me. I told them they would have to answer me if I caught them picking on him again. Like I said, I don't like bullies. I can tolerate them picking on me, but I can't stand when they pick on someone else. I found out that day that some kids were actually scared of me. I paid it no mind. The next day, the kids went back to bullying me. It didn't bother me. The kid that I helped out thanked me. He never got picked on again.

Always be the bigger person and walk away. Say something or do something if you see someone get picked on or if something is not right, even if you must call the police. Greatness is within you. Everyone has a hero in them. How many times have you seen something that wasn't right, but you did nothing? And now you wish you could go back and change it. We can't go back and change anything, but we can prepare ourselves for the future.

Life is full of surprises. You never know what will happen from one day to the next. Most people take life for granted and don't even know it. I take advantage of life. You have to stop and smell the roses. Some people take that metaphorically. I take that literally. If I'm walking, I will pick a flower just to see what it smells like. I sit in the backyard with my eyes closed just to hear the birds chirping. I walk on the beach shoreline just so the waves can hit my feet. I go to the mountains just to see how beautiful nature is. I take advantage of what most people take for granted. Most of us even take our bodies for granted. I have seen people treat other people badly because they are blind or deaf, or in a wheelchair. That's not right. I tell those people who pick on or take advantage of someone who is blind to wear a blindfold for a week, wear plugs for a week, or get around in a wheelchair for a week. Let's see how you feel after a week in another person's shoes. You should never treat someone badly because they are different. Many awesome people have disabilities. Some people become successful despite a disability. They do not let their disability stop them from achieving their goals. People like Stevie Wonder, Andrea Bocelli, Ray Charles, Clarence Carter, Willie Walker, Trischa Zorn, and the group The Five Blind Boys of Alabama. They did not let their disability stop them from becoming successful. They became singers, songwriters, musicians, and athletes. There are deaf people like Marlee Matlin, Nyle DiMarco, Beethoven, Millicent Simmons, Dr. Philip Zazove, and Linda Bove, who became actresses, actors, models, musicians, doctors, and teachers. They did not let their disability hold them back. Helen Keller was blind and deaf and became very successful. Helen Keller became an author, a disability rights advocate, and a political activist. She did her bachelor's in arts. There are people with Down Syndrome, Parkinson's disease, Autism, and Epilepsy who are very successful. People like Sujeet Desai, Isabella Spingmuhl Tejada, Jamie Brewer, Muhammad Ali, Michael J. Fox, Lewis Carroll, and Harriet Tubman. These people were musicians, designers, actresses, athletes, actors, authors, and activists. They didn't let anything stop them from moving forward in life. You have people with dwarfism, including Peter Dinklage, Zelda Rubinstein, Verne Troyer, Tony Cox, Herve Villechaize, Linda Hunt, and Brad Williams, who have become successful. Just to name a few. They have become actresses, actors, and comedians. They became very successful. Some people are born or later get paralyzed and still become successful. Some people become paralyzed after success, but it doesn't stop their success. Franklin D. Roosevelt, Stephen Hawking, Esther Vergeer, Frida Kahlo, Barbara Jordan, Teddy Pendergrass, Tanni Gray-Thompson, Daryl Mitchell, Aaron Fotheringham, and Christopher Reeve are some of the examples. None of them let their disability stop them from chasing their goals. Even some amputees have become very successful. People like Zion Clark, Oscar Pistorius, Caleb Smith, and Kyle Maynard. These are just some of the people with disabilities who overcame adversity.

Many more people didn't let their disability stop them from succeeding. Those people changed lives. Those people had heart. Those people are amazing. Those are the people who inspire me to keep moving forward. Odds were against them, and they didn't quit. I think that is so awesome. The first coach I ever had was paralyzed and used a wheelchair. He was a tee-ball coach. We won the championship that year. His son was a little person and became one of my best friends. He was awesome. There was a guy who was a family friend, and he was an amputee. That never stopped him from working every day. He was a great guy. There was this woman who was blind and was also a family friend. She didn't let her disability stop her from doing anything. She was a wonderful woman. There is another guy who is a good friend of my brother and mine; he is deaf. He didn't let that stop him from achieving his goals in life. He is very successful. He is amazing.

Most people without a disability give up on their dreams before they even try. How do you know you are good at something if you have never tried anything, if you never take a risk? Fear is what holds most people back from achieving. Most people are afraid of failing. Failing is what makes you stronger and more knowledgeable. If you're trying to succeed at something but fail at it, try it again, but the next time you try it, you know what not to do. Everyone is not going to succeed the first time they try something. They may end up trying it over twenty times before they get it right.

Sometimes, things take longer than expected. You cannot compare your journey to others. Maybe because you don't have the finances right now, or it's hard to contact the right people to help you get what you are trying to do off the ground. I wrote my first book in 2012. It didn't get published until 2022. I didn't give up. I kept at it until I got it right. You must know what you want from life and get it. Some people try something one time and fail, and then just give up on it. Then, they move to the next thing. They try it one time and fail, and then just give up on it, too. Why keep trying different things? You should remind yourself that attempting something different is good, but only after you have given it its due time and effort. If it's something you're good at, keep trying. Eventually, you will get it right. You will be successful. Never give up on yourself. You're the only one who is the key to your success. You have to have a strong will and self-discipline.

A strong will is not spending unnecessary money on things you don't need. Strong will is not being tempted to do things that will prevent you from accomplishing your goals. Self-discipline is knowing if you need to focus, exercise, eat right, practice, rehearse, go to bed late, get up early, study, be on time, or whatever it is you need to do to accomplish your goals. If you want to be an athlete and be great, you need to focus, eat right, exercise to stay in shape, and practice. If you want to be in the entertainment industry, such as in music, acting, comedy, magic, or whatever you want to do to entertain others, you must focus on it. Be on time, be up late, have rehearsals, and if it's acting, you must study scripts. Whether you just want to go to college for the job you want or just want to work a normal job, you have to get up early. Be on time, study, and focus on what you must do to achieve what you desire. You can do whatever you want to do. Just get enrolled and work hard. Some people will tell you that you can't do it. Some people will tell you not to listen to them. Let that be the fuel to your light, the fire you need to light the way to your success. You have nothing to prove to anyone. If you do anything, do it for yourself.

Always have a good attitude. A good attitude goes a long way. Negative energy doesn't attract anyone. No one wants to be around someone who is grouchy all the time, especially if you're in customer service or even in the public eye while working. Grouchy people complain too much. Have you ever noticed that the people who complain are the ones who don't get their work done? If grouchy people work more than they complain, they just might get some work done. Always remember. Just do what you have to do, and don't engage in what the grouchy people say. The world is too beautiful to be grumpy, mad, hateful, or selfish all the time.

People who are selfish always end up alone and grouchy. Selfish people don't want to share anything. They want to keep everything to themselves. If it's material things, selfish people will keep and not use them, and won't let anyone else get them. Selfish people won't even share their love. Selfish people will not share anything with anyone. That's why they end up alone and grumpy. I can't say being selfless is a great thing all the time, either. It's a good thing most of the time, but there has to be a time when you have to say no. When people are taking advantage of your selflessness, just say no. Be careful of those types of people. People who always ask for things. People who can help themselves but do not try to help themselves. They will use you until you have nothing left. Then, they will just move to the next person. I call them leech people. They will suck you dry of everything. Be careful out there. You can be selfless. Just don't be used.

Self-love is the most important thing. Self-love is being strong. It is self-discipline. It's setting boundaries and knowing when to say no. It's knowing to stay optimistic even when you fail at something. Pick yourself up and try again. Self-love is not giving up on yourself. Self-love is knowing your worth. It's taking care of yourself. That means looking out for your health as well as your hygiene. Self-love is knowing how great you are without people telling you. Don't get me wrong. It's good to hear when other people compliment you, but if you don't believe it, the compliment is useless. Self-love means no matter what, you have to keep breathing and moving forward. There's nothing wrong with high-fiving yourself when you do a good job and accomplish something, even if it's a little thing. There is nothing wrong with patting yourself on the back every once in a while. You are great. You are awesome. Don't become the person that negative people claim you are. Be the positive person that I know you can be. Be the positive person that you know you can be. I know staying positive is hard sometimes, especially when you fail at something. Just keep faith and keep moving forward. You will succeed. Always remember when you fail at something, make a mistake, or do something wrong. Just remember, if you are still breathing, you still have time to fix it. So ask yourself, "You breathin', ain't you?!"

Chapter 2

Love

LOVE IS NOT SUPPOSED TO HURT! Let me say that again. ***LOVE IS NOT SUPPOSED TO HURT!*** It does not matter if you are giving it back or receiving it. It simply MUST NOT hurt. It can include anyone—grandparents, parents, siblings, uncles, aunts, cousins, or even your kids. Love must never hurt. Love is a universal language, one that everyone can speak without knowing the words. You don't have to "speak" the same language to give love or receive love. You could be blind or deaf and yet would know what love is when it comes your way. Everyone is born with love in them. It is an inherent feature. On the other hand, no one is born with hate. Hate is taught! It is learned. I will delve into that subject later in this book.

Anyone can say the enchanting words, "I love you." Merely words are not important or meaningful. After all, it's not what they say; it's what they do. The thing is, you have to notice how they treat you and whether they are doing what actually matters. You have to hear the things they say to you candidly and unknowingly to know if they love you or not. You have to be vigilant and alert. Why? Because sometimes, love will blind and deafen you, and you won't be able to see it or hear it right away. You might even ignore it, even if it is glaringly obvious. But other people around you who truly love you can and will see it and hear it. They will try to warn you, but sometimes, love or the beguiling façade of love has a way of making the truth seem like a lie. You might end up thinking people are against you or, worse, maybe are even jealous. And falling in love, you can start thinking that the person who is treating you wrong, feeding you all the lies while pretending to tell the truth, is the person who truly loves you, and maybe they are doing it to fix you or make you better. Well, you will be wrong! Dead set wrong! People who truly love you tell you what you NEED to hear, not what you WANT to hear.

Suppose someone comes up to you and tells you, with all the confidence in the world, that you are going to hit the lottery next week. Are you going to get excited and go on a spending spree with the money you don't have yet? I can answer that question for you. No, you will not. You would probably label them crazy and tell them to buzz off and shoo away. Now consider another situation! If someone comes up to you and tells you that "there is a small chance" for you to hit the lottery next week, with a little explanation of how a lottery works, you would pay them more heed, won't you? You will consider them a normal person who is trying to warn and educate you on how the lottery works. That's the thing. That is what true emotion is like. You have to notice the difference between what you *want* to hear and what you *need* to hear. There is a world of lying, treacherous people willing to tell you anything, especially the things you want to hear. They will sell you all these hopes and dreams and lies that will not come true. Emotional scams and frauds. That is where you have to be vigilant! You have to pay attention to the *wolves in sheep's clothing.*

Let me be honest. Some people are only out for themselves. And they are prowling for people to take advantage of. You really have to be careful of people. And don't ever think that they are always strangers! It could be a family member, a so-called friend, or worse, even someone whom you might pick as your amorous partner. That's why you have to be careful and cautious about who you call a friend or who you pick as your love partner.

Yes, I know it's hard to tell who is truthful and who isn't. No one is a telepath or a clairvoyant who can read minds or look through time into the future. But there is a way to know the truth about people. And it is simple. All you have to do is you have to take your time to get to know a person. Don't rush into things and relations. You have to watch what they do. Over time, a person will tell you who they really are if you take your time. Just sit back and watch their actions. People are dynamic and unpredictable.

Here is an example. Imagine catching up with a person you haven't seen in a long time. You might think you know them because you have known them for a long time. You might think they are still the same loving person. But no! You meet them and discover that they are someone new entirely. People change every day. The person you knew may no longer exist. You have to get to know that person all over again.

I ran into a person I had known over fifteen years ago. I thought I knew her. Apparently, I didn't. I wasn't even close. The first time she and I talked, we reminisced over the old days. We talked about what we did over the years. She told me that she had kids. I told her I had kids, too. She shared nuggets about her life and how her life went after we lost contact with each other. I talked about how life was going with me. It felt like a connection, something instant and real. She told me everything I wanted to hear in a woman. All the answers and discussion felt right. I fell for it. Everything seemed good. As time went on, we decided to start dating. Well! To be more accurate, *she* decided to start dating me; I didn't even know I was in a relationship. That should have been my first warning, but I was giving her the benefit of the doubt. Not very smart on my part. Time went on some more.

One day, I got the news that my sister had passed away. I was on the phone with my mom and my other sister. In between the conversation, I see another call incoming. It was her. I didn't answer right away because my mom was in the middle of a conversation. We were discussing the funeral arrangements and other necessary stuff. Plus, my mom was grieving, too. What could have been more urgent or necessary, right? Still, when my mom took a pause, I told her to hold on. I wanted to answer the other line so I could tell my *girlfriend* at the time that I was on the phone with my mom, but by the time I was about to answer, she hung up. I was on the phone with my mom and sister for merely ten minutes.

Instantly, I called her back. Without a "hi" or a "hello," she started arguing with me because *"I didn't answer the phone fast enough."* I tried calming her down, explaining that I was in the middle of a conversation with my mom, and we were discussing the funeral arrangements for my sister. But she wouldn't listen. She rebuffed my explanation, saying she didn't care. On top of that, she demanded that whenever she called me, I had better answer. I got mad at her but didn't say anything. I didn't feel like aggravating the situation, so I decided to just let it go. I swept that under the rug.

After that, this became a regular practice. Everything I did, she had a problem with it. If I cleaned the house, she didn't like the way I cleaned. I would have *missed something,* or it wouldn't have been *clean enough.* If I cooked for her, she didn't like it. At times, she would brashly throw the food away in the trash. No matter what I did for her, all she did was complain. My mistake? I thought I knew her because I had known her fifteen years earlier, but she was nothing like she was those fifteen years back. She had changed into someone I didn't even know. Because I knew her back then, it didn't mean that I knew her.

People change every day. You need to take your time and get to know someone. Don't just jump into relationships blindly and without mindful analysis. That is a big mistake. At times, the biggest you can make. Take your time. Go out on dates. Not just special ones, but casual ones too—ones where you two are meeting more to spend time and getting to know each other better. Talk about each other's past, present, and future. And what is important is that you are both being honest. Both of you should hold nothing back. And when spending time, don't just buy everything they are saying, trusting blindly. Be mindful. Notice how that person interacts with other people. If they are treating other people mean and have no respect, that should be all the sign to not take the relationship further.

If they have kids and you level up to that point where you can meet them, notice how they talk to their kids. Notice how they treat their kids. If you find them being lackadaisical, making excuses for why they are not doing things with their kids or for their kids, that should be a sign not to take the relationship further. When they are around their families and are being disrespectful and mean to their family members, bail. In fact, run. It is a glaring sign that they will treat you the same way. If they can't love their kids or family, what can possibly make you think they will love you?

If they are always making excuses for why they are not getting things done or always complaining about everything and everyone, it is a clear sign that they are a miserable person, and if you get with them, be prepared to be miserable as well.

I have learned, quite exhaustively, that everyone shows signs of who they really are. Most of us don't see the signs or ignore them until we are in a much-developed relationship with that person. The signs were alarming us, giving us a loud and clear heads-up that the person was not a good person to be in an intimate relationship with, but we refused to notice them. Sometimes, when you really like a person and really want to make it work with the person, you will not see the signs, even when you do see them. You would keep on thinking that person is good for you. You might even force yourself to believe that they are a good person. After the breakup, however, you start looking back, and you start discovering how they were from the start of the relationship. You start thinking that you shouldn't have got into the relationship in the first place.

Sometimes, you only see the things you *want* to see. We are all human. We all make mistakes. I have made these mistakes, too. Multiple times, to be honest. Some women told me things I wanted to hear in the beginning, and I ignored all the bad signs, the obvious and the not-so-obvious-but-out-in-the-open ones. The result? I jumped into a relationship that ended in heartbreak. But on the bright side, eventually, I learned to look for the bad signs.

And I am glad I did. Here's another story. I met this lady on a dating site. At first, she was telling me everything I wanted to hear, but I wasn't falling for it this time. I had become a veteran of some sorts, you know, I knew the rap. We kept it simple. We talked on the phone for about a month. She told me she had kids and that she was in between jobs. Being a bit more wise, I didn't think anything of it and didn't rush into things. At that time, we were in a recession. Plus, I had decided I would make use of the option of "Dating" to its full extent before committing to anything.

What makes the date night so special is that you give each other time to miss each other. Being together all the time can make both of you bored with each other. The next thing you know, both of you are on your phones playing games or on social media and not giving each other the time that both of you need from each other. Eventually, you find yourselves drifting apart. After a while, both of you might start arguing with each other, feeling like you are being neglected. Then, because of the neglect, cheating will creep into your relationship. And trust me, that is the last thing you need in a relationship. So give each other time to miss each other. That way, neither of you will get bored with the other.

I didn't see any bad signs when talking on the phone with her. Nothing out of the ordinary. Until one day, we decided to meet up. That is where it went wrong.

The 5Ls

We were supposed to meet up for dinner. An hour before we had to meet up, she called and informed me that she couldn't make it. I was okay with it and asked, "What about next week?" She agreed. The next week came around, and the same thing happened. She cancelled the plan, but this time, too, I didn't create much fuss about it. As if to make up for it, she asked me why I didn't just come over to her house. Foolishly enough, I agreed. What I should have done was tell her no right away, but I was giving her the benefit of the doubt.

On the decided day, I went to her house. I knocked on the door, but no answer came. I thought I got stood up again. Furious, I got back in my car and called her, to which she promptly answered. I told her I was outside. She became apologetic and told me she was sorry and couldn't pick up the phone because she was in the bathroom. In no time, her son came and opened the door I was invited in. She told me she'll be out in a second. I was happy to wait, given that I had successfully met her and wasn't stood up. While I waited, I saw three boys and a little girl walking in the yard. I guess they were just coming from down the street after playing with the other kids. The oldest boy looked at me and said, "You must be here for our momma." I said,

"Yes, I am." Just as I said that the front door opened and four more kids were standing there.

The oldest girl said, "Momma said come in and sit down."

Now, to the people who are reading this, that's eight kids. I should have gotten in my car and left then, but no. I went into the house. I guess at that point. I was curious about what was going to happen next. I went to sit down. The room was crammed. There was no place to sit. There were clothes everywhere. The oldest boy told the oldest girl to move the clothes out of the way. She responded with a swift no and instead told him to do it himself. Next you know, the kids started arguing. Their mom came out of the bathroom, hearing the rumpus. I was gobsmacked. She had a huge stomach. No, she wasn't fat. What she didn't tell me was that she was pregnant. I was sitting in wild bewilderment as she got the kids in order. She told them both to move the clothes, then ordered the other kids to go into the room and to take the toddler and the infant with them. Yes, two kids that young!

I innocently asked her, "You have two more kids," to which she nonchalantly said, "Yes. I have ten and one on the way." I was thinking to myself, *Maybe I should have asked her how many kids she had.* I also was thinking, *she didn't just have kids; she had a tribe.*

To top it off, she told me that's why she hasn't had a job in five years. I thought to myself: *That was a long 'in-between jobs.' It was more like a five-year vacation.* While we were conversing, and I was trying to come to grips with what I was seeing, we heard something outside. A squabble of some sort. It was three guys outside her house arguing. She goes to the door to see what was going on. To my surprise, it was three of her kids' dads outside arguing. She goes outside to stop them. I saw it as a window, and just as I was trying to leave, one of the men stopped me and interrogated me about who I was. In my defense, not wanting to get pounced on, I just told him right away, "I was not the father."

I got out as fast as I could. I never called her back. I dodged a bullet with her. All the signs that I got from her weren't good.

You have to be careful when you are getting into a relationship. You must not just jump into it, especially with these dating sites being in trend these days. Sometimes, the person you want may not be the person for you, no matter how good a match you both are on the digital platform. And here is the funny thing. There is no certainty that you have to GO OUT THERE and look for someone. Sometimes, the best person for you might be the one who is right next to you. Sometimes, as humans, we want what we want. In that, we become wishful. That is what leads us into something that is not right for us.

And we might like or dislike the notion, but more often than not, the person you need in your life might be a friend that you kept in the friend zone and never gave a chance to be with. That person might have been there every time you needed them. They may have been that shoulder you needed to cry on. That person probably gets along with your friends and your family. And above all, that person probably treats you with the utmost respect, but you kept that person in that friend zone. What is more funny (or should I say not-so-smart) is that you might keep them in that dreaded friendzone for foolish reasons. Maybe because they didn't look the way you wanted them to, maybe they didn't make enough money. No matter what it is or was, this person that you kept in the friend zone, you probably are missing out on or already missed out on that person who was right for you. You have to recognize the signs. And that is no conundrum, I tell you. The signs to look for are respect, care, compassion, personality, and unconditional love.

There are some people who do not know how to love someone. Yes, it's true. Some people think, to love, they have to force their love on you, and they force you to love them back. Some people think they have to control you to love you. While there are those who think you have to talk down to a person to love them. Some people even actually think they have to be mean or negative to a person to show a person love. All these schools of thought are wrong. On the contrary, if you love someone, you have to show them respect. Utmost respect. This means you have to respect the life they had before you got with them. You have to respect their family.

Even when they are not around, you have to show them respect by not talking bad about them.

Show them that you care about them—about their interests. Show them that you care about their well-being. Show that you have compassion for them. More importantly, show them that you have compassion for their feelings. If they are sad, hurting, or sick, show them that you are there and will be there. Show them real compassion. Show them that you will have unconditional love for them and that, owing to this unconditional love you have for them, you will be there through their ups and downs. Show them that you will be there no matter what the circumstances are. Love is not complicated if you know how to love the right way.

I was dating this woman once. In everything she did to me, she was mean and did it with negativity. One day, she got mad at me just because my brother showed up to say a mere hey. She demanded that I make him leave. And for no reason, she almost went mad, breaking and crashing much of my personal stuff. Things I can't replace. To make things worse, she went through my phone and erased all my family members' pictures and phone numbers. And if that wasn't enough, she deleted all my kids' photos. Everything that I had gotten from my family was gone.

Even though she didn't know my family, she decided that she did not like them. On top of that, she wanted me to shut them down.

She didn't want me talking to my family, including my mom and my kids. She showed no respect whatsoever for my family.

One day, my brother was admitted to a hospital. The very next day, my mom got admitted to the hospital too. My son called and informed me about both of them, which got me worried—two of my dearest people in the hospital at the same time! I called my brother and was able to talk to him. He told me he was going to be okay, which allowed me some relief. But when I called my mother, I couldn't get in contact with her. Immediately, I decided to take the trip to the hospital to check on her.

As soon as I got back from the hospital, my girlfriend started arguing with me. Why? *Because I went to the hospital to check on my mom!! Can you imagine?* She showed no respect for anyone that I cared about. I was so mad that day that I tried to leave her at that very moment. But she stood in front of the door and said I wasn't going anywhere. She tried as hard as she could, but eventually, I made it out the door. As soon as I got to the car, she shouted, threatening that if I got in the car and left, she would take all the pills she could find in the house and kill herself. Stupidly enough, I took the bait and went back into the house. I really didn't want to, but I didn't want to take the chance of her killing herself. The whole situation was crazy. No one should have to go through that.

That wasn't the end of it, though. Her making my life miserable was becoming a routine. Every time I wanted to buy myself something with my money, she would always fuss at me and make me feel bad because I wanted to buy myself something, *WITH MY MONEY!* But every time she spent money on herself, nothing was said. Note that a lot of it was my money. I couldn't even buy the things that I needed without having to hear her argue and make a fuss.

One day, I got really sick. I was tired of her not showing any compassion. I had the flu, a sinus infection, and a headache. I felt like crap. I was coughing and sneezing a lot. I could barely move. Instead of attending to me, she started a rumpus because I couldn't give her a massage and got mad because I couldn't cook dinner. Here I was, barely moving, but she didn't care. The only thing she cared about was getting what she wanted done. She didn't care about my well-being at all. I used to feel like she didn't care if I lived or died as long as I got done with what she wanted me to do. I felt like she didn't love me *unconditionally*. She was selective, only counting being loved as love. She only loved me when I could do for her what she wanted. She only loved me when it was convenient for her to love me. When I was sick for that week, I got to sleep a lot, so I had a little bit of peace. I didn't have to hear all the complaining and arguing. She tried to start one of her argument rants, but I would just fall asleep while she was arguing.

The next week, when I got better, it went back to the same thing—lots of complaining and arguing. The next weekend, we went out of town to visit her family. We stayed the weekend at her brother's house and visited her mom, sister, and uncle. I treated her family with respect, not once showing any disrespect. I saw her family as my family because I was with her, in a relationship. But even with me setting an example when we came back home, nothing had changed. She was still being mean to my family.

A month later. My mom ended up going back into the hospital. This time, instead of hearing my girlfriend fuss, I decided not to tell her anything about my mom. I waited until the next morning so I could make my move. My girlfriend had to go to work. As soon as she left, I packed my bags and left and never looked back. I just couldn't take it no more.

Some people only have selective love. They only love you when it is convenient for them. That's not love. They are users. No matter what you do to make them happy, they always want more. They love everything you do for them as long as you are giving. When you do more, they love you more. When you do less, they love you less.

That is why you have to be careful. Don't confuse being loved with being used. In fact, test them. Just say no to a person who claims to "love" you and see how they treat you. See if that starts an argument. Be watchful of how they are treating you. For someone who truly loves you, if you tell them "no" or "I can't do it," their feelings for you shouldn't change. *UNCONDITIONAL LOVE DOESN'T CHANGE.* Unconditional love understands when you can't do something for them.

You should never put up with someone who is selective when it comes to love. Your partner should always make you feel loved at all times. If you get into a relationship with someone who doesn't want you to have good, positive things for your family or doesn't want you to have a good relationship with them, you don't need them in your life. Mind you, you don't have to take things too far. Some people go too far to help a family member, even going to the point of hurting their partner while doing that. Don't do that. Please! Some of you might be confused about what I just said. Let me break it down.

For example, let's say if your partner is getting mad because you took some soup for your mother because she was sick, or your brother's car broke down and he needed a ride to work—something that doesn't hurt you, your partner, or the kids—your partner should never get mad at you.

On the other hand, for example, if your sister is on drugs or your brother has a gambling or drinking problem, and all you are doing all the time is giving them money, that is when you are wrong.

Never take from you, your partner, or your kids for a family member's addiction or a recurring problem that your family members are not trying to fix. In this case, your partner does have the right to step in and tell you that you are wrong.

Now let's get the conversation going. If you and your partner have kids by other people, you and your partner should always respect each other's kids, no matter how old the kids are. You should never treat the kids badly, even if they are grown. Also, your kids should never treat your partner badly, too. And if someone is treating your kids badly, even when your kids are trying their best to respect them, you should do your kids a favor and leave that person alone.

Let me share another experience. I was with this woman. For the first year, it was going good. There were no bad signs as far as I could see. I was good with her kids, treated them with respect. I loved her kids like they were my own. Since things were smooth, we moved in together. After that, she flipped.

One day, my son came by to visit. I answered the door. It was my son and my granddaughter. At the time, my granddaughter was an infant, and my son had brought her by so we could see her. We were chatting and everything when my girlfriend came down, having a mean look in her eyes. I asked her what was wrong. She said nothing, so I just let it go and turned my attention back to my son. We got back into our chit-chat, and he handed me the car seat with my granddaughter in it. She was so beautiful. I picked her up, and the feeling was so awesome. My love for her instantly went through the roof.

While I was playing with my granddaughter, my girlfriend was sitting back, looking mad. I had no clue what was bugging her. After about two minutes, she got up and snatched my granddaughter out of my arms. I could not make sense of her reaction. I was just hoping she would just stop being mad. It didn't work. All of a sudden, she mockingly said that the baby didn't look like my son. She kept repeating the same thing, trying to insinuate that the baby wasn't his. She turned to me and asked, as if for confirmation, whether the baby looked like my son. I shot back that she did.

She got really mad and told my son to excuse us as we had something to do. My son knew that it wasn't true, but he left anyway so there wouldn't be any trouble. I was mad, but I just let it go. The very next weekend, my son brought my granddaughter so I could see her again. This time again, my girlfriend told him that we were just about to leave, so he must leave. He knew she wasn't telling the truth, but he left without saying anything. Two weeks later, it was raining really bad. Thundering and lightning crackled, and the wind was lashing the rain on the porch. My daughter came over and brought my grandson to see me. This time, my girlfriend went too far. She didn't even let my daughter and grandson come into the house. With all the downpour, my girlfriend had them wait for me on the porch. She came upstairs and told me my daughter was downstairs. When I came down, I saw them sitting on the porch, almost soaking wet. I confronted my girlfriend about why they were on the porch, to which she coldly replied that she didn't want them in. I was fuming. I went out on the porch, gave my daughter a hug, and was about to bring her in when my girlfriend appeared and lied to them that we were just about to leave. My daughter knew it was a blatant lie, too, but she left anyway. Every time my kids or any other family member came over, my girlfriend would come up with a reason for them to leave. I couldn't take it anymore.

I tried talking to her about the situation, but she wouldn't listen. She would just turn it into a yelling rampage for no reason. Even her oldest daughter started jumping in, but I never said anything to her. She even threatened me with a knife once. I was thinking to myself, *What in the world did I get myself into?* If that wasn't enough, one day, her oldest son got into it too. He got in my face, fussing at me, throwing a fit, and threatening me. At this point, I was getting very angry, but I remained calm. Eventually, the situation died down. I knew I didn't want to be with her, but being me, I stayed. What a big mistake!

Two months passed with no signs of improvement from her. One day, her son's car broke down. He came to me and asked to borrow my car. I handed him the keys, no questions asked. Eight hours later, we are in bed asleep when we get a phone call. It was her son who informed me that he had wrecked my car. I was hurt, gutted to the core, but I let it go. That was round one.

Four months later, my girlfriend and her daughters went out of town. It was just me and her son at home. Her son, for some reason, was acting really weird. He was acting paranoid. I didn't think anything of it; I didn't have a reason to. Plus, I was used to his mother acting weird, so I barely registered it. He came to me and asked to use my phone. I gave it to him, and next I knew, he called his mom, saying how he was going to slap me. I was dumbfounded. We haven't had any argument or even a discussion, which might have turned into an argument. Nothing had transpired that might warrant such a rage. He just came out of nowhere, saying he wanted to beat me up. I couldn't make sense of it, but at that point, I was so furious that I wasn't worried about making sense of things anymore.

I told him to give me my phone. He said no and tried to go out the door with it. I stopped him in his steps and snatched my phone out of his hands. He turned around and grabbed me. I grabbed him back. He tried to pick me up but couldn't. I, on the other hand, could. I ended up picking him up and went to the floor with him. I hit my head on the coffee table and broke it. I was furious, but again—me being me—I let it go. We got up off the floor. He realized he was going to get whooped, which calmed him down a lot. I then tried to talk to him. He was still acting paranoid, but was now acting calm. I let all that go.

A few days later, my girlfriend came back home. The next day, I received a call from my daughter, telling me that my son got sick; his appendix had flared, and I needed to be with him. The moment my girlfriend heard that, she got mad. She started fussing at me, but this time, I had had enough of the disrespect. I immediately decided to move out. If someone can't accept your kids, you don't need to be with them.

Your partner should love you unconditionally and your kids unconditionally, and vice versa. You shouldn't have to be unhappy to make someone happy. If that is a feature in your relationship, I am sorry, but you are with the wrong person. True unconditional love should go both ways and should be wholesome. If someone is claiming to love you, they should love or at least respect what or who you love and accept and embrace them.

Additionally, there should always be trust in faith. Without trust, a relationship is miserable. If your partner doesn't trust you, or you don't trust them, there is no reason for you to stick around. Without trust, you and your partner would always be arguing. You and your partner will always be paranoid, and you both will always be accusing each other of cheating. Trust is a primary factor upon which a relationship relies heavily.

Now, it shouldn't mean that a good relationship has trust from day one. You have to let it grow. Some people don't trust because they have been mistreated for so long that they really don't know how to trust. That is where you heal them with love and give them a chance. Love and trust go hand in hand. If you don't have trust, you don't have love.

It may sound crazy, but I will go on to say that a whole relationship has to start off with trust. When you first get with someone, you start off with just a little trust. You might start by giving your phone number. You trust that they will call you. After that, you take it to the next step, perhaps a date night. Now, with a relatively intimate interaction like a date, you are trusting that person. You are trusting them not to do anything wrong to you. If everything goes down well, you give them a little more trust. You start telling them little personal things about you. Here, you are trying to discover whether or not they will use what you tell them against you or treat you any different after you tell them something specific about you. Then, as time goes on, you give them a little more trust and let them meet your family. The next thing you know, you and your partner are officially in a full relationship.

Everything that you and your partner did, started with trust. If someone doesn't trust you, leave them. If you stay with them, you will surely cause yourself a whole lot of problems. Trust issues lead to insecurity issues, making you vulnerable and shredding your confidence. Insecurity issues are big problems you need to stay away from because they break you down slowly but holistically, and repairing yourself becomes quite a challenge.

I was dating this woman who had trust issues. In everything I did, she didn't trust me. I couldn't take a shower or brush my teeth without her saying I was going to see another woman. If I went to the store, she would ask if the cashier was a woman. If I told her that it was a woman, she would interrogate me about what I said to her. Every time I watched TV, I couldn't watch anything with women on it, which was almost everything. Darn it! I had to watch cartoons! I couldn't run an errand without her being suspicious. If I went to check the mail, she would always say I went outside just to try and look at the next-door neighbor lady. Even if I received a call, she would want to go through my phone to make sure it wasn't a woman. I was miserable. Every time I came home from work, instead of asking how my day went, she would start an interrogation, asking me if there were women working at my job and if I had any conversations with them.

I couldn't go to the store, I couldn't go to work, I couldn't watch TV without being questioned. I felt like I was going insane. She made me feel guilty about things I wasn't doing. I found myself mostly staying in the house, not going anywhere with friends or family. I even dreaded answering my phone. No one should have to live like that. What was more infuriating was I could barely talk to my mom and my sisters. She had to be there listening. I just got to the point where I concluded that the relationship wasn't going to work. She was just too insecure for me, or for anyone, for that matter.

You should never be miserable in a relationship. In fact, it should be the exact opposite. If you find yourself miserable, talk to your partner and see how that goes. People need space. Yes! Even in a relationship, people need space. I call it "Spouse Space." It doesn't matter if you are married or in a regular relationship; you and your partner NEED SPACE.

Some people are always up under each other, meddling in all areas of their partner's life. Most of the time, you will find these people arguing all the time. Sometimes, you and your partner are around each other so much that you don't have anything to talk about. You find yourselves sitting in a quiet room, having absolutely no topic of conversation. In fact, this might be an indicator that both of you need space.

I'm not saying both of you should NEVER be around each other, or maybe avoid each other's company deliberately. All I am saying is that you need to regulate things and not be glued to each other ALL THE TIME. Give each other time to miss each other.

Women! If you are with a man who has hobbies such as playing basketball or fishing or hunting with the guys, let him go and let him go without you. Give him that space. Give him time to not just miss you but celebrate his own personal existence, too.

Men! If your lady wants to go out with the girls for drinks or to hang out with the women, let her. Give her time to miss you and, more importantly, let her enjoy herself. Both of you need space. That makes coming together much more special when both of you miss each other and are also happy after you have engaged in something that you enjoy in your exclusive sphere, such as hanging out with friends. Good company tends to elevate your mood, and when you return to your partner with elevated spirits after a good time spent with your friends, you automatically enjoy each other's company more.

Additionally, both of you have things to talk about with each other, maybe sharing the events of the day with your friends or your outings. Also! It also makes date night with each other that much more special. It is like a cycle. You go out with friends and return to a date in a positive mood. You share that positive mood with your partner. Add to that the love you have for each other. That surely will add to the positive air. With that same refreshing air brimming with positivity, you will later go out to work or with friends and will share that positive air with them. Your friends will go home to their partners with elated spirits due to the positivity you shared with them at the table, and that will start another chain reaction of good spirits being shared.

Smothering can kill a relationship and lead to breakups. No one wants to be smothered. It just isn't in human nature to be smothered or suffocated with constant interrogations. Be careful of that. To ensure you are not being nosy, always talk to your partner and find out how they feel about the way you interact with them, or even tell them how they are making you feel. Make sure that you or they are not feeling miserable or smothered. If all of this doesn't work and they are not willing to change their ways, like one of my girlfriends I talked about earlier, let them go.

Now, you might come across confusing ordeals when you meet people. For example, you meet someone, and you find that he/she is a truly good person, someone who might be the right fit for you. You and that person get together, but then you both discover that you can't compromise on a lot of things for each other. Understand this: Just because both of you are good people, that doesn't mean it's going to work. It only means both of you are good people in your own ways.

Sometimes, people can be good people, just not good together. Don't let that discourage you or send you into a mental crisis. All it means is they are not the person for you. It in no way means that you should give up on finding that life or that "everlasting love" is not out there. It simply means that you should keep looking and hold on to faith.

In fact, you can even find a partner in someone whom you might find to be troubling or "not your best fit" when you first meet them. You might meet someone who has faced troubles in the past or someone who is going through some rough times when you meet them. That experience might be making them bitter at the moment, making them appear to be someone you wouldn't want to be with, when, in truth, they are absolute gems. Don't judge or decide people on just a few instances of meeting them. One or two instances don't define a person. It doesn't mean that the person is bad.

That person might be your lifetime. You never know who will be your lifetime and your happily ever after. That person might be that everlasting love you have been missing. Some people are good people; they just make bad decisions, ones that often spiral out of control. That doesn't make them a bad life partner. Maybe you come across a person who smokes and smoking might not be your thing. Before you dismiss them, give them a chance; that person might be so devoted and dedicated to you that they might even be willing to quit smoking just to be with you. People change every day. Some are just looking for a reason, a chance, or just someone to believe in them. If a person is willing to make a change, that too a radical one, simply to make sure things work out between the two of you, that person truly wants to be with you. Mostly, when people genuinely have feelings for someone, they are ready to make a grand change.

If you are with someone who does something that can harm them in the long run or can harm you, and they aren't willing to give up that foul habit or practice, let them go. They don't seem to genuinely make things work out with you. There is no promise between the two of you.

On the other hand, if someone notices and realizes that a certain practice or habit can harm them or harm you, and they are readily willing to change, they are people you can and should give a chance. And I am not saying to surrender to them. Gauge their commitment. If they keep saying they are going to change but don't put forth any effort, just simply let them go. All you have to do is be careful. Many people say a lot of things but come up short in delivering.

Then there are people who are very controlling and bossy. These are the kind of people you should never put up with. You are your own person. Being a partner is just that—a partner! That means you and your partner are a team. You are equals. No one is better than the other. You both have weaknesses and strengths, and must complement each other.

For example, if you have a boyfriend or husband and he loses his job while you still have yours, that doesn't make you better than him. If you have a girlfriend or a wife and you pay all the bills, that doesn't make you better than her in any form or manner. That's what you are supposed to do. Working together is what a relationship requires to survive. Neither of you will win anything worthwhile by bringing the other down.

Some people think the only way to show someone you love them is to control them. That's not true at all. It is completely practical and possible for you to love someone and have a relationship where the two of you are equal. If someone is trying to control you, let them go as soon as possible. You don't need anyone trying to make you a slave to their needs; that is not a sign of a healthy, functional, potentially successful relationship.

And I speak from experience. I was with someone once who always wanted to control everything I did. She wanted to control what I would watch, where I would go, what I would eat, all the way down to what I would wear. I couldn't even check the mail without her approving it. If we went somewhere, she chose the clothes and forced me to wear them even if I didn't like them or didn't find them apt for the occasion.

It got worse. After work, I would come straight home. She would tell me to clean the house and cook dinner. Before I would go to work, she wanted me to cook her some breakfast. I wasn't even allowed to watch the news. I had to watch what she watched, and that was after the fact that we had multiple TVs. Everything I wanted to do, she controlled it, and every errand, big or small, she needed done, she'd have me do it.

One day, I just wanted to just crash a little, relax and watch some football. She immediately shot my idea down. She told me that I had to cook and clean. I tried to protest, so she unplugged the TV and told me I wasn't going to watch anything unless I did what she wanted. I always avoid altercations and feuds, so I obliged. I cooked as quickly as I could, hoping to catch what was left of the game. After I had spent a few good hours cooking, she told me she really didn't want what I cooked and was instead craving BBQ. I was fuming. I told her I'm not doing it, but she was adamant. She said, "Well, you won't be doing anything until I get my BBQ." I knew there wasn't any winning against her. Plus, I couldn't have stooped to her level. I just put my head down, went outside, and started the grill. But that was also my last straw. I sat there thinking, *I can't do this anymore! I had to take a step.* After I cooked the BBQ, I cleaned the kitchen and made sure the rest of the house was clean too. By that time, she had heartily eaten the BBQ and went to sleep. I saw a window. I picked up my keys, checked I had taken everything necessary, and left. I didn't want to be controlled or bossed around anymore.

Most of us want to love someone and someone to love us. And we want that almost desperately. In that unchecked desire, we tend to accept almost anything. Some people stick to a relationship even though they can clearly see what wrong their partner is inflicting on them. They foolishly cling to the hope that everything is going to get better. In reality, things are only worsening. People even stay with cheating partners, and when someone tries to tell them, they refuse to believe it. They prefer to stay in denial. Worse, they start blaming themselves for why their partner is cheating or, sometimes, make up lame excuses trying to justify the disloyalty. The truth is, there is and never can be a valid reason to cheat.

Then there are people who take things up a notch. Being afraid of getting dumped, they make do with their partners verbally and physically abusing them, and even make excuses or justifications for why their partner is verbally abusing them. They either blame themselves or downplay what their abusive partners are doing.

And there is no scenario where this can all be considered right. To all such people going through such abuse, I say this: *STAND UP FOR YOURSELF!* Be that person who says, "ENOUGH!!" Enough of the cheating! Enough of the verbal abuse! Enough of the physical abuse! You are better than that, and you deserve nothing less. You should be treated with greatness. But first, you have to believe in yourself that you actually are great. My words won't matter if you don't. No one deserves to be mistreated. Everyone deserves happiness. If your partner is treating you badly, it is about time you tell them, "ENOUGH!" You have taken enough, and that stops now.

I press on it so vehemently because I have been through something similar. When I was younger, I was dating a woman who was violent and abusive. When I first got with her, there was a calm about her, and she gave no hints of being aggressive. But about six months into the relationship, one day, I accidentally knocked a glass cup on the floor. It shattered everywhere.

She looked at me and barked, "Watch where you're going, stupid!"

I was taken aback at first and said, "What?" thinking I might have misheard.

She coldly replied, "You heard me."

I told her it was an accident, to which she remarked dismissively, "If you wasn't so clumsy, it wouldn't have happened."

Her attitude was vexing me. I said, "Really?! Is that how you feel about me?"

She didn't say anything else. She just smirked and walked off. Even though it was weird and unusual, I didn't think much about it. I just cleaned the glass up. I should have spoken up for myself, but I didn't. I just let it go. Two weeks later, I was getting groceries out of the car and suddenly, one of the bags ripped open, and all the items went scattering on the ground.

Before I could even react, she reached me and slapped me hard and then ordered, "Now pick it up!"

At this point, I was just standing there, dumbfounded by the reaction. I gathered myself and started picking up the groceries.

While I was picking things up, she rebuked, "Next time, watch what you are doing."

I quietly took the groceries into the house, and she followed without lending me a hand. I confronted her for the slap, and without a hint of guilt, she said, "'Cause I can, and if you keep talking, I'm going to slap the hell out of you again."

"I don't like violence," I shot back, holding myself back.

She nonchalantly replied, "I don't care what you like," and walked off. This abuse, physical and verbal, went on for months. I really don't know why I stayed, but I did. I guess I wasn't brave enough to take a stand until I did.

One day, I came in from work and found her standing at the door. Just as I was getting inside, she literally punched me in the face. Confused, hurt, and in disarray, I asked, "What are you doing?!"

She yelled, "Why didn't you call me on your break?"

I told her I didn't get any during the day. But without relenting or understanding, she kept throwing fists at my face. Trying to defend myself, I moved back but tripped. She moved from punching to kicking me in my face. With much difficulty, I managed to get myself up and immediately dashed out the door. She ran after me, hurling whatever she could grab at me. I ended up tripping over a root outside. She quickly caught up with me and started kicking me in the face again.

But suddenly, she stopped. I lifted my head up and saw the police pulling up. I quickly got up, collected myself, and went into the house before the police could get out of the car. As soon as I got inside, she slapped me hard again, blaming me for calling the police. I foolishly tried to explain to her I hadn't, to which she yelled, "You ran out the door, and someone else might have called them!"

That was when the police knocked on the door. She gave me a glaring look and ordered me to go to the room. I complied. She went and answered the door. The police asked her what was going on and told her they had received a call about a domestic fight. She tried assuring them that it was nothing, but the cop knew something was off.

He said, "We gotta call about a fight," and then asked her where her boyfriend was.

She lied that I was in the room, lying down asleep.

The cop was adamant, "No ma'am. I just saw him come into the house when I pulled up," and then asked if he could speak with me to make sure everything was alright. She came into the room and warned me not to say anything. She instructed strictly, "If they ask what happened to your face, you tell them you got into an accident at work."

Scared, I went to the door. The police asked me what was going on, and I told them exactly as I was instructed: that it was an accident at work. The cop could have sensed I was shaken and scared; he said, "The bruises look fresh."

I nervously replied, "I just made it home."

He told me to step outside. As I was about to, my girlfriend made an attempt to intervene, but the officer ordered her to stay put. The other officer stood at the door to make sure she didn't come out. The officer then took me aside and said, "Look at me." I raised my head, and he conducted a cursory inspection. Then, sternly, he asked, "Do you want to press charges?"

I said, "No, sir."

He tried to talk some sense into me and said, "You shouldn't let her do this."

Another officer pulled up. The officer who was instructing and inspecting me asked him to get our names and run them. My girlfriend gave them a fake. I found that oddly confusing and weird. By that time, another police officer pulled up. He walked straight over to my girlfriend and called, "Hey (HER REAL NAME)!" The officer who was instructed to run the names heard his fellow officer and was instantly alarmed. He remarked, "That's not the name she gave me," and quickly ran the name his fellow officer had used to call her—her real name.

Come to find out, my out-of-control girlfriend had a warrant for arrest for domestic violence assault. The officers immediately put her in handcuffs and took her to jail. The one talking to me said, "You don't have to put up with that. No one should ever have to put up with that." He proceeded to tell me something that I eagerly want this book to convey. He told me that men get abused also; most just don't report it. He then assuringly told me that if I needed anything, I could call him. He gave me his card and then left. I packed my bags and left the house. I didn't know if she would return or not; I just wanted to get out of there.

After about a year, she called me again. She told me she was going through counseling and anger management. I always believe that people deserve a second chance, especially if they are trying to work on themselves and make themselves better. So I gave her another chance. That was a mistake.

The first month was good, but by the third month, she was back at it again. In fact, this time, it was worse. She had started hitting me again, and at times, I wouldn't even know what she was mad about. She would just bash me and wouldn't stop. Even if I tried to physically restrain him, she would pull loose and punch me in my face.

One day, she was throwing one of her rage fits and hitting me hard. Before I knew it, I had balled my fists up. With my fists up and merely a few inches away from her forehead, I ordered her to stop. Dismissively, she slapped me, but this time, I struck her back. It wasn't hard, certainly not as hard as she used to punch me, but there is no excuse; I shouldn't have done that. I should never have hit her.

She looked at me with rage fuming in her eyes. She just started swinging wildly. I grabbed her arm, twisted it to restrain her a bit, and yelled, "Stop hitting me!" While I had her by the arm, I pushed her on the couch and left. I found myself getting angry enough to put my hands on her, and that was a line that I never wanted to cross. I realized that her attitude was inducing in me regretful lows. That's when I said, "Enough!"

I wasn't going to put up with it anymore. That wasn't who I was or ever wished to be. I'm not perfect; I get angry. It is only human to be angry, but I put my hands on a woman. And that is the kind of low I never would accept for myself. I'm not proud of that at all. That is a regret that I have to live with. I made a huge mistake. It happened over twenty years ago, and it never happened again, but

I still feel bad about it whenever I think of it. I keep a reminder of it so I would never do that again, and that is why I have become more conscience and cautious of how I carry myself with people and what kind of people I seek for an intimate relationship. Most of you reading might be thinking *she got what she deserved*. I would say, "No, she did not." There were many options, much less violent and sensible than raising my hand at a woman. I should have left and never come back. A man should never hit a woman, and a woman should never hit a man. Violence should not beget violence. How can we be any different from an abuser if we reply back with the same abuse we hate? The best thing to do in a violent relationship is to leave and not go back—ever.

Everyone deserves love. Everyone deserves respect. These can be rightly considered as birthrights. If you are in a bad relationship, you need to punch out, and you need to do it now! I can't stress this enough because I have seen people suffering, hanging on to an abusive relationship for the weirdest reasons. Some lack the grit to get up and get going. Some think they cannot find another partner. Worse, there are some who believe they deserve the abuse.

For such people, I say this: First, getting up and going is the most rewarding thing you will ever do, and it doesn't require bravery of any kind. You can be scared of the tantrums or the rage fits your soon-to-be ex might throw. What if I tell you, you don't have to face them? You just can sneak out when they are not around. Yes, it's that simple! I have done this and it worked for me just fine. Secondly, to those who are miserably mistaken to think they cannot find another partner or deserve abuse, I can say, hand on heart, that the world is full of good people who know how to treat a person right. There is always someone out there who will love you the right way. Love is not hard to find. Maybe sometimes, it's hard to maintain, but I can assure you that true love triumphs and can face any challenge. All you have to do is that both of you have to be committed to maintaining that same love that both of you had when the relationship began. And trust me, committing to a good person is far easier and fun and less painful than hanging on to an abusive partner who is hell-bent on making your life a living hell.

Finding love could be hard if you make it. What I have discovered after observing many people is that many times, love is standing right in our faces, but we don't recognize it. The only thing you might have been looking for might be standing right in front of you, and you either don't see it or aren't ready to claim it simply because you are holding onto a misplaced, exaggerated fantasy, or maybe, as I have seen it, you are not sure.

Trust your heart. It is as simple as that. Some people try to find love with their eyes. Our own eyes can be deceptive. They might convince us that someone good-looking is what you want. The heart doesn't do that. It doesn't tell you lies; it simply allows the real feelings to settle in. So if your heart is telling you someone is the right person, there are good odds that they actually are.

Even though we have enough evidence to prove that just because a person looks good doesn't mean he or she is actually a noble soul, for reasons unknown, people keep forgetting this valuable lesson. Or maybe they don't forget; they just don't heed it. So I thought I would remind you again. "GOOD LOOKS" does not mean "GOOD PEOPLE."

"But how do we judge, man? It ain't that easy!!!" I can hear your protest. And I have a simple way to deal with it.

Whenever you are dubious about someone, just put that person in the friend zone and look within your heart. And by that, I don't mean dismiss them, but hold them at a distance for a bit and let your heart do the investigative work it is so good at. If you make this a practice before mindlessly getting intimate with the first good-looking person who comes your way, you will truly find the one for you.

And when you find that one, make sure you keep them. I can promise you that your heart will only say yes to the most genuine person—someone who will be the best fit for you on all fronts. So don't waste a good opportunity. There will be times when things might not seem to be sailing smoothly. If you and your partner find yourself drifting apart, go back to the thing that made both of you fall in love with each other in the first place. Revisit your fond memories and the reasons why your HEART convinced you to be with them in the first place.

Moreover, it is not always an internal rift that drifts two people apart who were once truly in love with each other. Sometimes, it is someone from outside. You and your partner should let no one come and intervene in your relationship—EVER! Guard your relationship as your most valuable treasure. You should be well-bonded in everything—the heart, the mind, all the way to the soul. It is good to mix up God in all of this, too. In fact, it is brilliant to seek God and His assistance in things relating to your partner because, I can say it with absolute certainty, that if the Heavenly Father brought you together, there is no chance anything or anyone will break it. Keep intruders at bay and protect your relationship. Stand strong against negativity, together.

Making love enduring is an easy job. You don't require anything fancy as much as the world or any fancy love odyssey might have you believe. You can express love with the simplest of things. Love each other with every word you speak to one another. Words have the most profound effect if you use them correctly. Use gratitude towards each other. With each heartbeat and each breath, be generously thankful and appreciative of your partner. Always think as "we" rather than as "you and me." Don't leave any room for any kind of negativity. Be as one, and you will have a long-lasting love.

Men pay attention! Treat your woman like she matters because she does. She should be your number one, no questions asked. And no, it doesn't mean being childishly obedient. No good woman will expect or want that from you. A good woman will just expect you to value her opinion and preferences in decisions you two make for your life together. Put her first always. Don't go consulting friends and family about decisions that impact YOU TWO.

To the party animals out there: if you are in a relationship with a woman, always come home at night. There is nothing, and I mean nothing, in the streets, bars, or clubs. Don't commit to a woman if you want to spend your nights raving while she waits for you at home at the dinner table. That is not fair.

Men, I know there is this wave of materialism out there. You are being told that your worth is how many digits you have in your bank. I declare that to be an ugly lie, and there are enough happy men out there to convince you just that. Women have this tendency to love holistically without asking much in return but love and respect. When a woman truly loves you, it's not about what car you drive. It's not how big your house is. It's about you and the love that she has for you. There are women out there in the world who are homeless with their men right now, and you won't find them complaining or scoping for other men. It is not that they don't have anywhere to go. Women, compared to men, always have takers to cater to them. They don't leave simply because they genuinely love their men.

To have such a woman, you need to treat your woman right at all times, and it takes nothing extra to do that. Chivalry is not dead, and it shouldn't die either. It is what separates men from boys and gentlemen from cavemen. Open doors for your woman. Bring her flowers for no reason. When you and your woman are walking down the street, walk on the street side. Protection and security shouldn't be mere jobs, but being protective of a good woman should be an honor.

Be expressive to your woman and sing her praise. If you think that is flirting, maybe it is. What is so wrong with flirting with a truly genuine woman? Look in her eyes every morning and say, "I love you." Before you go to bed, tell her that you love her. For no reason, tell her how beautiful she is. Words are potent, and they can leave the most lasting impressions. Let your partner know how much she means to you every day. Appreciate the work she does for you. Give her the attention she needs, but don't suffocate her. Do things that she might not expect from you. If your woman works, have dinner ready when she comes home. Cooking goes both ways; there is no man or woman in it. Times change, and we should adapt accordingly. Plus, food is one of the most genuine love languages. Make sure she returns from work to a HOME and not another office with a different job waiting for her. Run her a bubble bath and rub her feet when she's been through a hard day. Show that woman comfort and do it constantly.

When you two talk, make sure it is a conversation and not a speech. Listen to her instead of talking all the time. I know it's hard to express all the time—it can be draining—but there are times and moods when a woman needs to hear "I love you" every day. And in return, you shouldn't want anything from your woman but happiness. I know it sounds rather illogical to just give, give, give and not expect anything in return, but I know what I am saying. With the right woman, you don't have to ASK or SAY anything to get your actions and feeling reciprocated. Because when a woman loves you, she will readily do anything for you without having you ask for it. She would go through hell and high water for you. She will stand by you through thick and thin. If you are down, she will do anything to lift you up. If you go broke and homeless, such a woman would be right there by your side, making a home out of whatever scanty dwelling you are in.

When I say if a woman truly loves you, I can bet a grand that that woman will stand with you through all storms and all cataclysms the world might throw at you. And trust me, you won't see her budge from your side or have a wrinkle when she looks at you. A woman who truly loves you wants to see you at your best, and if you are not there, she will give her all she has got to get you there. A woman's love is one of the best things a man can have. Never take her for granted. Be everything she needs in a man, and then be some more. Be her Superman. Love her unconditionally. The best feeling for a woman is knowing that she is loved by her partner with all his heart and soul. Women love it when they have the assurance that they enjoy a position in a man's heart that no one else shares. And the little praise when you tell her that she is the most beautiful woman adds value to everything you say and do, and lightens her up more than we men can comprehend. Protect her and make her feel like a woman, but not as someone who is weak and can't protect herself, but as someone who is worth protecting and someone you want to protect because you are too afraid to lose her. A woman's love is the greatest feeling a man can get, and taking it for granted can be the dumbest thing a man can do.

Women, pay attention! Politeness isn't dead. Have morals and respect, not just for others but, as it seems to be dwindling these days, for yourself too. You don't have to dress half-naked to get a man's attention, and such attention is not worth having, period. If you dress half-naked, the only "men" who will approach you will have one thing on their mind. You don't want that kind of attention. Especially to the women who feel lonely or think they lack attention, I say this: You don't have to have sex with a man for him to like you. No real man wants their woman dressing half-naked for the world. Just be you, and the right person will come along.

And when that man comes around, do everything to keep him because he will do it too. For men, even the smallest gestures of care matter. If your man is working hard in the yard, bring him something to drink and see if he needs anything. There is nothing wrong with having a man's dinner ready when he comes in from work. It is the most simple yet effective and wholesome gesture of love and care. If he had a hard day at work, rub his back and let him know how special he is to you. Let him know how much you love him, and respect and value him for the hard work he does every day. Let him be the head of the house. Your man doesn't want to be in charge; he just protects and takes charge out of care and a sense of protection. Give him the attention that he needs, but also give him the space that he wants. If things in his life are going downhill, stand with him through it all. Be that woman he can count on in his bad times and who pushes him past his limits in a positive way. The greatest feeling for a man is knowing that his woman has his back. It's knowing that she will stand with him no matter what. If a man truly loves you, he would battle Satan himself just to protect you. When such a man loves you, he will sell his soul to provide for you. There is nothing that man won't do for you. Women need to understand that some (most) men have a hard time expressing themselves. They would rather show more than they say. So, if you don't hear the magic words too often, just look at what he does—the love will definitely show.

Now, I'm not giving men any excuse for not expressing their love exclusively in words. I already counseled men a few paragraphs back to do just that and to do that every day. All I am saying is that sometimes, more often than you might think, men want to be just nudged into such an expression of love. Just talk to him and let him know that you would love to hear it more. A man who truly loves you will surely change everything for you, even the way he expresses himself.

Be the superwoman your man needs, and before you dismiss it, saying that it is too much work, I can affirm to it, hands on heart, that there is a superwoman in every woman out there. Be that woman he would love to come home to every day. Be the woman he comes to when he is stressed, knowing that even when the world is against him, you are there for him.

Men and women pay attention! I told you in my first book, and now, here I am, doing it again in my second book because it is a message that can not be repeated enough. A relationship is easy to maintain.

The key to maintaining the relationship is: Just don't do what you don't want your partner to do to you. That's it! If you don't want your partner cheating on you, don't do it yourself. (And don't give them a reason to either.) If you don't want your partner to treat you badly, don't treat them badly. If you don't want your partner to be out all night doing only God knows what, don't be out all night doing only God knows what. If you don't want your partner dressing half-naked and flaunting their goods, then don't dress half-naked flaunting yours. It goes for both men and women, maybe to different extents, but the notion remains the same. If you wish to be respected, respect your partner. In fact, with the way you treat your partner, you show them how you want to be treated.

Some people sit and watch as their partners struggle with life for reasons that have no merit. Do not be that person—ever! To help you understand what I truly mean, I'll share one of my unfortunate experiences. I was with someone who watched me struggle while I was dating her. It was a trying time for me. I was working, but the money wasn't very lucrative, yet I paid all the bills. I usually wasn't left with any money after all that, but I never used to complain. She worked too and freely did what she wanted with her paycheck. I didn't have a problem with that, as I thought, as a man, it was my obligation to look after all those things—bills and all. I don't mind that ever.

The problem came when, one day, I needed an oil change and a new tire for my car. I mostly ensured to maintain all these things out of my pocket too, but this once, I didn't have any money left with me, so I asked her to help me with the two things. She flatly refused. That was every bit hurtful to me. I started to realize the pattern in everything. Whenever I asked her for help with something, especially monetary, she wouldn't budge. She would watch me struggle but never try to ease things for me. It was every bit hurtful, I can tell you that.

Helping, money or otherwise, goes both ways in a relationship. If you and someone are partners, you don't sit on the sidelines while the other one struggles. You help each other move forward. I'm just being real with you. I might sound bitter to many, especially those who do such a thing, but I think it is necessary to put the truth out. Like I said before, I am a friend, and I say everything with corrective intention. I'm going to tell you what you need to hear, not what you want to hear.

Do not let any kind of negativity make way in your relationships. If you had a bad day at work, your partner isn't the one responsible for it. Don't take it out on your partner. Don't bring external negativity into your alliance with your partner. In fact, encourage positivity in your relationship that is so strong it diffuses all the external negativity that makes its way towards either of you.

And all of the above is possible if you are patient. Remember, good things take time. If you haven't found that special someone yet, just hold on a bit more. They will find your way to you and you to them. I understand that everyone wants to be loved, but in that endeavor, I see people rushing things and making mistakes. Only some people wait for love to find them; others usually look for love frantically. I always urge people to be patient, and while you are at it, learn what you have to know it's real. You will be surprised to know how little people really know what they truly want. Most people look for someone to be their husband or their wife and think that is what love is. Yes, marriage should be the end result of love, but marriage doesn't need to make love happen always. Being husband and wife is okay, I guess, if all you want from your partner is to be just married. Most of you who are probably reading this must be thinking, *What could be better than making the person you love your husband or wife?* Well, I'm here to tell you there is more to it than meets the eye. I know scores and scores of people out there who are married, and both are ready to leave each other in the blink of an eye. Some of you out there are ready to split up, and you know damn well who you are.

I see this as a problem—one of the biggest, if I may, being married and just making do. The reason for this is that you didn't give yourself enough time to find that one person in your life. That one person who, for you, is worth spending the rest of your life with. The way I look at it. Being a husband or a wife or a girlfriend or a boyfriend just isn't enough for me. Tags don't matter. For me, I want to be with my "lifetime." You came across this title earlier in the chapter. What do I mean by "lifetime"? Well, boyfriends and girlfriends break up. Husbands and wives divorce. You see what I am trying to do here? A "lifetime" is there forever, or should I say, "must be" there forever. This lifetime is going to be there, standing with you, no matter what. He/she will be there through everything you go through. He/she will never hurt you. A lifetime will give you the time you need and the space you want. You would never have to worry about your lifetime cheating on you. A lifetime comes with positivity, happiness, trust, honesty, faith, compassion, compromise, sacrifice, patience, understanding, and unconditional love. Can you see the pattern? What I am trying to say here is that a "lifetime" is a wholesome package. A package of care and good intentions, a package of love and consideration and positivity.

"And how do I identify a 'lifetime'?" you may ask. Well, you just will know, mostly by how you feel when they are around. Being with a lifetime person is a wonderful thing. It feels right. A lifetime is going to be there with you from the moment both of you say your first words to each other, all the way until you take your last breath. And that is an energy that is difficult to miss.

I don't just want a wife. I want a lifetime. That's how you should feel. Don't just settle for a husband or a wife. Settle for a lifetime. I know, learned the hard way, that it will take some time, but you will definitely find one. And I assure you that a lifetime is better than any ordinary husband and wife. A lifetime comes with love that is enduring and lasts forever in everything: the emotions, the attentions, the respect, and the will to uplift you in your most trying times.

Chapter 3

Laugh

Many people say laughter is good for the soul. I agree! But what leaves me dumbfounded is though many are aware of such a valuable nugget, rarely do people follow it.

I truly feel that laughter is not just good for the soul; it is holistically healing and relieving. And I can prove it—right now, right here, as you are reading these lines. Ready? Picture this. You are alone and sad, mad, or even hurt. You pass by the TV or the radio, and you see or hear something hilarious. For that split second, all your problems seem to have gone away. For that split second, you feel you don't have any worries in the world. Relatable, right? That is how potent laughter is.

Laughter is an amazing antidote. In its effects, it is contagious and doesn't just heal you but heals everyone you share it with. I am sure you have experienced this that when you are with someone you care about, and one or both of you are upset, and something funny happens, the funny thing seems funnier. That shared moment of laughter feels not just funnier but even comforting. It makes you feel better instantly.

Here, I will take a little detour. I asked you something in my first book, and now I'm going to ask it again: Has anyone told you that they love you today? Have *you* told anyone that you love them today?

Being loved by family and friends is one of the greatest feelings. I used to think to myself, *What if I were born and my mother gave me up as a baby, and I had to live in foster care all my life? What if I moved from home to home until I was eighteen, never having a family to call my own and never making friends?* I used to think that if that happened to me, I would have grown up without any pain of loving someone like a family member or a friend, and then those people dying on me. The idea of being so helpless used to haunt me. I used to think that if I were all alone in this world, my heart would be free. I wouldn't have to care about anyone. No family or friends to let me down and hurt my feelings when I really need them. I would be pain-free. The idea seemed remarkable! Having no one to worry about except me and me alone. Yes! No worries at all.

You must be wondering why exactly I have detoured into a whole other discussion out of the blue. Bear with me.

Before I could conclude the life of a loner with no one to care about as the ultimate life, I was troubled (or should I say blessed) with a few questions. Would that really be the way? Do I really want to be lonely? Laughing by myself would have been okay, I guess, but the people that I have laughed with over the years, wasn't that more fun than laughing alone? The laughs I had with my grandfather, who made me feel worthy and that I mattered no matter what others might say; The laughs I had with my dad, whose friendly company and mellowed spirits made me feel protected; The giggles I shared with my loving mom who would always ensure that even if the world ran out of love for me, with her, I could find an abundance of it; The laughter I had playing with my kids; The cackles that roared through our house between sibling cousins, uncles, aunties, and my friends on dinners and many holidays that made me feel that I belong—to people, to a place, to a family. These questions and reminders made me realize that I wouldn't take all of those back for absolutely nothing in the world.

Everyone who is or was in my life made me who I am today. A question that troubles people quite often in one part of their life or another is, "What is the meaning of life?" Well, I am no sage, but my answer is love. Love with a little sprinkle of laughter here and there.

Be loved and give love. Remember when I said no one is born with hate? Hate is taught. That is a fact! And I can spend days debating anyone who says otherwise. When a baby is born, the baby has no sense of judgment that might make him or her interrogative or overcritical about anyone. All that a baby is, is curious. And all the baby wants is to be loved and nurtured. You ever heard the saying, "Sleeping like a baby?" That is because the baby is not stressed about anything—no worries about race, no worries about hating someone because they are different, no worries about cheating or defrauding others. Nothing. The baby doesn't have a worry in the world. And that stays with the baby for quite a while. When that baby is a toddler, they still are free of those worries. They still are filled with love. You take that toddler to a daycare or a park, what does that toddler do? That toddler will get there, see other kids of a different race, and start playing with them. The toddlers simply don't see colors. What they see is playtime. Even the other toddlers have no qualms welcoming a total stranger into the group, simply because they all share positive energies towards each other and don't expect any harm from each other. No hatred plagues their hearts.

When that baby gets a little older, that is when trouble begins. When the child enters the three-to-five-year-old range, that's when dark things such as hatred usually start to seep like the poison they are. Why do you think that happens? Do children magically turn on their HATE button after they turn three to five? No.

That happens because that is the age when children start hearing and understanding the things that come out of their parents' mouths. And mind you, it is not just what they hear but what they see their parents do. Now, I am not singularly blaming parents or all parents for that matter. The reason I say parents is because that's where everything starts from.

If a parent is loving, nurturing, and caring, the child will see them and imitate exactly that. Understandably, he will be loving, nurturing, and caring. If the child sees and hears positive things, that child will do and say positive things. If that child sees and hears hateful and hurtful things, well, you know where this is going.

I remember back in the 1980s, when I was in the fifth grade, it was me and two other students in the whole school who were of a different race. Everyone else was Caucasian. This particular day was the infamous Valentine's Day. The ritual was that all the students gave out Valentine's Day cards to each student, meaning that everyone got a Valentine's Day card. Sounds fun, right? Well, for the usual kids, it was. Everything was going well until I got this "Valentine's Day" card, which expressed anything but love. A couple of students got together and gave me a card that read:

The KKK is coming for you!

Horrific, you might say, but I didn't know what it meant entirely back then. As I opened and read the card, I was confused. The kids who had devised this vile plan might have seen me in a boggled state and started laughing at me. Imagine that! Fifth graders range from ten to eleven years old. Imagine a child devising a racism and hate-fueled prank! Abhorrent, to say the least.

But luckily for me, I didn't know what any of that meant. My parents and grandfather had never brought any such thing to my attention. I guess they shielded me from the hate as I grew up. All they taught me was, *"Right, don't wrong nobody."* They had always taught me to do the right thing no matter what. They taught me that hating is wrong in any form and manner and, more importantly, that I would never reply to hate with hate. As I read the card, one of my classmates heard me. Apparently, she knew what it meant, all of it. Understandably, she got really mad—fuming. She asked me to give her that card, and seeing her enraged like she was, I complied without much protest. I must add that I was still clueless about the meaning and the subsequent rage. She showed the card and its content to another student, who reacted in the exact same manner she did. The boy took a much sterner step. He immediately took the card to the teacher.

The moment the teacher read it, all color faded from her face, and concern took over. The reason I said "concern" is because that was the only emotion that I saw at that time. She stood up and quieted the class down with one stern command. Immediately, she interrogated who gave me that Valentine's Day card. The class was stupefied; no one said anything. She asked again, much louder this time. Again, not a single reply. Then, addressing me directly, she asked about the envelope the card came in. I surrendered the envelope, still dazed by the sudden change in attitude on such a pleasant day. She read the name on the envelope, demanded that the student step out the door, and marched outside. The kid followed, scared out of his wits. I don't know what was said, but I could hear it was strict and commanding. After a few minutes, she ordered another student, the friend of the first one, to step outside. He, too, went outside and joined his friend without any protest. About ten minutes later, the second student who was summoned out by the teacher came back in and made a beeline for me. Before I could make sense of the thing, he started what felt like a heartfelt apology. He told me that he didn't write what was on the card of his own accord; it was just the other student who dictated the words on the bus while on the way to school. I told him it was okay. About five minutes later, the teacher and the other student, who had given me the card in the first place, came back into the classroom. He came over to me and apologized, and it sounded sincere. I accepted his apology, too. Next, what happened was something I could have never prepared myself for. After the student was over with the apology, the teacher came over and apologized to me. She seemed more apologetic than the two kids. Of course, I told her it was absolutely fine. Need I reiterate, I still didn't know what the big deal was. To finally kill my curiosity, I asked the teacher what the matter was and why everyone was apologizing to me when all they had done was give me a Valentine's Day card.

She looks at me and says, "You really don't know, do you?"

I said, "No, ma'am."

She looked at me for a while, gauging whether she should or should not explain it to me. She took a deep sigh, sat me down, and started explaining some things to me. It wasn't a long explanation. She didn't go into too many details but gave me enough to get an idea of what was so wrong that it demanded an immediate apology.

But that is not the worst part. Later that day, as I sat and ruminated on the goings of the day, I realized something. I recalled that all the students had brought the Valentine's Day cards from their homes. I did some more thinking and realized that the card was not in his handwriting. Come to find out. His parents helped him write those cards!! Can you imagine!? That was when I started getting curious about what my true identity was.

The very next week, we started learning about the Silver War. She really didn't teach us about the Union side. We mostly learned about the Confederate side. The classes further piqued my curiosity about my heritage. I started self-teaching myself everything I needed to know about history, and whatever I learned then, I still keep revising to teach my kids. And before you object, I will try to explain why.

Having kids can be stressful. It can be hard at times (or most of the time). When you have a child, your life is your child's life, or the child's life is your life, whichever you prefer. You are no longer allowed to get tired. When that child is a baby, they demand nurturing and a lot of care. They have to be fed and changed regularly. Then, when they become a toddler, they require attention. They have to be watched at all times. Now, not only do you have to feed them and change them, you have to be vigilant all the time, making sure they don't sneak something in their mouth, making sure they don't pick up and play with sharp objects, making sure they are playing in the yard and not running onto the road. It's a lot of work. Next comes the school years. When school starts, you have to make sure they get dressed all prim and clean. You have to become a student yourself and learn their school lessons to help them with homework later. More importantly, you have to teach them right from wrong because now they will be making friends and interacting with people. You have to participate in school functions. As the child gets older, these school functions grow in numbers. There are games, bands, chorus, etc. No matter how old your child gets, you never have the luxury of getting tired and relaxing. You have to keep moving forward and working hard for the child and with the child. And this all starts from the day the child is born.

A child's social education begins as a toddler. No kids are born bad, hating and rebuking their fellow humans. They just go by what we teach them. If we teach them to be good, we will get good. But more often than not, we teach them bad. I know many of you might not agree with me here, but look around, and you will see that many things wrong that a child does, you will see their parent(s) doing something similar. What's worse is that when they do something bad, we punish them, as if it is their fault.

By all means, we should avoid punishing them because, whether we like it or not, they are only doing what *we* taught them. And if we wish to punish someone, we must punish ourselves for teaching them anything vile they did that *"brought shame to our family."*

That kid who gave me the Valentine's Day card wasn't born with hate. He was taught hate. Where exactly will a fifth grader even learn about the KKK?! He had absolutely no reason whatsoever to hate me. There is no natural cause that might make you hate a color. He didn't hate me because I did something bad to him. He didn't hate me because I did something bad to one of his family members. The only plausible explanation is that he was *taught* to hate me just because I was of a different race. And nothing about such a hateful lesson is cool.

Those who teach their kids abhorrent things like racism and such have no idea how it can scar a child, theirs and whoever other who is victimized. And this last one is coming from experience. Every day after that Valentine's Day, I played with that kid to show him that I was no harm to him. I felt like I was a threat. Plus, did he get that message? I don't know, but what I do know is that he shouldn't have been taught that in the first place. Why should any young soul have to bear such a strong burden when they haven't done anything wrong? Why should any child feel he might hurt someone simply because he is of a different color? No, no one can give me any answer that might make sense and have even a shred of logic to this question.

We as adults teach kids hateful things, and then when they do or say these hateful things they were taught, we get on to them and punish them. If there is someone to be punished, it is the adults. The kids only mimic us, only doing or saying what we did or said. How is it fair to punish them for a vice we inspired in them?

Through the actions of adults, kids learn to disrespect others. They learn to do grown-up things. Kids are not born with hate, disrespect, or any similar despicable problem towards their fellow human beings. I'm going to say this again now and might do it again later because I don't think anyone gets what I am saying.

Kids are not born with hate!

Kids are not born to disrespect!

Hate and disrespect are taught!

If your child goes to school and curses the teacher out, the first thing we do as a parent is say, "They must have learned that in the streets," or "They must have gotten that from the other kids that they play with." As parents, we blame everyone and everything else when our children do wrong, but we never blame ourselves. We are always looking for excuses for our children's misdemeanors. But the sad fact for many parents is that our children's learning starts at home. We teach them many of these foul habits. If not directly, then maybe through our actions. It's not the neighborhood kids teaching our kids to misbehave, nor are classmates teaching them anything vile. It's we as parents teaching them bad habits. They learn from us. Even if you protest to this, saying that you didn't teach your child all those cuss words, I would remind you that you might not TEACH your child cuss words, but you surely teach your child the KIND OF LANGUAGE they should pick up at school or the playground by simply using the language at home with your partners, if not with them directly. So, this one is still on you, sorry.

We need to do better. Kids always listen if you teach them properly. You don't tell them specific things, but instead, you give them the general idea of bad and foul on the whole, along with the specifics.

I remember when I was a kid, my grandfather kept his gun under his pillow. Yes, exactly, under his pillow, that's it, not in a lockbox. Moreover, he didn't even lock the trigger. He kept it under his pillow for safety for years. Now, I know some people may think that my grandfather was irresponsible. He actually wasn't. All of us kids knew that gun was there, but none of us dared to touch it. We knew if we messed with that gun, our grandfather was going to tear our butts up, no questions asked. He told us the gun was there, taught us how dangerous it was to use it (for us and others), and that's that. We never once went near that pillow. When my grandfather spoke, we all listened. In fact, we not only listened, we obeyed.

And it was not just about guns. That was simply an example. My grandfather taught us almost anything and everything there was to know about morals and about being respectful. He taught us to always respect people irrespective of rank or color. He taught us *Yes ma'am, No ma'am, Yes sir*, and *No sir*. He taught us not to be in the grown people's conversation. Now, he didn't turn us into mindless robots following instructions. He let us be kids and do everything kids did. He just taught us to stay in a kid's place and never cross the lines the grown-ups defined.

My grandfather was tough and firm, but he was also loving and kind. He never called us bad, derogatory names or titles, or nicknames with disparaging meanings. He taught us we don't need to be in a gang to be strong or recognized, but we need to stand on our own two feet and be our own strength. We worked a lot in the fields, but that taught us to embrace hard work. Whenever he got a chance, he would talk to us, teaching us the values of life through his many stories. As kids, we knew and respected the boundaries the adults would set.

That is exactly my point here. I know that with age and time, generations differ, but they don't differ such drastically. Kids today are in many ways very similar to us when we were kids. Kids listen to their parents. It is just that we need to talk more to our kids. I know sometimes they don't want to hear it, but when they get older, they will appreciate the talk. This simply means that what we say to our kids will help them, later if not now, and they will have some guidance to mend their ways with.

Now, when I say TALK to kids, I mean it in the best way. Don't talk down on your kids. Don't talk AT your kids. Talk TO your kids. Stay tough and stay firm when necessary, easy when not. They will listen. They are hardwired to listen to their parents.

And while you are at it, remember to let them be kids. Don't raise them up too fast or too slow. Show them that you love them every day. Tell them you love them often. Give them daily hugs and appreciate them when they do good. Let them know how proud you are of them. Positive reinforcement (not harsh punishment) makes your children value what you teach them or ask them to do. It makes your lessons and warnings worth heeding, enough to make them do what is right even when you are not around. In other words, how your kids act when you are not around reflects on you.

Sometimes, we raise kids to grow so fast. Again! Let them be kids. What I meant by that is that today, we are taking all their imagination away from them. How, you might wonder. Well, we let TV and music teach our kids instead of letting the kids explore and learn things through our practice. Some of you might not like what I'm saying, but I'm always going to tell you how it is. I'm being real honest right now. That, I believe, is the only way to send a true message across.

When letting your kids access TV and other digital entertainment, especially music, listen to that music yourself first. Some music is okay, but most of it out there has things in it that no kid should be listening to. Even the local radio stations have things on it that kids shouldn't be listening to. It's bleeped out, but everyone knows what they are saying, even the kids. I have listened to kids all the time singing along with the radio, and trust me, most of those kids fill in the bleeps—so much for censoring.

More so, even TV has gotten bad for kids. There are no more Saturday morning cartoons, and yes, I know what you're going to say: That cartoons are on all the time. Yes, that may be true, but they don't seem to attract kids as much as they used to back in the day. Instead, kids today have social media to get caught up on "entertainment" of various kinds, such as all the latest reality shows that showcase the most questionable content. Most of these reality shows are not for kids.

And exposing them to content that isn't age-appropriate, we have taken all the kids' imaginations away. Worse, parents themselves are robbing kids of innocent and fun rituals and beliefs under misplaced notions. For example, I have heard and seen parents competing against Santa Claus. They tell kids there's no Santa Claus, and it was them who bought those gifts. Imagine that! What was so harmful about the whole notion of an old, happy man with a flying sled and reindeer bringing kids presents for being nice? I cannot understand. Some parents are okay with their kids imitating things that they see on these vile reality shows, but won't let them have an imagination. And mind you, this imagination has the potential to induce good habits and practices in your children.

But you can change that and save your child from such an atrocity. You are the parents. Kids are expecting you to teach them. More importantly, it is your responsibility to check and allow access to the useful kind of entertainment and content, one that will nourish their mind and intellect without taking away any innocence. Your kids are always going to love YOU, irrespective of whether you bought the gifts or an imaginary friend called Santa. Seriously, if you are feeling insecure about Santa, you need to reevaluate your parenting. I see no reason to take Santa Claus or the Easter Bunny away from them. Let them keep their imagination. Remember when you were a kid and the way you felt on Christmas. Remember how you used to play with your toys and imagine they were alive.

Remember how you used to play with the Thunder Cats or G.I. Joes, and you went on an imaginary adventure with them. Recall the fun-filled days with the Care Bears or Barbie and the imaginary adventures you went on with them. Remember how you used to wait and exclusively dedicate your time to sit down and watch the Saturday morning cartoons and go on an imaginary adventure with them. Did that introduce any kind of problems for you, or did that give you some fine memories to look back on? If anything, at least for me, all those things taught me some important things, such as the value of time and punctuality, and earning what you want rather than being handed it out. I am sure many of you adults reading this book will remember doing chores or homework beforehand so that your parents would allow you to watch those cartoons. Now, when you look back, do you think that it was cruel of your parents to do that, or do you think it taught you discipline? I rest my case.

We need to stop taking away our kids' imagination. Imagination is not wishful thinking, it is creativity unraveling. And ask anyone who knows a thing or two about the mind, and they will tell you that creativity is one of the most required resources for children to succeed. We took away love songs and songs about camaraderie and friendship and gave them randy, sex songs filled with obscenity and graphic lyrics. We took away fun party songs and gave them songs that downgrade and degrade women. We took away uplifting and motivating songs and songs that encouraged unity and replaced them with violent ones. We took Santa Claus from the kids and gave them *Love and Hip-Hop*. We took the Easter Bunny and gave them *Housewives*. We took the tooth fairy and gave them *Jersey Shore*.

I'm not saying take them shows off the air or take them songs off the radio. I don't have anything against the shows or songs, and I know there is an audience for everything. If that's what you want to watch or listen to as a grown person, by all means, do it. This isn't moral policing that I intend. You are grown and free to make your own choices. But if you let your children watch and listen to those things, and they act on them, you shouldn't have any right to punish your kids. They are only doing the thing you showed them. It's not their fault. They are only doing what they are *taught*. And yes, this time, I am being critical because it is about saving our kids. All I am trying to say here is just be vigilant and responsible about what you allow your children to consume.

Be that parent to say no. I know it might be hard because of how much we love our children, but it is also necessary. Learn to say commanding sentences such as "No, you're not going to listen to this" or "No, you're not going to watch that." That's what separates them from us. That is also what our job is: to decide for them what is right and what is wrong. They don't know that. We need to worry about the grown-up things and let the kids stick to the kids' stuff. If you look around your neighborhood, you won't find many kids playing outside. Whatever you might find playing, that will be a small number, and that too will be for a very small amount of time. The parks and the basketball courts look like a ghost town.

Some of you might be responding to this: At least I know where they're at. Yes, you know where they're at. They are somewhere in the house exercising their thumbs on the Internet with only God knows who. So, sorry to say it so crudely, but parents today are more into the unknown than the parents of the old days. Today, you have to monitor the Internet as well, which is way too difficult. One has to have at least some technical knowledge of how to check and ensure that the things the child is accessing are safe. I understand that the Internet can be very useful, but it is also highly dangerous. And I can only say this in the simplest of ways: *PROTECT YOUR KIDS!*

If you love your kids like you say you do, protect them. You can take the high road, being all vigilant all the time, keeping an eye on everything, spending money on expensive security equipment and resources, and being on edge all the time about what your child is doing on the Internet. Or you can take the easier road by simply letting them be kids. There is no rush for them to grow up fast. It doesn't mean that you can be less vigilant if your kid goes out to play instead of sticking to a screen; vigilance can never be compromised. But at least it is easier to keep an eye on actual people your kids are playing with than keeping an eye on what they are doing on the screen. This is just one of many examples.

There are young kids out here who know everything about sex but don't know their country's history. There are kids out there who know everything about where to buy a gun and how to shoot, but don't know the safety of a gun and the proper way to manage and maintain it. There are kids out there who know drugs in alphabetical order, what the drug looks like, and how much it costs. They can TEACH you how to roll a blunt, but they don't know their math. And trust me, it is not the kids failing. It is us—the parents, the guardians, the adults—who are failing them!

I remember one day, I was sitting with a friend, watching a football game. He had gotten a phone call. As soon as he hung up, he asked me if I wanted to ride with him. I was at his house, and I didn't want to be there by myself, so I said, "Sure, I would ride." We got in his car and drove to a friend of his. When there, he went up to the door and knocked. A woman answered the door. She must have seen me sitting in the car, so she told my friend to ask me if I wanted to join them. At first, I said no, but my friend insisted and told me it would be quick, so I agreed. As I was going inside, I heard music coming from inside. I realized it was a weird song playing. It had a lot of sexual lyrics. As soon as we got in the house, I saw a little girl, no more than four or five years old. My friend asked the woman, "What did you call me over here for?" The woman told us she needed help to put up her new bed. I looked at my friend and sarcastically said, "This is going to be quick, huh!" Needless to say, I agreed to help.

While working on the bed, we needed a screwdriver, but it was missing. My friend asked his friend if she had a screwdriver, and she answered in the negative. He had to go to the car and get one of his screwdrivers. As soon as he left, one of her little kids came into the room to see what we were doing. The kid couldn't have been no more than six or seven years old. He looked at me and asked, "What y'all doing in my momma room?"

I said, "We helping your mom put up her bed."

He said, "Oh..." Then he looked at me and asked these exact words. I will never forget it, and I was shaken to the core when I heard the words come out of a six-year-old's mouth. He asked, as if it was not a big deal, "Where the weed at?"

I said, looking at him dumbfounded, "Huh!?"

He said, "You heard me."

But it was as if all words had escaped me.

He asked me again, this time a little bit louder, "Where the weed at?"

This time, I shot back, "I don't know where the weed at. I don't even smoke weed."

"You're lame," came the response, leaving me stupefied again.

But I tried to feign composure. I said, "What!"

He said, "You heard me." Then, before I could muster the words (or the courage), he added, "That's why I can roll a blunt better than you."

I looked at him, and in my head, I said, "I bet you can." I didn't say it out loud. His mom was standing right there listening to the whole thing, and by the looks of it, the conversation had absolutely no effect on her, as if it were a routine conversation for her.

When my friend came back with the screwdriver, the little boy turned towards him and inquired, "Where the hoes at?"

No matter how hard I tried to process the information, I couldn't. What was more unsettling was that his mom stood there laughing. And while I was still trying to make sense of things, in came a pregnant little girl. She looked to be no more than twelve to fourteen years old. She asked the mother when she was going to cook because she was hungry. The mom told the little boy and girl to get out of the room and that she was about to cook.

The entire scene was discomforting and unsettling. I urged my friend, "Let's hurry up and get this bed fixed so we can get out of here." He seemingly shared my discomfort and agreed. We quickly finished and darted out.

On the way home, I narrated the conversation I had with the little boy. My friend, though equally stumped, said, "I can believe that because when I came back in the house after I got the screwdriver, her teenage son was talking about how he wanted a gun."

I said, "What?!"

My friend repeated, "Yes, a gun."

I asked him, "What did you tell him?"

He said he straight-up told the kid it wasn't a good idea and that he should instead think about school. And when he mentioned school, my friend told me, the teenager walked out of the house.

It is sad, entirely dismal, that we as parents think things and practices like that are okay. I'm not saying all kids are doing things like that, but a lot are for us to be comfortable. If you ask me, not even a single kid should be living a life like that. We have to make a change, but that is only possible when we start changing ourselves.

And while on the subject of change, another thing that we need to tweak is our attitude towards bullying. Before you say that no parent teaches their children to bully, I would ask you to look again because that is another thing that we ARE teaching our kids, quite open, whether we like to admit it or not. Some of us don't even know we are teaching our kids how to bully.

Like I said in the "Life" chapter, bullying is never cool. Lots of parents invoke violence, which, in many ways, leads directly to bullying. Okay, answer this: What's the first thing you tell your child if someone is picking on them?

You tell them to beat the other kid up, right? I'm sure you might say it in a different way—maybe in more discreet or less direct words, but the gist is the same, right? I have always told my kids: if another kid is messing with them, they should report directly to a teacher; if that teacher doesn't do anything, they should tell the principal or the counselor; if that doesn't work either, they should come and tell me. If the teacher, principal, or counselor doesn't take corrective action, then it's my turn to go up to the school to talk to them.

I have always strongly believed there is always a way to fix things and avoid violence. Kids should be taught not to bully, and that begins with a "no violence" rule. They should be taught not to disrespect and talk back to the elders, especially teachers. Believe it or not, most people have disrespectful kids because they are teaching them how to be disrespectful, and they don't even know it. Again! No child is *born* to disrespect someone. That misdemeanor is taught. When you get into it with the next-door neighbor or if you and your partner split up, you start teaching them that they don't have to respect the neighbors or maybe their dad's or their mother's partner. You're indirectly allowing the child and telling them that they can disrespect grown people. Some of you may disagree. To them, I ask you this: Where do you think children learn to disrespect grown people? Are you going to make excuses by saying they learned it in the streets or from other kids? There is no valid excuse that you can churn up—certainly, the blame game isn't going to work.

Kids learn from their parents. Often, when kids get a bad grade or do something wrong at school or on the school bus, and the teacher or the bus driver gets on them for acting up, your children come home and tell you their version of it. Many of you believe what they say before questioning the full truth. Then what do you do? You go to the school or the bus stop with your child and reprimand the teacher or the bus driver. Some parents even curse the teacher or the bus driver out in front of their child. Moreover, some parents even take things far by directing their children that if the teacher or the bus driver says anything else to them (which is often a corrective scolding), the children should report it directly to them. Addressing such parents, you just taught your child that he or she could disrespect anyone, and you will be there to take up for them.

My suggestion is that before you react to what your child says, look into the situation first. There are cameras at school. There are cameras on the bus. Find out what your child did before you jump into super-parent saving the day. Find out what the actual events were and why exactly the teacher or the bus driver reprimanded your child.

Some of you will skip this first part and just believe what your child tells you. That is a grave mistake. There are plenty of men and women who have been to jail for fighting the bus driver or the teacher because they jumped into action based merely on what their child told them. I urge you to analyze. Or maybe at least think over this once: Who's going to take care of your child when you're in jail?

Most of you don't believe your child would do anything wrong. The worst things I have heard people say are, "Not my child," "My child won't do that," or "I know my child." In actuality, you don't know your child. You don't know what your child is capable of. That is why I urge you to first find out what your child will and won't do before you start saying, *"Not my child."*

That's why you have to teach your child right from wrong. If someone says something about your child, especially a teacher, a principal, a bus driver, or a counselor, you have to look into it. You should never just assume, as a verdict, that your child didn't do anything wrong. Don't get me wrong. I am all for loving and defending your child. Teachers or elders are every bit as capable of being wrong. I'm not saying your child is wrong all the time. All I am saying is to take all the information, consider all perspectives, and listen to all sides of the story. That way, you will know how to approach the situation and solve it in a non-aggressive way.

Here is another thing! Parents curse each other out in front of their kids, especially if the parents are not on good terms or maybe no longer together. You should never talk bad about the other parent in front of your child—and I am saying this not for your partner's sake but for the sake of your child and his mental development.

When I was five, my mom and dad split up. In the earlier days of the split, I often heard my mom say bad things about my dad. I think she was hurt over the breakup. But after about a year, she stopped saying anything bad about my dad again entirely. I never heard my dad say anything bad about my mom. I remember that whenever my mother would launch a tirade against my father, it would affect me deeply. It would feel sad and hurt when my mom would talk bad about my dad and would ponder over things she said for hours. Imagine your child sitting alone, processing hurtful words and expletives hurled at someone he or she gravely loves. Not a pleasant thought, is it?

This helpful point I have been trying to make for the past few hundred words is inspired by my grandfather. My grandfather was a beacon for me when I was a child. He always made me smile. He would often say, "You should never put your child in the middle of a break-up." And trust me, my grandfather knew a thing or two about excellent parenting.

Today, some parents even use their kids for leverage or try to teach their kids to go against the other parent in a breakup. I cannot assert entirely how damaging that is for the children.

Women! Stop talking bad about the child's/children's father in front of your child/children. Men! Stop bad-mouthing your child's/children's mother in front of your child/children. The only thing you are doing is hurting the child/children. When the child's mom starts dating someone else, and they start getting serious in the relationship, many men will tell the child not to listen to their mother's boyfriend. When a child's dad starts dating someone else, and they start getting serious in the relationship, many women will preach to the child not to listen to their dad's girlfriend. Despite what you believe you are accomplishing, the only thing the child is learning is negativity and disrespect.

This bad-mouthing or not respecting your ex's partner soon translates to the child feeling that he or she doesn't have to respect grown people. You start something inside your child that shouldn't be there, and it is extremely difficult to stop or eliminate.

I know your love prompts you to safeguard your child, and there is nothing wrong with that. In fact, that is your job. You should always have your child's back, but you should NEVER put negativity in your child because you have issues or you don't like what the other parent is doing. That is not you protecting your child, that is you protecting your ego—and that is nothing but selfish. Keep the children out of the middle of grown people's issues.

Some parents are always trying to be their kids' friends. At the cost of sounding controversial, that is also a big mistake. Kids will always have friends. They have schools, playgrounds, and other avenues to make *friends*. What they need is parents.

You cannot appease your child in all things. Here is a fun fact—you don't have to. Of course, they are going to be mad when you tell them they can't have something. That is what kids do. The notion of being *a friend and a fun parent* shouldn't make you agree to everything. You are the parent. You should raise them to the best of your abilities and must ensure they grow up to be individuals who are able to utilize theirs.

One of the biggest mistakes is to let kids have an option. What I mean by this is: Don't let the kids tell *you* what to do. Don't let the kids tell you what they are going to do in *your house*. Don't get me wrong; I am not asking you to be THE DICTATOR of the house. What I am trying to establish is that as a parent, you need to stand strong and stay firm. Your directives towards your children should carry weight. When you tell them no, you should mean it! And the kid must know that you mean it, too. Of course, moderation is a must. You cannot always be the ORDERING or DICTATING. It is your home, not an army camp...

Another mistake a parent makes is that they start disciplining a little late. They start saying no between the ages of six and ten. That age bracket is a little too late (but that doesn't mean the opportunity has gone). A better age to start is in the toddler stage. Yup. The earliest years matter the most. Whenever I present this discussion to people, I hear a lot of parents dismissively say, "He/she is only a baby." BIG MISTAKE!!

Toddlers are already learning. They are making observations and learning to interact, act, and react. At this stage, being firm will register with the most impact. Your command will settle in your child's mind, and they will grow with it. By the time they make it to the preschool stage, they will know what you are going to put up and what will set you off. Thus, I always suggest two things: one, start your positive teaching when they are at a toddler stage, that is when they are learning. And two, always remember to be a PARENT and not your child's FRIEND.

Your child looks up to you for protection and guidance—that is what a parent does. A parent is supposed to love their child unconditionally and teach their child everything they need to know to grow up the right way. And yes, sometimes you want to buy things for your children because you love them. I am not against that. All I emphasize is that you have to maintain a balance and teach your children to earn things rather than just handing them over. The world is not going to hand them everything they want when they grow up. Why, then, do you, as a parent, hand them everything they want when and set the wrong standard for them? Is it not your job to train them for the real world?

If you want to shower gifts on your kids, do that for a reason. Like, for example, when they do something good. And simultaneously, when they act up, you should punish them with a matching strictness. It's just that simple. This will instill in them the values they need to succeed in life.

It is understandable already—When your child grows, does the right things, like work hard and honestly, they will ultimately have a great life. On the contrary, when your child grows up, spends time doing all the wrong and negative things, like maybe breaking the law, they will have a dangerous and disastrous life. If you love your child like you say you do, why would you want your child to grow up in that bad life? And before you get confused, your uncalled-for pampering and spoiling are steering them in just that dangerous direction.

Love your child, but not without teaching them the right ways of life. Yes! Sometimes teenagers do stray, mess up, and do something wrong. My suggestions are not a foolproof, hundred percent efficient method. But as parents, we have to take the right preemptive measures and hope for the best. And starting disciplining our children as toddlers, teaching them the right positive way from the get-go as a preemptive measure is our best bet. Plus, it can be said with certainty that if you use discipline in your child-rearing in the earlier stages, tweaking their behaviors in a later age will become easier and more manageable. Your teen will always correct their mistakes and do the right thing when it's all said and done if you had made them obey your commands as toddlers.

This brings us to a subtle concern. When being strict or maybe commanding, we have to be careful that we are not disrespectful towards our child. And I know that is a thin line to tread. Never belittle your child. Never talked down on them. Never curse them out and call them disparaging names. Sometimes, when angry over a child's attitude, your emotions might get the better of you. When that happens, you have to ensure that whatever comes out of your mouth is strict and reprimanding but never demeaning or disparaging.

If you are not careful about that, all you will do is hurt your child. You will make them bitter and resentful instead of corrective, mindful, and careful. Cursing, cussing, berating, abusing, and the like aren't corrective measures, they are belittling and negative scars that will only imprint on a child's impressionable mind. If you exhibit negativity towards them in any form or manner, negativity is what they will reciprocate with. You don't want to do that. If that's something you do very often—curse and cuss and use abusive language—I am sorry, but you should never have kids in your possession. I will suggest you let the kids go to a better family that will treat them like they should be treated.

Some of you readers might want to object: Donquies, aren't you the one who just said a few lines back that we should be strict and must discipline our kids?

Yes, I am who suggested that. I'm the type of parent who does not spare the rod. I got my butt torn up when I did something wrong as a kid. I do the same with my kids and give them a good round of spanking when they act out of line. My go-to method is putting my kids in the corner, but every now and then, I would give them a spanking if that becomes necessary. They don't get a spanking all the time, at least not as much as I did when I was a kid. They should be happy for that.

Most people think you should spare the rod. I don't think so. And the reason for that is simple, which many of you might object to. Hitting your kids doesn't do as much damage to their mental health and development as belittling them using words. It goes without saying that when I say "hitting your child," I obviously mean in a manageable way and not slamming your child's head against the headboard. That is abuse, and that is something I am entirely against.

Building on that, what I don't like is when someone hits their child across the head and simultaneously belittles them using disparaging words like calling them stupid. I don't approve of (or preach, for that matter) someone just picking up anything and hitting their child anywhere mindlessly and over aggressively. I almost detest it when a child makes a mistake and their parent curses them from head to toe, hurling profanities even adults shouldn't have to listen to. What I don't like is when a parent uses a disparaging word as a name to call their child out. What I mean is when parents use a curse word as a name. To me, that is a disgrace. A child should be disciplined by all means, yes, but disgraced? I don't think so. For me, such parents don't need kids, or, more correctly, don't *deserve kids*.

Let me share an experience that is hard to erase from memory. I met a woman on social media. After about two months of talking, we decided to go on a date. She wanted me to pick her up. I drove to her home. When there, I got out of the car and knocked on the door. A teen boy answered the door. The kid invited me in and told me that his mom was in the room getting ready. All of a sudden, I heard a voice coming from a back room. "Who opened my damn door!"

And without a chance for the kid to explain, the woman came out of the room and started hitting the child across the head and calling him stupid for opening the door. She saw me sitting there, but that didn't bother her one bit. She didn't even offer a mere "Hey." Next, she turned to the two other kids and started cussing them out for not cleaning up the place. The crazy part is that the house was clean. I couldn't spot one thing out of place. What a nightmare of a woman! She started calling them vile names along with some expletives—B this and MF that! Sorry for the abbreviations, but I just didn't want to spell the word out. I hope you get what I am trying to say.

Well, the woman spent five minutes just cussing the kids out. For the first few minutes, I would have been confused, but for the rest, I am sure I was heated. If you had put an egg on my head that day, it would have fried.

After her rant subsided, she turned to me and said, "How you doing?"

Well, not very well, you grumpy woman! But I didn't say that. I said I was doing okay.

She said, "Sorry about that, but these stupid kids know better."

By this time, I had had enough. I didn't care if I ruined my date. I looked at her—straight face—and said, "There is no such thing as stupid kids, and if there is such a thing as stupid kids, they must have gotten it from their parents being stupid."

She was taken aback a bit, but quickly got into her aggressive mode. She said, "So, what are you trying to say?"

I didn't say anything. I simply walked out and threw the flowers on the ground that I bought her on the way out. My only regret was not doing much for the kids. I wanted to, but I didn't know what to do at the time. I quickly rushed to my car, making sure I didn't do anything in a fit of rage due to the woman's off-handed behavior. I got in the car and started pulling off.

Almost on the road, I was about to pull off when I noticed another car pulling up. A guy from that other car waved and stopped me. I realized it was a friend of mine I hadn't seen in years. Though inside, I was still fuming, I was excited to see him. He asked me what I was doing on that side of town. I told him everything, including the foul experience I had with the lady. Then he said something that transformed all my rage into sheer sadness. He said the family I had just visited was his, and that woman was his children's mother. Those were his kids in the house, and he was coming to get them. I just couldn't believe it—the idea of having such a bitter woman as a partner and a mother to your kids!

He told me about what he and his kids' mother were going through. He said he didn't like it either, and they were going to court to get the kids in his custody.

I said (prayed), "I hope you do." And I said it all earnestness. I couldn't imagine such innocent children living with such a woman.

We exchanged phone numbers, and I even befriended him on social media later. I left and went home, hoping and praying that everything would go well for my friend and the kids. A month later, I opened up my social media page, and the first thing I saw was a photo of him with his kids. The post with the photo read: *Thank God I have my kids in my custody.*

That was awesome. I couldn't have been happier. From that day forward, every time I opened my social media page, I was always treated to a post from him sharing something positive about his kids. He did right by those kids, saving them from a mom who would launch a barrage of expletives at the slightest mishap.

It might have ended well for those kids, but I can tell you there are a lot of kids in the world who don't have the luxury of such a happy ending. There is a dire need to preach and establish measures that can be used to save kids from abusive parents. People have to stop punishing their kids just because they are kids. Abusive parents mistreat their kids not because they do wrong things, but simply because they are kids and cannot do much to save themselves. That is where we, as a society, have to act and intervene.

Kids shouldn't be treated badly. They shouldn't be used as avenues to make money; they are not paychecks. There are people out there who are embroiled in legal battles, holding young ones in their custody just because these kids bring low-income and welfare benefits and favors like food stamps in the form of child support. If you are one of such people, you are dead wrong.

There are people out in our society who don't give a penny's worth of damn care about the kids. Pardon my language, but such people deserve reprimand. There can be no sensible or pardonable reason to abuse kids who have no share in the blame. These people only care about the income that the kids bring. More often than not, these people will buy themselves new clothes and shoes and eat real good with the money they get as child support while their children roam around in raggedy clothes with shoes full of holes and hungry. Tell me, how is that right by any measure of ethics or morals?

If someone treats a kid like that, they are nothing but selfish people, and we as a society should have no qualms about punishing them or holding them accountable. Kids are God's little blessings. We should treat them better than what we have been doing in modern times.

If you are one of those people who were beaten, starved, and talked down to by your parents as a kid, why are *you doing it to your kids?* How is that fair? You know you didn't like it back when your parents did all that? Why would you think your kids would like it? How does that even work? If you lived through something so foul, shouldn't you do the exact opposite—end that vicious cycle?

I'm not saying I'm perfect at raising kids because I'm not. I'm not saying I know everything about raising kids because I don't. But I can still say that kids shouldn't be treated badly because calling out a parent abusing their children because they had a similar, bleak past doesn't require me to have any kind of perfection or knowledge—that is basic common sense.

Adding to an already troubled situation, some people let rife with their ex-partners mess up their parenting and their relationship with their children. If you and the other parent are not together anymore and you get on with someone new, you should never let that new person come in between you and your kids, in any form or manner. That is a mistake as big as it gets.

You should never let your new partner keep you from your kids. More importantly, you should never allow your new partner to ill-treat or misbehave with your kids. If you are seeking a new relationship, both of you must always treat each other's kids with love and respect. And it works on reciprocity. If your new partner has kids, you should treat their kids like you treat your kids, and they should treat your kids like they treat their kids.

In fact, you can use this situation to gauge your new potential partner. You can observe how they treat kids they have from past relationships. For example, if they neglect their own kids or when they do see their kids, they treat them badly, you shouldn't be with them in the first place. That should be a red flag—no question asked.

Trust me, I've been there. I was with a woman who didn't want me to get my kids. Needless to say, I didn't listen to her. But that was a bit of a dangerous decision. Every time I went to work, she treated my kids badly. I treated her kids with love and respect— the thought of ill-treating them not even once crossing my mind because they were another man's kids—but she treated my kids like trash. I'm not going to lie, I got a little lousy there. She got away with it for quite a long while—three years, to be exact. Three years of my children being bullied and abused.

But I woke up—a little late, but I did. I realized that this is not the relationship for me, but, more importantly, not for my kids. And from that day forward, I decided that I would not let another woman—UNDER ANY CIRCUMSTANCE, NO MATTER HOW LONELY I MIGHT BE FEELING—treat my kids like trash. I decided I would not put up with it, and since I have seen my kids suffer, I am pressing that you shouldn't either. No matter if you are a man or a woman. NEVER LET SOMEONE TREAT YOUR KIDS LIKE THEY DON'T MATTER. You'll only end up hurting your kids.

I am so sure about this because I happen to have been on the other side too—The child side. I still remember being ill-treated by a foul partner my dad had. I loved my dad dearly—hands down, a great father—but the woman he chose to be with treated us kids horribly. She treated us like we had wronged her somehow, something none of us could figure what.

Back when I was a kid, we were poor with next to no food to eat. My grandfather did what he could to keep food on the table, but he couldn't do it all the time. My dad lived nearby; a few minutes' walk, tops. We used to walk up the street to visit him, which wasn't very often because of the partner he was with. She would always treat us kids badly every chance she got. In fact, she treated us like crap and got away with it for many years.

On this one particular day, when I was nine, I walked up the street to see my dad. I was really hungry—Hadn't eaten for about two days. I was looking for hooks to go fishing down to the river and wondered if Dad. When I got to my dad's house, I smelled food. Needless to say, my two-day-hungry stomach rumbled. I observed that Dad was gone, but my stepmother was there warming some food she had cooked the night before.

I knocked on the door and out came my grumpy stepmother to the door. She looked at me and asked what I wanted.

I, trying not to say anything to incur her wrath, said, "I was wondering if my dad had any hooks so I can go fishing."

"No," came the reply, followed by her characteristic foul-mouthed insult, "Tell your momma to buy you some hooks." With that, she started laughing in my face. But I was used to her. Plus, I was really hungry, and I could smell food, so I made do with her snide attitude. I asked her if I could get something to eat until I found some hooks to go fishing with. To my astonishment, she said, "Come in."

I went into the house, happily thinking I was going to get something to eat. She went to the kitchen, pulled out all the food she had cooked the night before, looked at me, and asked, "So you want some of this?"

"Yes, ma'am."

You might be thinking she had a change of heart. That is what I thought too. We both are wrong. What she did is abhorrent, to say the least. She looked at me, put all the food in one big bowl, and then took that bowl out the back door and threw all the food to the dog she had in the backyard. And if that wasn't enough, she turned, looked me dead in the eyes, and told me to tell my momma to feed me. She just laughed in my face. I didn't say anything—just walked out the door and walked home feeling more insulted than hungry.

Later that day, my dad came to our house to see us. I pulled him to the side and asked if he had any hooks so I could go fishing. He told me he *did have* some. 'What evil woman...' That's what you are thinking, right? Well, it was what it was. Me and Dad walked back up to his house. On the way, I told him I was famished. He assured me he would have some food at the house that he could give me.

My stepmom was sitting on the couch when we got there. My dad made a beeline for the refrigerator. When he looked in, he saw that all the food was gone. He asked my stepmom about it, to which she lied that the food had spoiled, so she threw it out. My dad looked at me, a mix of angry and sad, I could tell. I think he knew she was lying. Immediately, to avoid another one of her snide rants, he took me outside to his shed and handed me the hooks. Then he said, "Come with me." I am sure he would have been heartbroken when I told him that I was hungry as hell and he couldn't give me anything.

He grabbed me by the hand and led me directly to the store to buy some food for us. Not just that, he dropped the food off at our house, and then me and him went fishing. And that was a great day of fishing. We caught some decent fish. But it wasn't great because of that. My dad bought food; we had a great time together. The fish we caught, my dad cleaned them and gave them to me. Like I said already, hands down, a great father, just caught up in a relationship with a very wrong person who just couldn't stand his kids.

The best thing about it all, despite everything that my stepmom did, we didn't HATE her. As kids, we were cool about it because we had come to terms with what she was. My dad or grandfather never taught us to HATE anyone. I believe that is one of the best things they did. When we grew up, we didn't hold a single misdemeanor against her. We saw no point in that. After my dad died, she ended up living terribly. She lost her two legs and an arm to diabetes, and we couldn't even think of letting her be by herself in such a dire condition. Me and my family took her in as family, and we helped her in her last days. There is no merit to being vindictive I believe. I can say with absolute certainty that letting go is far more peaceful than revenge. In her last days, we did as best as we could. We fed her, my mom helped her in the restroom, and none of us treated her badly. We did what we could to do right by her. But the lesson out of all of this is that just because you are with someone doesn't mean you can treat their kids badly. Life can turn around, and trust me, it more often does. I think I have driven the point home, so let's hop on another concern—a rather grave one. Nowadays, if your child is acting up—throwing a tantrum, not listening, etc.—you might run them to the doctor, and they will want to push a pill down your child's throat. They will even assure you that your child will be good once the pill takes effect. No disrespect to our professionals, but no, they will not be good. Maybe, for the time being, they might display positive symptoms, but the moment the pill wears off, the problem will return. The child will go right back to acting out and being unruly.

I understand we want the best for our kids, and thus, listen to a doctor who apparently has specialized in the field and is well educated on the subject. When such an accomplished professional says our kids need the (ADHD) medication, we readily believe them. Now, again, no disrespect or our doctor friends—I am not saying that they are always wrong—but not every child needs that medication. At least not in the number that we see and hear today.

Here is what I feel. I feel there is a whole different ball game at play here—One with sinister ambitions. I feel that the various pills being administered to our kids under the pretext of different mental health concerns are to get them used to drugs. And I have good grounds to come to such an incriminating and controversial conclusion. Think about it. What do most drug addicts tell you? What is the main reason drug addicts take drugs? Ask any and they will tell you, they take drugs to escape reality—to forget about their problems, but what happens when the drug wears off? The problem persists. Doesn't that sound like what they are doing to our kids?

Drugging them up for the moment to get rid of the problem, only for it to reappear once the pills flush out of the child's system.

They tell us parents to throw away the belt, and counsel us that the pills will do the job the belt does without the "violence." In reality, the pills are way more harmful than good. Why and how? I'm glad you asked! That's because, even though the pills give you seemingly a few hours of quiet time and a disciplined child, in reality, they are damaging your kid's brain—almost irreparably, might I add. To substantiate my claim, consider and notice the side effects of the pills—insomnia, delayed growth, loss of appetite, ticks, moods, and irritability. These aren't normal symptoms EVERY CHILD HAS. Also, you will notice that when the pill wears off, the child gets irritable, in some cases even more than they used to be before. Their attitude gets worse.

That doesn't add up to me, and the only conclusion I can draw is that giving kids pills doesn't solve a problem; it only worsens it. What these pills do is they subside the problem for the moment, but they don't fix or solve the actual problem permanently. They make your kid a shoo-in to be an extra on the show The Walking Dead— They turn kids into zombies. What adds to my skepticism around the use of the pills is how they are marketed as a long-term solution. They say that with these pills, your child will calm down as they get older. That doesn't make any sense. Your child calms down anyway as they get older—pills or no pills. That is just how a human being naturally is. When they are babies, they sleep a lot. When they are toddlers and kids, they like being physically active, and they play a lot. In middle school, they start getting a little rowdy. But by the end of high school, your child starts having a better handle on their emotions and subsequently calms down. That's it. That's the balance of nature. Not to sound old, but back in my day, parents fixed everything with two very important and effective things—love and belts. These two fixed most problems.

Now, don't misinterpret me. In this book, I'm not preaching to just mindlessly and aggressively start spanking your kids whenever you want to discipline them in one thing or the other or when they act up. If it's not your thing, don't do it. I know not all parents are okay with spanking their children. For such parents, love can be a go-to tool. As parents, you do need to show children a lot of love (carefully, maybe—maybe not too much, but…). With love, you can build a strong foundation of discipline and manners that can take care of attitude problems on its own. You can teach them morals and values from the very beginning, counseling them with love and care. You can use the time they spend with you as an opportunity to teach them many things about good behavior. You can let them play outside and even join them and use that interaction to teach them important lessons. If your child loves to play outside (as most children naturally do), you can use that as a bargaining chip to make them listen to you and act in a certain way you want them to.

I know some (many) of you may disagree, but spankings did work back in the day. Think about this: How many kids were acting up and being unruly and obnoxious (even with adults) back then, compared to today?

Of course, there were kids being rowdy back in the day, too. But I think it can be said as a fact that it was nothing like it is today. We didn't need pills; we had parents who knew when to love us unconditionally and when to use the belt.

In 1999, two teenagers shot up a school. I'm not going to go into detail about it because we would stray from the point. Just hear me out. The two teenagers were diagnosed by multiple psychiatrists. They examined the case thoroughly, and all came to the same conclusion: one of the teenage boys had depression and suicidal problems, and the other was psychotic. Those are some very serious problems in a teen. What if those teenagers were taking medicine for their problems? Would the medication have fixed them and made them better, or would the medication have been just a temporary fix? Something to think about because it can be argued, based on observation, that as soon as the medication would have worn off, the problems would have returned, and the two teens might have resorted to their aggressive ways. Medications wouldn't have fixed the problem, but the doctors talked like they would. I'm not going to sit here and make excuses for those teenage boys. I'm not going to say what their parents should have done or not done, for that matter—I never am judgmental or assume the moral high ground to tell what a parent should or should not do in their child-rearing. I believe all parents care for their children. What I am saying is this— To teach your children manners and save them from behavioral issues, take the time out to learn and know your child instead of letting them rely on medication for you.

Let's take a detour for a moment and allow me to give you a little history lesson. In 1944, Ritalin was made in the labs and was being experimented on; 10 years later, in 1954, it started being sold. It started out as a medicine for fatigue and depression. It was the ultimate ADD medicine. Then came a second stage for this medicine's purported and proposed effectiveness, around 1968. It started being used as a medicine for a mental disorder. Then came the third stage of this medicine in 1980. This time, the medicine was paraded as a cure for hyperkinetic behavior in kids. In 1987, they changed the name of the disorder to ADHD, and in 1990, all of a sudden, poof! Out of the blue, over 600,000 kids needed ADHD medicine. Do you see the pattern? It almost seems that every year, the medicine is upgrading in its supposed effectiveness, and so is its popularity. Every year, more and more kids have started to need the medicine, and every year, the drug corporations are getting richer and richer. Right now, 62% of kids between the ages of 2–17 are on some kind of (ADHD) medication. Let that sink in. A 2-year-old toddler is taking a medicine that is constantly changing in its uses and effects. Does anyone besides me see something wrong with that? Another important question I ask is: Why exactly is there a need to calm down a two-year-old in the first place? A 2-year-old is *supposed to be* hyper. That is just how a normal kid is.

They say spanking your kids is what messes with them mentally when they get older. I don't think so. Everyone I know who has gotten a spanking is as sane as it can get. No one is mentally messed up at all. In fact, they look back to those times as fond memories, as all they do is sit and laugh about the things they did that got their butts torn up.

I know hundreds of people my age and older who never once even considered any heinous idea, such as shooting up a school or a courthouse or a church or a store, just because they got a spanking as a kid. In fact, they will surely claim not to have any such wild ideas because of *that very spanking* they got as a kid.

Let me make something very clear. There is a difference between spanking and beating. Some people confuse the two. A spanking is a few licks across the behind. Even though some people don't agree with that, and that's okay, but I do. What I don't agree with is beating a child. Beating comprises violence, abuse, and ridicule and includes punching, black eyes, broken bones, burns, or bruises all over the body, which is an overkill and entirely uncalled for in the job of child-rearing and disciplining. That is something I never agreed to and will never agree to. No child deserves that. I have talked about it once in this book, but I think this message needs repeating.

Such beatings can leave mental scars on children. And in child-rearing and disciplining, mental health is far more crucial than physical health simply because it has more lasting impacts on a child. Know the difference between spanking and beatings, and you will have a useful tool at your hand that can save your children from the horrors of medicine.

Don't get me wrong. I'm not saying there aren't *any instances* where a kid might actually require medicines. I am well aware that there are worst-case, extreme scenarios where a child's mental health is at *grave risk,* one where a kid might need medicinal assistance to function properly. But those are rare cases—extremes. To conclude that more than half of our kids need them is a ridiculous claim. If I were to estimate, maybe only 1 or 2% of our kids might need help and medical aid. That's it. And that's a big maybe. 62% of kids sounds to me like someone is trying to get rich. To me, that's a hard pill to swallow. In fact, it is as if someone is shoving this pill down our throats, and we are acting oblivious—Food for thought!!

Kids are naturally hyper. That's all there is to it. It has been that way since the beginning of time. Kids burn off energy as fast as they get it. Today, kids don't seem to be burning off energy like they are supposed to, like we used to back when we were kids. They are mostly glued to their electronic devices, plopped on a couch or a bed or a sofa, whiling away their time and mental resources on social media. They are sitting in one spot for hours. That doesn't burn the energy they are supposed to. A consequence of this pent-up energy can be seen in the classrooms. If you observe, kids today are unable to sit still in class. They are so used to using electronic devices at home, and when they don't have them at school, they can be seen being fidgety, using all that pent-up energy in their classrooms.

Nowadays, it is very common to see two and three-year-old kids being pushed in a stroller with a device in their hands. They know nothing about playing outside, but they know almost everything about social media and YouTube. Since kids are not burning energy in the amounts they should and instead are storing it up, the energy often comes out at the wrong time, like in class at school or church or at the doctor's office. And yes, not all kids are affected, but an alarming number of them are.

Back in the day, or should I say *"normally,"* kids used to wake up, eat breakfast, and dash to the bus stop. Waiting for the bus, they would play around some dumb but fun game, burning some good calories of energy. Then they would go to school, go to PE, and burn some more. After school, they would return home, complete their homework, and then go outside to play again, or they would horseplay with their siblings. And if this wasn't enough, they would come home again, eat dinner, play around the house some more, do chores in the house (which was yet another activity to burn energy), eat and play some more around for a little while, and then finally go to bed. The next day, they would do it all over again. It can be clearly seen that each activity they engaged in was physical, allowing them to burn the energy kids naturally have.

The vacations were a whole different story. If it were a holiday, spring break, or summer vacation, kids would want nothing more than to play outside and wreak all kinds of havoc—*ALL THE WHILE BURNING ENERGY* they are gifted with by nature itself.

Sadly, kids are not seen doing any such thing anymore. We have gotten lazy as a society. And I blame the parents for it. Medicine is raising our kids because *WE PARENTS* have gotten too lazy to do it for ourselves. Sounds harsh, but it's true. We have to reconsider our methods. We have to start asking the right questions. Questions like: Is that what we really want?

Today, we come up with a fancy, hush-hush way (courtesy of the money-centric corporations) of saying kids are too hyper and then, without any consideration for nature's way, we give them medicine to chomp and gulp. And we don't just stop there. Even the other consequences they have due to inactivity, we try to fix with medicines or by substituting routines that were far more beneficial for them with something that is damaging in the long run. For example, we say the kids are getting obese, and we have started to change the food at school.

The only reason they're too hyper or obese is that we are not letting them play. School food has gotten so nasty—in flavor and nutrition alike. Most kids throw away a lot of it and turn to the vending machines. Which, needless to say, is worse: Candy, cakes, sodas, and chips for lunch. Change the menu to something they are not going to eat, and give them access to vending machines out there so they can eat something unhealthier? It doesn't make any sense to me. And the solution for me is rather simpler and safer—let the kids go outside to play. They play outside, they burn fat, and they burn energy—nature takes its course. Easy as can be…

Here is the kicker: The key to your kids' happiness—something we are desperately looking for in our modern experimental ways—is love. That's it! All this brouhaha around disciplining kids and keeping them healthy and all, just boils down to one thing—Love.

Love them enough to teach them right from wrong. Love them enough to teach them morals and values. Love them enough to not hurt them or not let them hurt themselves in any kind of way. Love your child enough to let them be a child. Love is what amplifies the effect of all that you might do for your children. And most importantly, love your children without the world and money-hungry corporations telling you how. They are your kids, and no one can know what is best for them better than you—at least not these corporations.

Things in this world need a change. PARENTING needs a change. Kids are growing up way too fast. Or should we say, being forced to grow up way too fast? They are not being allowed to be fun-loving, adventure-seeking, naughty, creative kids—all that which nature wants them to be—and thus, their emotional growth is taking a hit.

Kids' suicide rate is on the rise every year. We put too much pressure on kids nowadays. What is adding to this is another grave problem that modern-day parents have to be vigilant about. Parents today are almost forcing (unintentionally and unknowingly) their children to mature faster than they should. We have to fix our ways not only by changing *their* habits or routines but also by how Moreover, if you believe in yourself, whether someone else does or does not becomes pointless., as parents, are interacting with them too. Kids shouldn't have to worry about adult things. In modern days, parents are letting children intervene in their business instead of letting them focus on being kids. Kids should never worry about where their next meal is coming from. Kids should not have to worry about anything adults worry about. But I often see parents discussing such things not just around kids, but *with* the kids. It seems like we have entirely misinterpreted the notion of *"Talk to your kids."* Talking to your kids is healthy, and doing it on a daily basis is excellent. But that conversation is for them to share *their* problems with you, not the other way around.

That is why I can't emphasize enough—LOVE YOUR CHILDREN. And one part of loving them is not letting them take the brunt of life. There is a time for that.

Hug your child and tell them you love them every chance you get. Every day, if that is possible. Nothing reinforces and reaffirms self-worth in children more than when they hear their parents telling them they are loved and valued. And in the world we are living in today, as God is my witness, children need that reaffirmation more than we ever did.

When having a conversation with them, listen carefully and intently. Listen with undivided attention and keep your ears peeled. Read between the lines if that is required, and find out if there is anything in their life that is troubling them that might need a little parental/adult intervention. As a parent, you must be ready to fix every such problem. When you pick up on such a problem, be there for your child and let them know everything will be alright. Children today are faced with an assortment of self-worth and self-image challenges. For many, it is difficult to navigate through them, which has all kinds of adverse effects on their vulnerable, innocent minds. Consequence? Children are developing complexes, which, if worsened, can lead them to subscribe to self-inflicting practices or suicidal thoughts and actions. No kid in the world should ever think about suicide. Always protect your kid, even if you have to protect them from themselves. *KIDS DON'T NEED YOU TO BE THEIR FRIEND!!!* Kids need a parent. A friendly parent? Of course, that can work, but the role of *parent* and not *friend* should always take precedence. Friends come and go, but a parent's title and their job never change. As my grandfather used to say, *"Right, don't wrong nobody!"* and I believe his golden words don't have any more relevance than for our role as parents.

I know full well that becoming a parent can be difficult. We have to deal with young, impressionable minds that can be capricious and attracted to the most dangerous things; we cannot talk them out of them with mere logic because they are only making decisions emotionally. That is what real parenting is all about, and that is where love comes in handy.

Again! I am not saying to put a damper on every adventurous thing they do or want to explore. Remember, we need to let our kids be kids. We cannot be extra and over-cautious and force them to be adults too early. We just have to be vigilant with the many negative things in the world that can have lasting effects. We have to ensure that they just don't engage in anything that might haunt them later and impede their chances of success in life. And we have to be careful with how we teach them about such things without them misinterpreting our intentions and throwing a fit.

Take tattoos and extra piercings, for instance. It is common knowledge that in the professional world, tatted people are seen through a lens of skepticism. Don't get me wrong. I'm not against tattoos and extra piercings. But—whether we like it or not—there is a stigma around them with consequences; we as parents cannot turn a blind eye to it.

Our kids see things and want to imitate them. The moment children turn 18 these days, the first thing they want to do is get tattoos and extra piercings. Which is cool, but here is the problem. If they get tattoos and extra piercings—neck, face, hands—they can no longer get accepted in respected professions such as the military. The corporate business world wouldn't want to hire them. That makes it really hard for them to get a good job. A simple reason for that reluctance is that tattoos and piercings are commonly endorsed by people like thugs, cults, gangsters, etc.—people who don't have the most trustworthy reputation—people who are not considered someone who makes good life decisions. Now, I am not saying that people with piercings and tattoos are just that. Some might like it as a style preference; others might be trying to undo the wrong decisions of the past and wanting to turn their lives around. But these things sure do cast the wrong impression, which is not favored in the professional world. It is a sad fact, but a fact nonetheless. And yes, the opinion around the stigma is changing (thank God for that), but that still is a long haul.

We need to educate our children on the world's expectations of them. We have to teach them that even though we cannot let the world dictate our every action, there will be instances where we will have to conform to its ways. Thus, when they grow up, they will know which way to go and which battles to pick. Again, and I cannot stress this enough: *I'M NOT AGAINST TATTOOS AND EXTRA PIERCINGS*, but the world is not as accepting as I am. I'm not saying not to get tattoos or extra piercings. All I'm saying is to be mindful of what you want your future to be. Parents have to suggest precautious measures for their children. They have to guide them because they are experienced with the ways of the world than the young children.

Many of you might say, "Come on, D, there are many successful people out there with ink!" Agreed—many famous athletes have tattoos and extra piercings, and entertainers have tattoos and extra piercings. But here is the reply to that: Those people have already made it. And once people become famous or successful, the world becomes accepting and receptive to their ways. It is an unfair bias (some might even say hypocritical), but it is what it is.

Our children haven't yet made it big. Our children have a long way to go. They can get all the piercings and tattoos after they make it to a successful level, and they are happy with their lives. But until that happens, it is only wise to conform a little so they can move about in the world without having to face hurdles—hurdles that can be avoided just with a few smart preemptive measures.

Most of what I have discussed and shared is roughly focused on what *parents should do*. I would now change the conversation a little and share what parents should make the *kids do*. A detour, yes, but bear with me. I firmly believe that one of the *tasks/duties* (in fact, I am going to go on a limb and call it an *obligation*—almost religious) of parenting is to strengthen your child's mind like a fortress and make them leaders and owners, not followers or mere side characters in someone's stories. Hear me out.

I taught my son to own the football, not run the football. I taught my daughter to own the basketball, not dribble and shoot the basketball. Get that? In other, much simpler words, I taught my children to associate value with themselves and not just merely add value to something that can be taken away. Consider this. If a football team wins the Super Bowl and they give the game ball to the star of the team, the owner of that football team can just swoosh into the locker room and rob the game ball away. What is the player going to do? Nothing. Why? Because he can't do anything. He doesn't own the team, the owner does. The company of that football

149

team bought the footballs, so in actuality, all that player did was get the winning touchdown with that football. That doesn't mean he owns it. The owner of the football team owns that football, so the owner gets to do whatever he or she wants with the winning game ball. I hope I have driven the point home.

Don't teach your child to play the game. Teach them to own the team and be in a position where the main reward cannot be stripped away. Be the man or the woman of your family, and teach your kids to aim for success that lasts and is valued more than small-time rewards and gifts.

Now, let's change the conversation again. Trust me, this discussion can be considered *the most integral part* of this whole book. You might have guessed it. This part of the conversation is about Family.

Family is very important.

I could have said this thing in a thousand different ways—fancy ways—but this simple statement holds all the value and emphasis I want to deliver. In fact, this isn't merely a statement based on opinion, I consider it to be a fact. A valuable fact, and I can't stress that enough.

To lead a successful and happy life, you should always love your family. Not just love them, but tell them that you do, any opportunity you get. And I say this because the benefits of such expression are countless and wholesome, more than we can imagine. Every time I talk to any of my family, I tell them that I love them. Not just to my grandkids or kids, but my siblings, uncles, aunties, and cousins, every time I see them or hear from them.

Having a loving family, one can sail through the bleakest of days and the most difficult of times—in every phase of life, at any stage. And for that reason alone, I think, along with a generous expression of love, forgiveness should be a feature of your relationship with all your loved ones. I believe there should be no grudge bigger than your family.

Me and my family were dirt poor growing up, but we had each other, and trust me, that helped a great deal. My family didn't bicker much. We mostly laughed and played games with each other; thus, not having many toys or resources for entertainment didn't quite bother us. Now, I am not saying that we didn't have wishes because that would be wrong. Like all kids, we wanted fancy things, too, but having each other made it easy, as we managed to frolic around with each other a great deal.

Before everyone moved out, me and my family worked for a guy who owned a barn. And since it was us siblings together, it was work and play for us. Every time we baled hay for him, we played in his barn. We would climb all over and throw the hay around, playing hide and seek. We would spend countless hours having the best time of our lives. There was no Internet, no social media. But it was the best time. We would enjoy actually doing things instead of being glued to screens like zombies. It was just us. We enjoyed being with each other. In the fall and winter, after we were done with the chores, we used to go out in the field located in the back of our house and build ourselves little huts out of the cluster of dead sticks we could find in the field. I would dash from one hut to another hut. Oh, what fine memories. It was all so much fun.

In the spring, since we couldn't afford to buy kites, we made our own out of sticks, old hay bale string, and old, used plastic that we found. Those kites were the best, and no, I am not exaggerating. In the summer, after our chores were done. We would go out swimming in the river as a family.

What I want you to observe here is that all of the fun we had, we had with no money and nothing expensive. Making huts with dead sticks, playing where we worked, making kites out of discarded plastic, these things didn't cost a dime. We had each other, and we had to be creative and inventive with what little we had. That's resourcefulness if you ask me. And I think we all can agree that it is one of the most valuable traits to have in life. Can we say our kids are equipped with that? I think we all know the answer to that.

Mind you. It is not about being a thrifter who doesn't want to spend money. In fact, it has nothing to do with money. It is all about enjoying what life gives you, being grateful for what you have, being inventive, and valuing family and love. If I take a look at my life today, I have all the money I need. I am sufficiently blessed, but what is it that I cherish the most, far more than the money? I can say, hands on heart, it is the love in our hearts and all the heart-warming memories.

I also stress this part enough because I actually and literally know the real value of having family around in difficult times. That is because I am the youngest of the ten. As my siblings and I got older, they moved out one by one; we stayed close to each other, but it wasn't like the bygone days, as they would be busy with their lives mostly. I was the last to move, and when all of them were gone, I spent plenty of lonely days by myself as a kid. For a while, it was just me, my mom, and my grandfather. That, too, happened on a few remote days. My mom worked a lot, so she was almost never there. She didn't have a car, so she pretty much lived in town, and it was just me and my grandfather mostly. It was this alone time when I felt the lack of resources the most overpowering. It taught me the value of having people in life and how valuable family is.

Back then, I had to spend a lot of lonely holidays, and I used to wish I had more money so I could just visit my siblings or have them over. On some holidays, when the whole family came out to my grandfather's house, I would make the most of them. Those vacations would be the most awesome ones I would have. So great that I still cherish memories in the present day.

And it wasn't just me who missed the family and our time spent together. My siblings, too, knew the value of our time together and missed it greatly. In fact, we would try to come up with ways we could come together at any opportunity we got. One such plan was that we started playing softball as a family on the weekend. And I cannot even count the many memories I have from that time. Moreover, it is not just about the emotional advantages. It is the wholesome effect it had on me and my siblings and the utility of relationships in dire times that make me want to emphasize the worth of family more and more.

So, what I want you to take from my trip down memory lane is this: Always spend time with your family. You never know when something might happen and when life takes you away from one another. You might not even get a chance to tell them how you feel or spend the time you want to spend with them. At the end of the day, family is all you have that you can count on.

Spend time with your family before it is too late. I know, sometimes family makes you mad. They get on your nerves and drive you crazy, but they are still family. What family doesn't get mad at each other? If you ask me, is it even a sibling that doesn't make you want to pull your hair out?

The 5Ls

Sometimes, one of your family members might make you want to wring their neck, and sometimes it would be the other way round, but you don't because you love your family and they love you. There might even be times when you may not always see eye to eye, but family should always stick together because today, tomorrow, a month after, or maybe even years after, there will come a time when you will find that the only ones who genuinely care about you are family. Life will show it to you, no matter how much you might not want to agree with me right now.

I remember one day, my oldest sister was out with my mom. I was around seven years old, and most of the family was still living at home at the time—three of my sisters had moved out, but the other two were at the house that day. They didn't have a car. We lived way out in the country, so it was hard to get around. My mom and my sister were out handling some business and had to go to an appointment while doing multiple other things in between. Since it was pointless, tiring, and costly to get home in between these errands, they just stayed gone until everything was done. Buses didn't come to the country area where we lived.

I was lying in my sister's bed. My other sister had fixed some food that day. I remember it because we didn't have food often, and when we did get food, it was memorable. As I was lying in her bed, I dozed off to sleep. When I woke up and tried to move about, I felt I was frozen. I tried fidgeting a limb here and there, but couldn't. I realized I couldn't move at all. All my limbs were limp. I felt real weak and immobile. Inwardly, panic was taking over. I didn't know what was going on with me. I can say the only thing that could be classified as a gadget or a tool we had was a phone. My grandfather kept a phone on because we lived too far out not to have a phone, and that day, he was right.

I could see and hear things, but my limbs wouldn't budge. I heard my sister call everyone to eat. I wanted to get up and get going, but my feet just won't listen. I guess she noticed I didn't come. She called out again, this time only to me. I decided I must shout a reply, but I discovered I couldn't talk loud either—my voice was weak and inaudible; the person next to me wouldn't have heard it. Everyone started looking for me. I could hear them calling for me, but I couldn't hint at my presence in any way. Then I heard the phone rang. My sister answered it. It was my mom calling and checking up on us. I heard her tell my mom that they couldn't find me.

Then, after some searching in and around the house, my other sister came into the room where I lay plopped. She is the youngest daughter. When she saw me awake, she asked, visibly annoyed, "Don't you hear us calling you?"

I replied, or should I say, tried to reply, "I can't move." A whisper would have been louder than my voice.

She irritably asked again, "What? I can't hear you."

I said it again, this time loud enough to be heard, "I can't move."

Quickly, she went and got my brother. He came rushing to the room and asked me what was wrong. I told him what I had told my sister: *I COULDN'T MOVE*. He ran to the room where my sister was already talking to my mother and told her to tell Mom that something was wrong with me and that I was unable to move and could barely talk. My sister couldn't process the information quickly enough and just handed him the phone. He told my mom I was conscious but couldn't move my limbs or anything else, for that matter.

Since we were way out in the country, the ambulance would have taken eons to reach me. My mom said she was going to try and find a ride, and she told my brother to call my dad. When he called my dad, he was interrupted by my stepmom, who did her best to stop my dad from coming over. She didn't want him to take me to the hospital. He told my brother to bring me outside. But I knew my dad wouldn't have listened to her in an emergency. He was on his way. My brother hung up the phone, came running to the room, and picked me up.

It was chaos all around. My body was limp. He took me to the living room. Meanwhile, my mom called back, asking all kinds of questions about the progress to take me to a hospital. My sister told her that Daddy was coming to get me. My mom gave her instructions to pick her up on the way, giving her all the details of where they could locate her. In no time, my dad pulled up. My brother was about to carry me outside to the van when Dad slammed in, pushing the door and making a beeline towards a limp me in my brother's arms. My brother instantly handed me over to him while my sister filled my dad in about where to pick up Mom from. My dad took me to the van, drove at a blazing speed, and reached where my mom was supposed to be. She was already standing on the side of the road. Worry and panic were evident on her face when she got into the van. Of what little I remember of the ordeal, my dad was driving really fast, and I don't think he heeded any of the signals that might have come our way. I must have blacked out because the only other thing I remember is my dad running with me into the hospital, panting and gasping.

When I woke up, I had an IV in my arm. My mom, dad, and sister were standing over me. While the situation seemed under control and all, I could read from their faces that they were worried witless. The doctor had revealed that I was dehydrated and suffering from malnutrition. Now that I've been a father myself, I can imagine what my dad might have been feeling. Nothing can be more heart-wrenching and vexing for a father to hear that his children are not well-fed.

I'd rather take a detour before I go on a monologue about a father's feelings. I don't think one book can cover that. Anyhow, going back to the hospital, I really don't know how long I was in there for, but I was surely happy that I was leaving. And so was my family. When my dad brought me home, I was surprised to see the whole family there waiting on me. I could tell that they were genuinely happy to see me with the way they hugged and kissed me, and inquired about everything.

And that is what the gist of my discussion is—that family is something one can depend on in the most dire of times. The way everyone left everything just to visit me, the way they all stuck by my side, I will never forget that. They all seemed ready to do whatever they could have done to save me, I was sure. Now remember, this is a family of people who barely had any kind of luxury at their disposal. But I can bet a grand that if I had asked for a three-course meal at the time, they all would have pitched in every penny and served me a platter of food I couldn't have finished in a month! That is what taught me that families are invaluable. They stand together no matter what. At least, that is what they are supposed to do—mine, at least, did just that, and I can't thank them enough for that.

Without family, where would you be? It is a question you all must ask. You will discover that you are not as thankful to them as you are supposed to be. I, for one, really don't know where I would be without my family. What makes families more precious is that every moment spent with them turns into a memory that acts as a healing balm for the blue days in life. I know some memories are bad, with a bad aftertaste, but given that most of them are sweet and warm enough to put a smile on your face even on the bleakest days, I will take the deal.

I have countless memories that I cherish to date. Like this one memory I have about me and my mom. Now, I will give a heads-up here: Only the older generation might relate to this memory, but I am quite confident that it can warm the hearts of even the younger ones reading this. So here it goes—I was around four years old. Mom had to go to the bank—she wanted to take some kind of loan, I am not sure for what. I joined her, too. Upon arrival, I saw that the bank had these rotating doors. Back in the day, they were a novel and exciting luxury—at least for a four-year-old. It was the first time I ever saw something like that. My mom walked straight into the bank. Needless to say, I didn't.

I just went round and round through the door. I would hop into one of the wing compartments every time someone came into the bank. I was loving it. I was having the time of my life with that rotating door. About fifteen minutes later, Mom called me over to her. She was waiting to talk to someone. I barely sat for a moment when I had an urge to use the restroom. I asked permission from my mom, and she told me to make it quick. I got in there and tried entering one of the stalls. I tried opening the stall door to the toilet, but it wouldn't open. Upon inspection, I realized that it was one of those fancy doors with a coin lock and that I would need a dime to get inside the stall. I went and told my mom. She didn't have a dime. She asked if I could hold it. I couldn't and told her just that with all the urgency I could muster. I HAD TO GO BAD.

She looked around, bent over towards me, and then whispered, "Climb under the stall door."

I looked at her, a bit confused, a bit excited, and asked, "Are you sure?"

"Yes, I'm sure," came the reply.

Like a soldier, I said, "Yes, ma'am!" and marched over to the restroom. When I saw a clear window, I started climbing under the door. As I was busy with the task, another kid came in and started doing the same thing I was doing. Apparently, he, too, had to go to the restroom—BAD!

After I was done, I went back to my mom and sat in her lap. A little while later, the man my mom was waiting for called her to the cubicle. I asked my mom if I could go to the rotating door again. Before she could say anything, the guy at the bank gave me a "Go ahead." Still, Mom's permission was a must. I looked at her, and she told me that I could. Without further ado, I dashed to the door. There, I found the same little boy—the one trying to crawl under the stall door—playing with the door. Like old buddies, we decided that we could play together, and that was just what we did. I can assure you that this camaraderie was based on our little mischievous rendezvous in the restroom. To the younger generation reading this book and wondering, the answer is yes. Yes, we had to pay to use the public restroom back then. Now, my mom didn't get the loan that day, but that little memory in that bank was priceless. I still remember that boy's face, and it makes me chuckle whenever I think about it. I wonder what he is up to these days—Hopefully, not sneaking into bathrooms anymore!

Here is another memory that I want to preserve through this book. Before my mom and dad got a divorce, I used to take every chance I got to spend time with Dad. One such precious memory is a routine my father had. I was four years old at the time. Dad would sit in his rocking chair watching M.A.S.H., HEE HAW, or one of the many other Western shows. He would be eating pretzels and drinking root beer, eyes glued to the screen. I used to sit there with him, sometimes on his lap or sometimes on the couch, and barely completed an episode before dozing off. To be honest, I never liked anything that would be on the menu—M.A.S.H., HEE HAW, any of the Western shows, pretzels, or root beer. I only loved being there with my dad.

On some Saturday mornings, Dad would take me to work with him. I used to sit on the forklift with him while he worked. I thought that was so awesome. When we came home, we sat down together and watched wrestling. That might have been the only thing my dad watched that floated my boat. I loved watching it with my dad. That routine is embedded in my mind and never fails to make me smile whenever I sit and ponder over the bygone days. It makes me appreciate the small things in life and reminds me that family is the most valuable asset I can ever have in life.

Even though we didn't have much when I was growing up, I loved every minute of it. Back then, my brothers were always roughing me up. Being the youngest, that was inevitable. And that too is a fine memory I wouldn't trade for anything. Before you think my brothers used me as a punching bag, it was nothing of sorts; it was boys just playing around in a way. I love all three of my brothers, Daniel, Darcy, and Doyle Sledge—Better known as Man-Man, Buddy, and Duck. They always looked out for me, even though I haven't ever been beaten by anyone as much as I have been whooped by them.

Me and my brothers would just be standing around, and next thing you know, without me knowing, they would start hatching a plan to get me. One would whisper something to the other, he would relay the plan to the other, and before I got a whiff of it, they would be off. I would be running like a hare running away from a fox because I knew what was coming next. But I wouldn't go very far, obviously. Two of my brothers would then grab me. The other one would climb on anything nearby and jump over me with an elbow to my chest. If they didn't have anything to jump off of, two of them would hold me while the other one would start punching me like they do in wrestling. It didn't hurt. Well, I'm going to say it didn't hurt all that much. After they tired themselves from beating me up, they would invite me to play checkers or cards or something that I would find fun and enjoy. Talk about bribing! My sisters, who I love dearly, were the opposite of my brothers. I love all six of my sisters—and I can't express this enough. Brenda, Sandra, Tracy, Sharon, Sheila, and Tina—each has a value unlike the other. But don't for a moment think that they were void of mischief. Nope. They would keep calling me a baby and try to make me a baby for real. I used to have to run from them and hide. But even though I was the one who was picked on the most, if I ever get to go back to those times, I would jump at the opportunity without a second thought. Those were some awesome times, probably some of the best, even with all the hardships.

Thanks to what I have experienced, I always tell people to value family over everything else. Some people take their family for granted. They never express themselves holistically to the very people who will go against the world for them. They don't tell their family that they love them. They don't help each other out when one of the members is in distress. I see many families today who are merely just a dictionary definition of the word—They just have a family; it's nothing more than just that. No emotions, no expression, no care, no memories, just a formal need-based interaction that seems forced.

If you have a family—mom, dad, siblings, children, spouse, grandparents, uncles, aunties, cousins—you have no idea of the treasure you have at hand. Some people don't have a mom or dad to talk to when they are feeling bad. Some people don't have siblings to joke around with and do things with. Some people don't even have grandparents, uncles, aunties, or cousins they can visit on the holidays. Dads and brothers going out fishing, playing pool, or going to play basketball, mothers and sisters going out shopping, to the movies, or to the salon together. These are all things that will give you the most wholesome treasures of your life that no wealth can ever offer. Trust me, I say this from experience; this is no emotional pep talk.

Let each other know how much you love each other. Hang together now because later on in life, it might be too late. Every time you get an opportunity to get together, jump on it. Don't wait for vacations, Christmas, deaths, marriages, or any other occasion. If you can, plan a meet-up and make all the memories while you can. Trust me, you will thank yourself (and probably me too later) for planning that movie night with your cousins.

And while you are at it, I will ask another favor that you can do yourself. Look around to see if you have relations outside of family that are worth celebrating. You might come across friends who fit the description. Some friends—the real ones—are good enough to be considered family.

I know a real friend doesn't come easy. Our world is a mean place, getting meaner by the day. But I am sure we can figure out some standards to separate the real ones from the lot. A real friend is going to tell you what you need to hear and not what you want to hear. A real friend won't let you destroy yourself. A real friend is going to stand with you through your ups and downs. Some people get "friends" and "associates" mixed up.

If a person comes to you only when they need or want something, that's an associate. If someone is always there when you need them, that is a friend. If someone wants you only to hear their problems and is not worried about what you've got going on, that's an associate. On the other hand, if it's someone you can talk to about anything, and they listen and respond with care and empathy and offer genuine solutions, that's a real one there. If it is someone who never encourages you to do something positive to make you a better version of yourself, that's an associate. In comparison, if it is someone who encourages you to always do the right thing and is always giving you positive vibes, that is a friend. If they only come around when it's a party or when it's time to go to the club, that's an associate. If they are there when you need help around the house or need a ride or help you get something important done and stick with you the whole way through it, that's a friend.

Again—don't get friends twisted with associates. You have to watch who you call your friend. Some people think they have a friend, and the next thing they know, they are getting stabbed in the back by their so-called "friend." This is a lesson I should thank my grandfather for—yet another piece of wisdom that wise man taught me. He taught me to be careful who I call a friend. I can truly say I only have six true friends. I am old enough to know friendships do not come easy. I know the number isn't a big one, but I can also say with absolute certainty that they are the true ones.

And I have good reasons for that. I can always trust them to be there for me if I need them. Shanti, Ron, Tammy, Chris, Tyler, and Kenny. All six have been there when I needed them for my ups and downs. They always tell me what I need to hear, not what I want to hear. They always lift my spirits when I'm around them. They always encourage me to stay on the right path and to feel better about myself. They always say positive things. They make me smile and laugh when I don't want to. They are real, true, and awesome friends I can't thank God enough for. Thank you, my friends, for being there.

Chapter 4

Let go

Are you still holding on to something from the past that is negative? If so, why? These are important questions you should be asking yourself time and time again. If the answer to the first one is yes, and the answer to the next one is some silly reason, you might want to follow up with questions like, "Is it worth holding on to someone who doesn't care about you?" "Is it worth holding on to a grudge?" "Is it worth holding on to anything that is blocking you from moving forward with your life?" If the answer to any of these is a "Yes," I want you to do something for me, or I'd say something for yourself.

I want you to go outside and walk straight for 100 yards. It could be on the sidewalk or in a park where you go for a stroll, or even the road if that floats your boat. It doesn't matter where you walk. I just want you to walk. But here is the condition. You have to walk forward while looking back. You cannot look forward at all. You have to keep walking. I just want to see how far you will make it. Would you make it five yards or ten yards? I don't think so. My guess is you would not make it the whole 100 yards. You might make 5-10 yards, that too on a terrain you are familiar with.

Some of the things that might happen are: You might veer off the straight line. You might run into a mailbox. You might run into some playground equipment. You might run into a tree. You might walk in a puddle of water. You might step into a hole or off the curb and twist your ankle. You might run into a garbage can. You might run into a garbage truck.

Do you see what I am trying to show you? None of that which might happen is something you'd want, is it? What I am saying is that you can't live your life looking back and living in the past and expect to move forward into the future. You can try all you want. You can hold grudges, keep wallowing, keep overthinking, but none of them is going to help you *MOVE FORWARD* in life. Isn't that all we want? To move forward? To make some progress in life? How do you expect that to happen if all you are doing is dedicating all your intellectual and emotional resources to what has already happened and cannot be changed whatsoever?

Now, if you expect me to suggest some fancy meditation routine or some mindful journaling as a cure to fix all that, I am sorry, but I don't have anything to offer. Don't get me wrong, I don't have anything against all that. I just believe it doesn't require anything at all. All you have to do is accept what happened and then just let go. Whatever is holding you back, let it go. The only worst thing I believe can happen to a human being is death. Whatever happened with you, as my warrior-of-a-man grandpa would have said, *"You breathin', ain't you?!"* As long as you have life in your veins, you have all the chance to make something good out of it. You can take it from a man who has seen the lowest of the low life can offer and yet managed to make something beautiful enough to write in a book about.

I used to hold on to a lot of things. And now that I look back, I see how foolish I was to do that and how many precious moments I lost. Here is an example. I used to be with this woman who cheated on me. It wasn't a doubt; I knew for a fact that she cheated. I had enough evidence, but still, I didn't let her go. I was foolish enough to believe that she would mend her ways. Now that I think of it, she might have guessed that I was not very smart and was an extremely emotional human being. She was wrong to assume the former but was correct with the latter.

Anyhow, seeing that I was not giving up on her, she started treating me badly. Still, I didn't let it go. Eventually, she left me for another guy. This should have been my cue, but like I said, I am an extremely emotional man. I still did not want to let it go. I was a fool. I don't toy around with emotions; I simply can't. If I feel for someone or something, it is just hard for me to let go. I even tried talking to her, thinking I might get her back with words. That didn't work.

When my attempts to solve it with table talks failed, I tried to go long. I tried to create a rift between the two and break them up. Needless to say, that didn't work. Everything I did to get her back didn't work. It was crystal clear she didn't want me, but I was holding on to something I couldn't let go of.

It ate me up for months. I would sit wallowing, missing a great deal in life. The world was still moving forward, and I was standing still. I lost precious moments of life—Moments that could have given me a treasure box of memories. For example, I missed my little girl's birthday. I cannot explain how terrible I felt about that later. I still feel bad if I think about it today. I didn't even celebrate my own birthday. I just let time pass me by because of something I couldn't let go of. I was hurt. It got bad—in fact, worse—so much so that my family started to get worried. My oldest brother came to see me. And the moment he looked at me, he said, "You need to pull yourself together." But that was all he offered. He did not say anything else, worried that I might take things the wrong way or maybe overreact since I was already vulnerable and emotionally overwhelmed. Usually, my brother says something inspirational.

But I think his words, no matter how limited, hit home. I sat and thought about it. Was it really that simple? Was it something that deserved so much of my attention and time? Such questions rattled my brain, but I am happy that they did. Also, my brother not giving his usual motivational speech also struck me—in a good way. I came to the conclusion that he wanted me to figure it out on my own, which meant that he believed in me to do that. That was uplifting.

I drove to Pensacola. I parked down by the water at Palafox Pier. I sat in my car for a while. Then I got out of the car and sat on the bench for a while. I looked around for a minute. I saw an older couple walking hand in hand. The couple stopped and hugged each other and stood there looking out over the bay—Surely something I wasn't looking for. To distract me and not think about anything romantic, I looked away, but that did me no good either. My eyes landed on a young couple walking hand in hand while their kids were running around and playing. Shaking my head, I looked towards the water. There, I saw a man and his son fishing. His son had just caught a fish. The two were smiling and laughing. The son was beaming with an ear-to-ear smile of accomplishment; the dad was celebrating as the kid's biggest fan and cheerleader. They certainly were enjoying themselves.

I felt like there was a lot of emotional stuff going on around me, or maybe, since I was already emotionally vulnerable, I was feeling more than I should. I decided to head home. When I got up to go back to my car, I saw a mother and her kids eating ice cream and laughing. Then, I saw a group of people walking out on the pier, laughing, smiling, and joking around with each other. They seemed happy, as if there wasn't a worry in the world. Then there were these two people sitting under a tree reading a book together. That felt warm and comforting. Then, a few kids and their parents playing in the water sprinklers caught my attention. The giggling of the young ones felt like music to my ears, and even though I didn't know, I needed that—that feeling of comfort in the simpler things, the more valuable things that I had been overlooking. I also saw a group of people running and exercising with each other, and they seemed like they meant business—focused and ready. That gave me a nudge that shook me good. When I made it to the car, a couple and their three kids buzzed past me, riding their bikes. The whole scene—people enjoying life with loved ones, people taking care of themselves and looking ready to take life head-on, old and young couples enjoying the company of loved ones in a calm retreat—gave me a reality check I desperately needed.

Everywhere I looked, there were people smiling and laughing. While I was moping around, I realized the world was still moving forward, and it seemed genuinely happy to do that. I was worrying about things I couldn't change. In that very moment, I thought to myself, *What am I doing? It's not like she is putting her life on hold for me. She is living her life while I'm moping around, sad, missing important things in life.* That was the moment when I pulled myself together. I asked myself questions like, "Do these people have no problems in their lives?", "Have the old couple never fought?", "Have none of these people ever experienced a break-up or lost a loved one?" I knew the answer to that, and that served me well. It gave me just the push I needed.

I decided to let go. I let go of the hurt. I let go of the sadness. I let go of the wrong belief that she might return or maybe realize how much I wanted her. I let go of it all. From that moment on, all I wanted to do was move forward with my life. You know what I did next? You guessed it; I went to see my kids. I left Palafox Pier and, without thinking twice, steered my car to go meet my kids. And a great lot of peace that brought me. Meeting them was warm and healing. My kids put a big smile on my face that day.

If someone breaks up with you but you want to stay together, you start thinking, *What if I did better*? If you lose a job or don't get that promotion, you scrutinize yourself, wondering, *What if I stayed longer hours or maybe worked more on that presentation?* Don't focus on the what-ifs. What's gone is gone—what's done is done. The best thing you can do is let it go. Focus on your life and moving forward. I understand this can be easier said than done, but then again, that is exactly what makes it worthwhile. And I am not asking you to give up on the good things in your life. That would be a dire mistake and misleading. All I am saying is to turn your focus on yourself. On what you loved and what already loves you back—

Your people. Because I can assure you, everyone has a fair share of good things waiting for them. There will be someone who comes into your life who will love you better. If you lose your job, you surely will get another—maybe even a better one. Instead of focusing on the what-ifs, focus on working harder to get that promotion. Too many people focus too much on the what-ifs. "What if I had done it this way?", "What if I had done it that way?", "What if I hadn't shouted at him/her? Maybe she/he wouldn't have left me.", "What if I never went there?", "What if I had gone there?" Does any of that sound familiar?

When you start badgering yourself with the what-if thing, you start beating yourself up for something that isn't worth it. You can do it all you want, but you won't get anything out of it—Certainly not what you want. Because most of the time, things that are draining us and exploiting us are things that are never healthy for us, no matter how much we think we like them or love them.

The same thing applies to the things or people you can't change. You might not like to hear this, but some things and people are really beyond our control. We might want to have some control over them, but we cannot, no matter how hard we try. The intelligent thing to do is to realize this simple fact. We can try once or twice, maybe even a couple of times more, but we must be smart enough to know what is beyond our control.

Don't translate this as learning to give up. Nope. I am never going to be the person who writes a book suggesting giving up on something you are passionate about. All I am saying is to better your approach to going on about things. Obsession, madness, and infatuation aren't quite healthy or fruitful. All I am suggesting is to be smart.

Don't focus on what you can't change; focus on what you can. If you fail at a life goal, focus on what you can do better and how you can improve your skills or maybe add to them. If someone doesn't love you and doesn't want you anymore, you can't change that. You can focus on being a better version of yourself and then looking for a better partner—a partner who shares your values, your dreams, someone who accepts and celebrates you for you. If you lose a job, there isn't much you can do. The world is a money-centric place, and the competitive corporate world doesn't allow much room for mistakes or show mercy. If you underperform, you are going out the door. But that is not the end of the world. As my grandfather would have said, *"You breathin', ain't you?!"* Focus on what you can do to get a better job, maybe learn a skill or further your education. If you were fired from a toxic workplace you worked hard at, celebrate. It may be hard for the moment, and you might be worried about the bills, but trust me, ending things with a foul workplace is the best thing that can happen. If you are hardworking and skilled, you will find a better job.

This attitude works wonders with everything. If you lose your home, focus on how you can get a better one. If you lose your car, focus on how you can get a better one, even your dream car. The idea is to go for better whenever you hit a slump in life, no matter if it is your job or relationship or some other life goal.

Doing better and aiming for better is a conscious effort, not fortune. It means working hard, moving forward, and focusing on your goals. As long as you are focusing on the what-ifs or the things you can't change, you are setting yourself up to be stuck in the past. And the longer you cling to that, the harder it will be to climb out of that rut. You can't move forward if you keep going backward. And each step you take in the backward direction, each minute spent pondering over the past and desperately trying to change that which you cannot, you are moving farther away from your happiness. You are moving farther away from your goals and friends and family—everything and everyone that truly matters.

And that is not even the worst thing. The worst thing about this kind of ordeal is that it can swallow you whole without you even knowing it. It can take you away from all the good things in life, and you won't even notice. The result? After a while, you find yourself walking alone. You might have scared or offended all your people away. Some more time spent doing that, and you won't be able to see your goals and your dreams. You have walked backwards for so long and so far, you can't even see where you were going, and now you are lost. And then, when every element and shred of happiness is robbed, you find yourself walking into a dead end—a wall. With nowhere to go, now you are stuck in the past, and your back is against the wall. At that point in your life, you'd have lost everything—Family, friends, goals.

You lost everything because you refused to move forward. There are some people right now facing the walls. And the next stage for them is depression, as it will slowly kick in and devour any chance of happiness. Everything they ever worked for is gone.

The reason I know what's going to happen next with such acute accuracy is because that was me once. I have been a part of this trap and know how it works and makes you feel—makes you feel weak and eventually lose all hope. I walked myself into a wall, and eventually, the wall collapsed down on me. I lost focus on my family, my friends, and my whole entire life. I lost everything.

But with as much accuracy as I can tell what will happen next in this cycle, I can tell that even with everything lost and gone, you can come out of it and make things right and then better. That is the good—you can always get it all back. You can come back stronger and wiser, ready for round two.

How, you ask? I'll begin with the most basic thing first, and I'll say it just like this: *"You breathin', ain't you?!"* That is the first thing you have to realize. You have to realize that the only end is death. As long as you are breathing, alive, and healthy, your chances of success are never gone. So this is the first step—to convince you that since you are still alive, you have a chance. With this belief, you will stand up, climb out from under that collapsed wall, and get your feet under you. Step one, done.

The second thing is you have to let go of the what-ifs and the things you can't change. No ifs, no buts. Let bygones be bygones. No looking back, reminiscing, and wallowing. Chin up, eyes locked on a happier tomorrow. Now, you're starting to walk forward away from the collapsed wall. You are no longer sad and depressed. All of a sudden, you will find yourself having a clearer perspective. Your goals will reappear, you will start liking things. You will start developing a focused outlook on life. With your chin up and head no more stooping, you can see where you are going. You are determined to move forward. Now, you're walking away from the collapsed wall at a steady pace. With a clear road ahead, you start focusing on your goals and dreams. And in no time, you will see that you are walking a little faster and away from the limiting wall. Another reward, and probably the best one, will be that you will start moving towards your family and friends. You'll no longer feel lonely. And that will only put more spring in your step and motivate you further.

And before you know it, you will be so focused on making the best out of life that you won't even remember how to get back to that collapsed wall. Remember, you don't just get back the things you lost. But with a little revamp of the mindset and a little hard work, you get back everything better than ever. Everything depends on focus. Focus on the right thing, and you will be scaling mountains. Focus on the wrong ones and you are getting back to that wall that surrounds you and robs every happiness.

Some people spend way too much time facing that wall and looking backwards. They waste energy on being mad all the time. They get mad at the big things, and they get mad at the little ones. Hell, they have this weird ability to get mad for no reason at all. And they can do it hours on end. They'll be just walking around mad all day.

Here is a simple question for them: Why? Why do you waste that much energy being mad? And before you answer them, please don't. This is a rhetorical question. There can be no logical answer to such a self-inflicting practice and attitude. I understand that some of you might have survived a world of hurt. You might have faced tragedies and setbacks—loss of loved ones, failure to get your dream job or house, seeing your dream fail, living life in absolute shambles—you might have poured your heart out to someone who would have stepped on it and left you hurt and sad. I UNDERSTAND. And in no way am I belittling your life stories.

On the contrary, I revere them and ask you to do the same. Look what you have been through and survived. Respect that. And finding that same strength JUST. LET. GO. Whatever is bothering you, don't cling to it. It's not worth holding on to.

Life can be hard sometimes, or should I say most of the time. But that is how life is. Sometimes we all get mad. In fact, sometimes it is okay, even beneficial, to be mad. But the difference between those who make it and those who lose themselves in obscurity is that some people focus only on the things that make them happy—irrespective of what calamity they are in—while others, the losing kind, fixate on the things that make them mad.

Focus on the things that make you smile. Focus on the things that make you feel better. Focus on the good you have rather than crying about what you think might have been better. Some people have great kids, a great partner, a great home, a great job, a great life, and they are still mad all the time. They might be worrying about something they cannot control, entirely neglecting the blessings they have. That's not good, only a recipe for disaster. After a while, people they care about often start pushing themselves away. And before they know it, such a person finds themselves alone and lonely. So the gist of it all: Don't waste time and energy being mad. Pay attention to what you have, not what you don't or have lost. Either let it go or work harder and go get it.

While I myself am not the grumpy kind, I have had quite an intimate experience with one. I was with a woman once who was always mad. Whatever I did, I couldn't do anything right for her. I once brought her home flowers, and she told me, "They're not going to do nothing but die anyway." I tried to be the gentleman and do small stuff like open the doors for her, and she would shoot me down, saying, "I got it." When I cooked or cleaned for her and asked her how the food was or how the house looked, she would tell me that was what I was supposed to do, and it was nothing special I did. A little appreciation wouldn't have hurt, right? Sometimes, when I'd cook, she would get mad at me because we didn't go out to eat, and if I took her out, she'd be mad I didn't cook at home. I was always in a mix of confusion and exasperation.

Even if I did something by myself, she'd turn it into a rumpus in some way or the other. Like one day, I was in the room watching TV. She threw a tantrum that I was glued to the TV and not paying her enough attention. The next day, I left the TV off and asked her what she wanted to do. And … you might have guessed it. This woman gets mad at me for having the TV off.

I simply couldn't win—or lose, for that matter. I couldn't do anything right. It got to the point where I would just wait on her to tell me what she wanted me to do, and even that wasn't good enough. She'd ask me to do something; I'd do exactly what she wanted me to do. And guess what? She got mad because I didn't do it fast enough. Here I was, huffing and puffing, and this woman had the heart of stone to say I wasn't quick enough. What?

I thought she was going to eventually blow the house down. The scary bit is that it was getting out of hand. It was taking an actual mental toll on me. A lot of times, I found myself taking sleeping medicine to go to sleep before she got home. I'd want to avoid her at all costs. I wasn't a fan of fighting over something petty every day. It was horrible living with her. It was an everyday thing.

She would go to bed mad and wake up mad. I tried talking to her about the situation. Yup… she got mad at that too. Needless to say, I just couldn't take it anymore. Even though it didn't happen instantly or even later than it should have, nonetheless, I left. There is no reason for someone to be mad all the time, and no mad woman was going to convince me otherwise.

There is also another kind—one who doesn't turn things bad intentionally but ends up doing just that. That is the fussing kind. There is no sensible reason to want to fuss all the time, and you are not convincing me otherwise.

And I have a pretty good reason for that. In fact, an educated, medical one, if I may. It is proven that "Fussing" over things actually raises blood pressure. It might not sound quite accurate, but there is ample data you can Google to read on it—all verified by trusted, authentic psychology and psychiatry experts. Fussing is considered a direct cause of the silent killer—stress. The problem with stress is that it doesn't have any unique symptoms that might qualify as an actual disease. But I and many doctors can confirm that it can lead to actual physical problems that can lead to a painful and slow death. I don't think there is a need for me to offer any more reasons why fussing is a dangerously stupid thing to do. I don't think you'd be thought of as someone smart if your tombstone reads: "Died because he lost a job and didn't apply for another."

The best thing to do when you get mad and want to fuss is to find a way to calm down. Yup, it is that simple. I know some of you might have a hush-hush routine or maybe a suggestion to *embark on a spiritual voyage to find yourself*; sorry, you won't find all that in this book. This book is a practical one.

It will only suggest practicable suggestions that I have either used or seen to work firsthand. Do what is easily accessible. For example, you can go to the gym. I am a big fan of this one. You can hit the gym and work out that anger—Give that rage a safe channel rather than spilling it around yourself and hurting your own people. Outdoors is also a good option. You can go for a jog or run. Or maybe, if you are not the adrenaline-loving kind, you can go for a walk—a small stroll in the park has many health benefits.

While it might seem like it, the idea is not to exert some physical labor to distract from the mental torment. The idea is simply to distract. Sometimes, when you get mad, all you need to do is just walk away from whatever is grinding your gears. When you start fussing, you transfer your negative energy to someone else. You get them mad, and now they start fussing back. Tensions escalate, and both of you start saying things you don't mean. Sometimes, other people get caught up in all this fussing—people who don't deserve it—Kids, spouses, parents, siblings, good friends. Before you know it, things turn into a big mess. Comments passed turn into taunts; taunts become arguments; arguments become feuds; feuds become brawls.

In fact, this is one of the biggest problems with fussing—how quickly a non-issue can turn into an all-out brawl. Things can escalate rather quickly. What might start off as a simple comment hurled at someone can turn into a slugfest in the blink of an eye. And before anyone can de-escalate the situation, someone ends up in jail, at the hospital, or both.

That's why the best thing to do when you have your mind racing with thoughts and you are overthinking many things at once is to walk away. Fussing does not do anyone any good. I understand that fussing is a difficult thing to control. Emotions are not the easiest thing to control. Then, there is a problem with how people communicate. Some people think the only way they can get their point across is to fuss. Which, needless to say, is far from any sensible truth. I can assure every reader of this book that plenty of people can get their point across without fussing and arguing. Many of you might want to say, "D, sometimes people can get on your last nerves." Aye, aye. I don't deny that at all. I understand full well that sometimes (more often than we like) people do things to make you want to fuss. But here is something else I know too: Such people are never really worth it. And thus, I always urge that it's best to calm yourself down and think rationally. Spending time in the pen for something trivial? I cannot think of one reason why that might be a sensible thing to do.

Before you say I am being rather optimistic, I can assure you that I make all these suggestions from a place of experience. I have gotten into my fair share of feuds, and it is precisely because of all of those feuds that I have learned to let it just go. It took me some time and patience, but I got there, and so can you.

Now, whenever I get mad to the point I want to fuss, I just walk away. For me, water has a calming effect, so sometimes, I take a drive down by the water and sit there and just think. I think of the reasons why I or someone else was fussing in the first place. I think of the consequences, and every other time, I see that the tension just dissipates over time. Even better, often, by the time I go back to where I came from, I forget what it was that I was mad at in the first place.

Give yourself some time to think. Grant yourself this really easy-to-access luxury because the consequences can be very costly. Fussing is a waste of time and energy. It also has an incredible capacity to turn into a "waste of life"—yours or someone else's, even someone truly valuable and important.

I understand that life can get frustrating, but keeping composed seems to be the most all-encompassing and effective antidote to that. In fact, you tend to think better if you are composed than when you are angry or worried. To craft a creative solution and climb out of your frustrating problem, you need a mind that is uncluttered and composed.

The more you stay, instead of walking away whenever you are frustrated or vexed, the worse things can get. I might be sounding counterintuitive, but it is actually true. You might want to counter me with something like, "Are you asking us to run away? How will that solve the problem?" To you, I will say this: you are fussing. I said no such thing. All I am saying is to step back, be analytical, and approach a problem sensibly rather than letting rage take the steering wheel.

I understand that inclinations and attitudes have a role to play in all this. We are all different people, with minds and moods of our own. And thus, interactions can be tricky. I know that there is a whole crowd of people out there who think they really have to get their point across. They just want to be right or maybe heard. If you are one of them, there is nothing wrong with that. I am not writing to judge. But I would say this, even if you want to get your point across, fussing only will do otherwise.

When you fuss and argue, the point you are trying to get across may not resonate in someone's mind at all. This is because all they heard was you fussing—they couldn't pay attention to your point, which might have actual merit. Consequently, what could have been a learning experience for either of you ended up only being a brawl or a feud, or an argument. If only you had walked away and later returned and discussed things calmly, maybe explaining your stance and listening to theirs, you would have enjoyed a higher percentage of them listening and agreeing with you.

Fussing and yelling solve nothing. I was lucky my oldest brother taught me that a long time ago. When I was in my teens, I got to witness the benefits of this firsthand. My oldest brother got into a confrontation with a man who thought my brother did him wrong. The guy was already a hothead. Contrastingly, my brother was the calm type. I don't know all the details of why the man was mad, but he was fuming. Me and my brother were standing under a tree at our sister's boyfriend's aunt's house. This guy came up to my brother and, without any preamble, started fussing and cussing. My brother told him to calm down and that they could talk it out. The guy wasn't having any of it. He was just jumpy and told my brother he wanted to fight him. My brother wasn't giving up either. He was constantly trying his best to calm the situation. It is worth mentioning here that my brother could have easily won the fight; he had the physical prowess and the gumption to throw fists too—he wasn't a coward. Yet, my brother decided to take the high road. The guy kept bouncing around yelling, but my brother was as cool as a cucumber.

I was standing there making notes. Then, after some to and fro, my brother said, "If you're not going to listen to what I have to say, I'm just going to leave." He even got ready to get in his car and leave. The guy was still being fidgety—fussing and cussing, and all. By this time, my brother was in the car, ready to drive away. He asked him one more time if he wanted to address the situation calmly. When the man showed no inclination toward a pacific solution, my brother closed his car door.

Something about my brother getting in the car ticked the man off. He might have assumed that my brother wanted to fight and might be looking for something to bash him with in the car. Quickly, the guy looked around and then ran and picked up a brick he was able to find. He charged with it towards my brother, saying, "Let's go!"

While my brother was all relaxed and in no mood to throw fists, I wasn't. I was ready to throw it down if things went south.

Plus, I was skeptical and believed that the man didn't understand my brother's peaceful stance and was about to jump him. As soon as he picked up the brick, I stood behind him and clenched my fist. Inside, I was all pumped up, and the only thought that raced in my mind was, *as soon as he tries to swing with that brick, I am going to knock his head off.*

My brother saw me and knew exactly what I was about to do. Immediately, he said, "Look, man, let's talk." It took some persuasion, but after a heated standoff, luckily, my brother was somehow able to convince him to go for a non-violent solution. The guy asked my brother about something and why he took it back. Like I said, I don't know the details on why the guy was mad, so I had no idea what they were talking about. My brother explained that he saw the known neighborhood thief hanging around the guy's house when he was about to drop off the object in discussion, so he considered it best not to drop it off but hand it to him in person. The guy calmed down and dropped the brick.

My brother got out of the car and walked to his trunk. He called the guy to come, and my brother handed it to him whatever the guy thought my brother took. My brother emphasized once again and said, "If you had just come and asked me what happened, I would have told you." My brother also told him that the neighbors, too, could have verified that he had been there for the drop-off if only the guy had been patient enough to ask around a little. In fact, my brother even narrated the whole conversation, which I remember still. He said, "I told your neighbor that I had something for you and to call me so I can meet you, so if you talked to your neighbor, you would have known that." The guy was now almost apologetic and guilty. He admitted that he hadn't talked to his neighbor. My brother said, "Exactly! That is what I was trying to tell you, but you was doing all that fussing, you didn't want to hear what I was trying to tell you." The guy apologized to my brother. They shook hands, and the guy walked away.

And this "No fuss" attitude has been quite a fascinating feature of my brother that I have always admired. I have never seen him get mad, throw a fit or a tantrum. He is always calm in a pressured situation and always lets reason and logic dictate his actions. He was calm as a cucumber back then, he is now, and for that and many other reasons, he will always be an awesome big brother.

One way to deal with fussing is to revisit the way we think and critically evaluate our thought process. Some people have a hateful way of thinking. They tend to develop a negative or aggressive connotation with everything. Hateful thinking makes people paranoid. They are always evaluating someone critically or negatively. I had this neighbor who always told me that I was going to do something bad to him. He would say that I might kill his grass with the weed killer, or maybe that I would break into his house and steal things. Hell, he even said that I was trying to hurt his dog.

Nothing he said was true. I can't even dream of hurting a dog, let alone killing one. He had the same attitude and stance towards the other neighbors. He always thought hateful things about almost everyone. And because of that, we always found him fussing and being grumpy all the time. I never understood why he always thought of doing terrible things; all I know is that just because he was always thinking foul and bitterly about people, he was always overthinking and in a constant paranoia that made him a bitter person to be around.

If you think good, you will do good. If you think hateful, you will do hateful things. It is as simple as that. Every now and then, you might think of something hateful to do to someone, but most of you don't act on it. And that, I guess, is okay to a certain extent. Oftentimes, we think hateful things because we are overwhelmed with emotions. But the smarter thing is to not ACT ON THEM. Some people are not that smart. When they have hateful thoughts, they don't dismiss or dispel them but instead always act on them. And you can always tell who these people are. These are the people who are always thinking that someone is conspiring and thinking of doing something harmful to them. They are people who are always skeptic and on their toes, thinking foul of others. The other person whom they assume might hurt or harm them probably would be sitting at home, not even thinking about them. Yet these skeptics would have some botched-up, made-up theory that would make no sense at all.

These people are always on the defensive, trying to inflict harm on the other person first because they strongly believe that the other person wants to hurt them; they think—building on their misplaced logic—that it is smart to hurt others before they hurt them. Hateful things only make things go from good to bad and bad to worse. If a hateful thought comes to your mind, what do you do? This is a question that every one of you should consider if you wish to suppress this scourge of unnecessary fussing that can steal your joy.

This is what I do if I ever have a hateful thought about anyone. I don't forcefully try to suppress it. I know it will only make it worse. What I do is that I get up—any opportunity I get—and I just go sit by the water. Understand that sitting by the water, taking in the nature and the serene rhythm of the place is my favorite thing to do. It brings me peace naturally and helps me calm my mind. If that is not possible for whatever reason, I'll watch something funny on TV. Humor tends to undo the knot in your mind and relax you; at least it does that for me. If I am really overwhelmed and looking for a strong release, I'll go to the gym. The idea is to either let something help you forget your foul thoughts, distract you from them, or channel them somewhere safe where nothing or no one gets harmed. I do what it takes not to let the hateful thoughts brew longer about anyone.

You might want to object to me saying that the world is a foul place already and that might be the only way to survive. I am sorry, but you are wrong. In fact, one of the reasons the world might be like this is that we let hateful thoughts brew instead of taking any action to dissipate them. Hateful thoughts can and will definitely lead you in the wrong direction. When you have hateful thoughts, it takes no time for these thoughts to invade your mind and make you take hateful action. Making baseless assumptions about someone wanting to hurt you without a reason is as stupid as it can be. Unfortunately, some people grow up that way. Some people grow up with parents who have this hateful paranoia. Such parents are always feeding vile and angry ideas, and they rub the same off on their young ones, making it a part of their upbringing as they grow. As a result, these kids end up doing the same thing when they reach adulthood, and the cycle continues.

Hate is so powerful and potent, it should not even exist in anyone's mind, reason or not. The best thing to do is to let things go and let them take their time. Whatever it is—people, work, life, relationships—just give them space and room and attention, and things will eventually fall in place.

The next thing, after self-correction and evaluation, to avoid hate, is to keep your surroundings peaceful. Keep company with people who think positively and never linger on negative ideas and beliefs. If you know someone who is always spilling out something hateful whenever they are around, either ask them to leave or get up and leave their space immediately. You don't need to be around any such person. I understand that they might be a loved one. And in that case, you can try to change them. You can preach them, guide them, and counsel them. You can even make room for them around yourself to allow such a person to correct themselves and heal from whatever hate is consuming them. But if they are failing to make an effort, let them go. Never let hate consume you. Never give it even the smallest space, because if you do, hate will, with absolute precision, ruin your life.

While on this subject, it is only logical to gauge avenues where hate can creep in. And if I have to select one, I'd say jealousy might be at the top of that list. You might be wondering, "Aren't jealousy and hate two different things?" Well, yes, they are, but they are in no form or manner not interrelated. Jealousy is something people need to let go of whenever they sense the slightest hint of it. Why be jealous of another person? Because they have a better car? Because they have a better job or house? There is nothing that you should be jealous of because there is nothing out there that someone else has acquired that you can't. No matter what it is, if you work hard, play your cards right, you can have what others have achieved. And in case of a remote possibility that you might not achieve that same particular thing, you can definitely achieve something better. Even in cases when rewards might seem natural—for example, good looks—one should understand that everyone has some natural gift that others don't have. That should be enough to convince you that there's no logical need to be jealous.

Now I will say here something that might not sit well with many. *Most people who are jealous are lazy*. It might sound like a stretch, but this is true, at least for things that can be acquired through hard work and sweat. Jealous people want to snoop into everyone's business and be judgmental towards others' achievements, but they never see the hard work one might have done to achieve what they did. They want what the next person has but don't want to work hard to achieve it. If someone buys a new house, there is no reason to be jealous. You too can get a similar house, maybe even a bigger one. All you have to do is work hard to get all that. And it doesn't have to be the same thing the person did to get a new house. I say this to not let the jealous people escape the truth using some botched-up reasoning. They might have said that someone got a house because he had support or some natural talent or maybe some advantage, or this or that. The person who got the new house might just be good at real estate; you might be good at accounting. Either way, both of you can achieve the same thing through working hard. The only difference is that they achieved something because they worked hard with what talent they had, and the jealous ones don't.

That is why whenever I come across people lamenting about how others have something they don't, I suggest to them to replace their jealousy with effort. Working harder is a potent antidote to jealousy. Another reason why I suggest people rid themselves of jealousy as fast as they can is that jealousy has great potential to turn sour and lead to fouler, more dangerous outcomes. Some people have gone on to hurt people just because they were harboring jealousy. When jealous people can't find a channel to let their jealousy and the resultant frustration out, they can turn dangerous. They hurt others because it makes them feel better about their life. The pain and hurt they inflict can be of any kind, physical or mental. They don't care, as long as they are venting their frustration in any manner. I know it makes no sense, and it is not right in any imaginable way. But then again, so is jealousy—it is devoid of logic.

Now it isn't necessary that people who turn violent when they feel jealous are just violent people or foul people by design. Violence is often a trait that has underlying roots. Roots that go deeper than we can imagine. Most people who resort to violence in the face of any inconvenience, such as jealousy, it is likely they have grown up in a home or a setting that was hurting them. They might have abusive parents or might have been bullied in school by other kids. Such people grow up with violence and rage as a "normal" in their lives. The result? They adopt it as a part of their own lives. They are hateful and angry towards everyone they come across. They bully their neighbors, they are angry towards their family—wife and kids—they are foul with their colleagues. Everyone they come in contact with, they are probably looking for ways to hurt them. That's how they grew up, and that's all they know.

Now, you might be saying, "Shouldn't they just stop with the rage and all?" I agree with you, but only partially. They should, but it is easier said than done. Breaking free from something you have grown up with isn't the easiest thing to do.

Having said that, some people who grew up like that were able to break the cycle. That is why I said I agree with you "partially." Because it is possible to do that. The ones who break this cycle realize the simple truth: Just because you grew up like that doesn't mean you have to do the same to others. And they let this profoundly liberating thought steer their way and break the shackles of a foul and bitter early life.

Don't let people who hurt you in the past dictate how you live your future. People hold on to grudges. Hell, they even hold onto misplaced grudges based on misinterpreted conclusions. And they just don't hold a grudge; they let the grudge dictate their moods and actions. This results in them being an overall grumpy individual who is always in a bitter mood, never easy to be around. I don't see the point in it.

Like I said in the first book, if you don't forgive, why would you expect God to forgive you? Holding on to a grudge, not forgiving whoever hurt you, has never and will never bring you the peace you are looking for. It will only hurt you inside and out.

On the inside, you will be stressing yourself. You will be engaging in rage-inducing thoughts, which will cause your blood to boil. More scientifically, it can and will lead to problems like high blood pressure, and I don't think I need to stress how that is dangerous, like actually dangerous, almost fatal for your health. High blood pressure is the single most effective silent killer; ask any doctor, and they will tell you the same.

On the outside, when you hold on to a grudge, everything around you is affected. Your work and career, your personal life. Everything you hold dear is in the blast radius—your family, your friends. When you hold a grudge against someone, you let them occupy an unnecessary position in your mind. That's not all. You lend them a position of certain control. You let their presence in your mind embitter your mood and influence your behavior and actions. For example, every time you are with your family and someone mentions that person's name, you instantly start brewing up negative emotions and thoughts. Consequently, what was supposed to be a jovial time with your family, kids, or friends soon starts to become sour because you are angry and spewing hate recklessly. You even let some of that rage spill on these dear ones around you. You might shout at your spouse or kids for being playful, or you might insult a friend, saying words that can never be taken back. As a result, your people, the ones who truly love you, start distancing themselves from you. Your family starts to push away from you because they don't want to be in the middle of whatever you've got going on. Your friends don't want to hang around you for the same reason. No one wants to get themselves hurt simply because *you* have a grudge that you can't let go of and walk away from.

It might sound like a stretch, but there are people who died, were murdered or maimed, or are serving time in jail because of a grudge they held on for too long, because they wanted to get revenge on someone for a mistake or inconvenience that might have occurred eons ago. There are many people who have suffered simply because of the inability (or lack of will, should I say) to just let go. I don't think you'd want to be a part of that statistic.

I know some of you might be seething, thinking that I don't realize or understand the magnitude, hold, or weight of a vengeful emotion. Trust me, I do understand. I get that you want to get back at someone who might have wronged you. But I ask you this, "What good would that do?" Will it be worth it? Do you think you would feel better if you got your revenge, or maybe worse if you didn't?

You believe (incorrectly, I'd say) that because someone hurt you, it is only logical that you hurt them, that it might be the only way to have some kind of peace. I am sorry to pop your bubble, but that is not the best thing to do. Or at least, something that might bring you peace. It might bring your relief, yes, a momentary calm, but peace? Nope. Never can rage and vengeance bring peace.

If someone does you wrong and yet you can walk away from it, that is what can bring the ultimate, lasting peace you desire. That is the best choice. It is power and control unlike any. It gives you control over your peace and happiness. Just imagine the control. That is a power that no revenge can bestow upon you. I know that what I am saying might sound far-fetched, but it is entirely possible and absolutely rewarding.

If you aren't already convinced, here is something I will share that might drive my point home. (I hope, fingers crossed) I have observed, more often than not, that revenge does more damage to the person taking it than to the one it is being taken out on. Now, it might be an innocent observation, but I have seen many times that the one taking revenge ended up in more trouble than the other one. In fact, I welcome you to ponder it too. Have you ever had someone do something to you, and then you did something back to them, but instead ended up getting yourself in trouble? Maybe not everyone, but many of you reading this book will be nodding heads in the affirmative.

One reason I can think of why that might happen to the one taking revenge is that their cognitive and reasoning skills are temporarily impaired. Rage does that to a person. When we are angry, we don't pay much heed to logic or consequence. This makes us vulnerable in the long run. The only thing we are focused on is inflicting damage to the person, and everything else is a blur. We might get the revenge we so desperately seek, but since we haven't paid any attention to the consequences, we end up inflicting more damage on ourselves than on the other person.

In fact, rage and hate can render us so devoid of logic that even when we have options that can help us exact revenge through a legal channel or maybe some other sensible, less self-damaging solution available to leverage, we will ignore them completely. Some people would rather get revenge than walk away. Some people would rather get revenge than call the police. Both of the solutions here—walking away or calling concerned authorities—are as sensible as it can get, but a vengeful mind won't heed them. I am sure many of you who are reading this right now might be feeling a little embarrassed since you might have done the same or something similar—suffered a loss that could have been averted if only you had acted rationally instead of taking your revenge.

Some of the gunslingers might want to shut me down with, "But D, won't that make us look weak? Backing away or not hitting back? Whatever happened to an eye for an eye?" To you, good people, I can assure you that there is no weakness in being sensible and smart. In fact, it is the purest form of bravery and strength to not be dictated by primal, animalistic instincts and to do what is right. Never once have I suggested anyone in these pages to be a sitting duck and just let people abuse and misuse you, or walk all over you. As God is my witness, I know there are people out there who deserve to be punished. What I am suggesting is that even if it is revenge you seek, seek it in a manner that doesn't inflict you more. Do it sensibly. Let the concerned authorities handle it. Walk away if the issue is too petty to be losing your cool over. Not every fight or feud is supposed to be fought; some you just sit out because they are not worth the peace of your mind.

I knew this woman. In fact, that would be an understatement. She was a *friend* of mine, a childhood friend from back in the day. We never dated or anything like that. She was in a relationship with a guy who always did her wrong. He was a selfish human being, the kind who always thought about himself and himself alone. He would cheat on her, abuse her, and beat her like a maniac. And for the most part, she made do with it for a long time. But one day, she had had enough. One day, she called me and told me that they had an argument that got out of hand, and he punched her in the face. She added that after the beating, he simply left and hadn't been home in two days.

Her narration infuriated me. She continued and told me that she was leaving a store when she saw him with another girl. Immediately, I told her that it was a good thing. Good riddance. But I could sense it in her words that she wasn't quite ready for "riddance." She couldn't just let it be. While a part of me understood why she was so mad, I still didn't want her to do anything foul.

Ranting and raging, she told me she wanted to hurt him like he had hurt her. I tried my best to calm her down. I suggested she just let it go and pleaded not to do anything she was going to regret. I knew it wasn't worth rattling your mental peace over a vile human being like that, but emotions had the best of her. To all my attempts at calming her down, she shot me down with reasons I couldn't argue against. She told me she was tired of how he was treating her, and she felt like it was about time she got back at him. I told her to just walk away and even reminded her that she could easily do better than that crap of a man. To that and my fruitless attempts at calming her down, she simply said, "Forget that." What she added to it was something that boiled my emotions too, for a while. She said her eye was swollen, she was hurt, and this brat was out there with another girl as if nothing had happened. For a while, I wanted to encourage her to beat the man to a pulp. Hell, I wanted to lend her a hand, but I knew better.

She said he had to pay, and I wasn't convincing her otherwise. Still, she was a friend, and I wanted to save her from anything dumb that she might regret later or might face grave consequences for. I pleaded, "Think before you do something you will regret. Let me come over and talk to you." Nope. She wasn't having any of it. She was done talking. I was almost halfway into asking her to allow me to come and talk her out of this when she hung up. Immediately, I redialed her number. She didn't answer. I couldn't give up on her like that. I had sensed she was angry; I could almost feel in my bones that something really dangerous was about to go down. I couldn't sit on the sidelines now, could I?

For almost thirty minutes, I kept calling her. Nothing—squat. After about forty-five minutes, my phone rang, and I jumped at it. I asked her if she was okay, to which she replied that she was. It would have been a complete relief until I sensed something sharp, almost menacing, in her tone. I asked her if she was ready to talk. She told me how to get to her. Without wasting another minute, I went to pick her up. Little did I know, I was in for a surprise.

As soon as I was at her doorstep, she came barging towards my car. She had a suitcase in tow with her, and she had a big, menacing grin on her face. Trying to make sense of her behavior, I took in the surroundings and glanced behind her. My eyes landed on a window of the house she had gotten out of. The window was brutally shattered. My eyes darted to the next window pane and discovered that that window, too, was shattered to bits.

I was trying to process everything, bewildered. By this time, she was at my car door and got in, all the while laughing. I asked her, "What did you do?" Instead of a reply came a loud roaring laughter. I sensed that she had done something really troubling; I just wanted to understand how bad it was. When she was done laughing, she looked at me and said, "I'm tired of him. He deserves everything I did." I was hoping the shattering of the windows was all the damage she had done. I was wrong. Before I could utter a word, I noticed smoke coming out of the backyard. I asked her what havoc she had wreaked. She had a whole list. She told me, grinning all the while, that she had punched and drilled holes in the walls, as many as she could. She had also taken ketchup and mustard and squeezed them all over the furniture. I could only imagine the horrific scene. She continued telling me that she had cut holes with a knife in a bed in one of the rooms. And to top all of that, she told me she took all the new clothes the guy had bought recently and burned them in the backyard.

Not gonna lie: for a brief moment, I, too, was terrified of the way she was laughing. I tried to calm her down and told her she shouldn't have done that. She was downright dismissive and brushed me off, saying she wasn't trying to hear what I had to say. She ordered me to drive and told me to drop her off at her sister's house. She then informed me that her ex-boyfriend was going to pick her up from there. All this time, I was trying to somehow talk some sense into her, which I knew had little chance of happening. I asked her, "Do you think this is going to be a good idea?"

Without a beat and as coldly as she could manage, she said, "Yes. I am going to hurt him like he made me hurt."

I countered, "Yes, you already told me that. Revenge is not a good thing." I even pulled out my grandad's golden words of wisdom, "*Right, don't wrong nobody.* You should have just packed your bags and left." But they didn't seem to have any effect on her either. She simply said, "It is what it is." I realized there was no convincing her. She had made up her mind, and she wasn't going to budge. I felt sorry for her, even a little worried too, but I was helpless.

With a sunken heart and a worried mind, I dropped her off. Two weeks later, I got a phone call. The number was of the infamous county jail. For a moment, I tried to figure out who that might be. But it didn't take me long. It was her. She was in jail, incriminated for criminal mischief. She told me that the guy she was living with, the ex whose house she had wrecked against all my convincing, had called the police on her for all the terrible things she had done to his house. I wasn't surprised. Not one bit. It was almost expected.

Despite everything, she was a friend, and I wanted to help her. She goes on to tell me that the bail was set at $2,000, but would come down to $200 if she had a bail bondsman. She asked me if I could be her bail bondsman. I could have been pissed at her for not listening to me in the first place, but I knew that I couldn't turn my back on her. Not right now, at least. If she had come to her senses, that was good enough for me. Plus, I thought jail was as good a lesson as one could get. I agreed instantly and went and bailed her out.

As soon as she got in the car, she apologized for acting the way she did that day and not listening to me. I told her it was okay. She said, "No, it's not. I should have listened to you and just left." I knew there was no point in going on another moral lecture. She had learned her lesson, even if the hard way.

I assured her, "There is no reason to dwell on the past. What's done is done. There is no need to worry about something you can't change. All you can do is keep breathing and move forward."

A little while into the ride, I asked her why she had called me to bail her out of jail instead of that other guy who had met her at her sister's house. Her response was a bit too sad. She said she did call him, but he had told her he didn't have any money and just hung up, saying he had to go. I looked at her smiling and said, "You really can pick 'em."

She looked at me and said, "You're the one to talk."

I was a little mock-annoyed. I said, "What do you mean?"

She looked at me and said, "Really?!"

I got defensive and started to explain, "I may have had one or two bad relationships."

By this time, jail had worn off her, and she was all giggly. She retorted, "More like thirty or forty."

I looked at her and said, "Ha-ha, very funny."

We reached her sister's home, and before she got out of the car, she took a deep breath, paused, looked at me, and said, "You did teach me something."

I asked her, "What's that?"

She said, and this is what I want people to take away from this story, *"That revenge is not worth it and to walk away and let go."*

I told her I was glad I could help. She thanked me for picking her up. The good thing was that the punishment she got was something manageable. She ended up with a year of probation and a $2500 fine, which she completed and paid. I was glad that she was lucky, as these things often blow out of proportion, with people ending up in jail for years and years. If only people are wise enough to realize that a little patience and restraint, and letting go can save them from years and years of trouble and a life of regret.

Letting go of something someone did to you is a lot easier than seeking revenge. I know it sounds a little too optimistic, but I can assure you that it's not just that. In fact, for me, it is more practical and logical than optimistic. Most people don't realize that and go too far with revenge. In worst-case scenarios, people transgress to the point of taking a life. Nothing is worth taking a life. No matter if it's money, gold, diamonds, or whatever, taking a life is not worth it and will never be.

We must understand that controlling rage is the single most important thing to learn. Oftentimes, when people are angry, they take the most outrageous actions on a whim, in a fit of rage, never lending a minute's worth of thought to the consequences. One example is, and I have seen many people do, buying a weapon or something similar. The worst thing you can do when you're mad or want revenge is to go get a gun or a knife or something of that sort. A gun is for protection. A gun is for hunting. A gun is for many things but *NOT FOR REVENGE*. In fact, that is the worst idea for revenge. Because it gives you absolute uncontrolled power, and uncontrolled power always reaps the worst results. It allows you to incur nonreversible damage and harm with the slightest action in the briefest possible time, making it an absolute worst thing to have when you are overwhelmed with emotions, when logic is in the backseat.

A gun solves nothing. You just end up in jail, and the only people you hurt are the victim's family and your family. And this consequence is entirely unfair. Neither the victim's family nor your family did anything to deserve the mental anguish, pain, and hurt. They didn't even want to hurt you. So, why then are they punished because of your actions?

If you are among those harboring any such idea and happen to stumble upon this work of mine, I'll plead with you this: *PUT THE GUNS DOWN AND LET WHATEVER IS BOTHERING YOU GO.* Think before you act. Because, even if it might not seem to be, even if you think your people will be fine without you, even if you think that you have no one to care for, even if you think your people will be fine without you, I can assure you that you are wrong. There are people who care for you, and no revenge is worth losing them.

Once you take a life, there is no taking back. And when you take a life, especially in a rage-induced breakdown, you are not taking one life, you are taking at least two—the one you are killing and yours. And neither is something you can get back.

If your partner hurt you, just leave. There is someone for everyone out there. You just have to be patient, and you surely will find someone who will love you enough to forget bad past experiences. If your friends did you wrong, don't hang out with them anymore. They are not the end of the world. If someone you don't know did something or said something wrong to you, walk away. They don't know you enough to have an opinion about you that might be worthy of any attention. They and their opinion do not matter. You cannot allow every other person you come across to rattle your peace. It is only foolish. Hell, it is entirely possible that they are bitter because they are dealing with monsters in their own lives, too. I am not saying that it is okay for people to be foul toward the world if they are going through a rough patch, but be the bigger person, not for their peace but for yours.

I used to be a bouncer in a club. I saw people get mad over the dumbest things. People used to come into the club and fight over nothing—petty squabbles would morph into full-blown brawls, and people would end up going to jail for nothing. I never could understand that—not then, not now. Fights would start over something as absurd as someone stepping on someone else's shoes. Imagine that! Isn't that crazy? You put your whole life in jeopardy over someone accidentally stepping on your shoes. The club is a packed place. What did they think was going to happen? I believe if they don't want their shoes stepped on, they should wear the shoes they like the least. How difficult is that to figure out, right? Or maybe, better yet, do not go to any crowded place at all. What madness is it that you go to a place that is brimming with a crowd and then get into a scuffle simply because someone stepped on your shoes? Whatever happens to common sense?

My foot probably got stepped on thirty times a night. I knew that people were drinking, and they were not purposely stepping on my shoes. They are intoxicated, they can't walk straight at the moment. Hell, even those who are not drunk can't walk straight because of the number of people. That is simple to understand. And honestly, I wouldn't blame the drinking for the brawls. What I noted was that mostly the ones who weren't intoxicated were the ones who were starting the fights and brawls. And what's worse was they were persistent. When they started fighting, we would intervene, break the scuffle, and kick them out of the club. That should've been it. You would think that, but that never happened. Instead of going home, they would stay out in the parking lot waiting for the person they got into it with just to fight with them again.

That is not even the worst case. The worst was when guns got involved. Sometimes, these brawlers would arm themselves, standing out there with a gun, waiting for the person to show up so they could even the score. Once they saw the person come out of the club, they would start shooting wildly and blindly, not caring who got shot. Most of the time, it was someone else who got shot and not the person they were shooting at. Now, they are on the run for murder. These people often forget that the club has cameras, so the police know the identity of the shooter. In no time, the police would get hold of them and take them to jail, book them on murder charges, and they would end up spending the rest of their life in jail. I ask those people, "For what? Because someone stepped on their shoes? Is that it? Is that reason enough to spend precious years of your life behind bars? Years that could have been spent with family, with friends, parents, kids, and partners? Years that could have been spent living a wholesome life?" Explain to me how that is a fair trade.

It never made sense to me. Just try to picture this. The person goes to jail for murder or attempted murder, and the one who they were shooting at, the one they wanted to "even it out with," where are they? They are at the club the very next week, probably having the time of their lives. That is not worth anything, and no one is convincing me otherwise. If the person had just let go, if he had been patient enough and practical enough to convince himself that he wasn't stepped on intentionally, but it was because of the crowd, he could have been home with his family. It's not that serious. *Let go of all the pettiness.*

I'll try to share as many stories as I can in this book to make my point; I hope you can relate to one of these and understand that pettiness is never worth a damn. Here is another. I was sitting in the parking lot in my car at this store one day. I had taken a friend to the store and was waiting outside. I was idling by when I heard a man yelling. Let's call him Guy 1. He was yelling at another man, whom we will call Guy 2. Guy 1 was yelling at Guy 2, saying that Guy 2 disrespected him.

Now, Guy 1 was parked right next to me and had his baby with him. Guy 2 was parked in a spot behind me. Out of the two,

Guy 2 had a relatively pacific stance and wasn't answering back much. He was trying to ignore Guy 1. He walked into the store, hoping that this yelling man might drive away. He got into a conversation with the people he brought to the store, maybe relaying the event. I thought it was over. It should have been, but I was wrong.

Instead of Guy 1 driving away, he waited in his car until Guy 2 came out. Yes, weird as it was, the guy simply waited so he could start the feud again. And the foolishness didn't stop just there. Just as soon as Guy 2 came out of the store, Guy 1 got out of his car, *his baby in his arms*, and started yelling again. I couldn't make sense of what was wrong with the dude. He literally waited for the guy to come out and was dumb enough to get into a fight while holding the baby. He was yelling, "You disrespected me, and now I'm ready for you." All this while Guy 2 tried to keep his cool, saying he didn't want to fight the man.

Another thing I noticed was that the two guys seemingly knew each other, but Guy 2 didn't know particularly why Guy 1 was so fuming. He asked Guy 1 what was the problem. Guy 1 shot back a confusing reply. He said, "You disrespected me."

Guy 2, having no clue what it was all about, asked, "How?"

Guy 1, without skipping a beat, gave the funniest response I could have never imagined. He said, "You took my PlayStation."

215

The conversation would have been hilarious if it weren't for two grown adults participating.

Guy 2 defensively said, "The PlayStation your sister gave me?"

Guy 1 shot back, "Yes, but you knew it was my and you took it."

Guy 2 said, "Your sister gave it to me. I didn't know where it came from."

Guy 1 wasn't having any of it. "I'm not trying to hear that. You got to fight me."

Guy 2's response was something that told me that he was far more sensible than the other one. Also, it seemed that he had made a rage-based mistake in the past and wasn't going to make another. He said, "I'm not fighting you. I just got out of jail, and I'm not trying to go back."

Guy 1 was still acting childish. "I don't care about that. I'll go to jail for my respect. I'll die for my respect." Yup, one of the dumb things people believe. I am all up for holding your own when it comes to respect and all, but the issue at hand didn't seem too momentous for me to end up in jail. With each word, Guy 1's rage was climbing up a notch. After a while of yelling, he decided he could solve the problem through a brawl.

I am not exaggerating when I tell you what he did next. It was almost 90 °F, and the kid was way too young. He was almost a baby. That man, despite all that, put his son down in the middle of the parking lot. He set the poor child on the hot pavement in the middle of the road, without an ounce of care. The baby sat there crying and would surely have felt the skin burning as he immediately started trying to crawl to his dad. His dad, on the other hand, was paying no attention to him whatsoever. He was walking towards Guy 2, still yelling, "I'll die about my respect!"

Even Guy 2 saw the absurdity of the man's action and was worried about the little, helpless child. He asked Guy 1 to get his son off the street. But all that mindless idiot could think of was rage. He said, "Don't worry about my son, but you just sit right there because I got something for you!" He went back to his car and reached for something in the backside, all the while yelling, "I'll die about my respect!!"

Guy 2 was part scared, part angry. He saw the man fishing for something and asked, "Now you are about to shoot me?"

Guy 1 snapped back, "Yes, I don't care nothing about going to jail. I'll die about my respect!" Luckily for Guy 2, whatever he was looking for, he didn't find. He surely would have killed or badly injured Guy 2 if he did. After searching rigorously, Guy 1 gave up, surely exasperated and exhausted. He walked over to his son, picked him up, and made his way to his car, yelling, "I'll see you in the streets! I'll die about my respect." Luckily for everyone, Guy 2, the baby, the bystanders, and, to some extent, Guy 1, he left without any critical damage to anyone.

This story is a prime example of exactly what I want people to learn. I want to show how mindless people can be when they are angry. They simply give up on anything when they are feeling vengeful. Guy 1 was the prime example of that. He didn't care about anyone or anything. He didn't even care for his son enough not to do what he did and what he was about to do in front of that kid. The kid surely would have been traumatized. The way I see it, he straight-up disrespected his son; he showed that the kid's comfort and safety were secondary to his rage and vengeance. That is the poorest parenting right there. He put his son in danger over a PlayStation. To have that much hatred in your heart is a disgrace.

On the other hand, Guy 2's behavior is what I want people to learn and embrace. He handled the entire situation with relative peace and sensibility. He could have infuriated the man easily; he could have hurled a few profanities his way or maybe thrown a fist or a jab his way. He wasn't even wrong, as far as I could judge from the conversation. He didn't steal or forcefully take the PlayStation; he was simply given that by the raging maniac's sister. But still, he kept calm and managed to keep himself alive and, very likely, Guy 1 out of jail.

I wish we all could be better men and women, and let go of all the hate and let go of all the negativity. I know it is a little too optimistic, but I believe we can at least try to achieve that. I am sure if we strive together, we will be able to douse much hate, if not all of it. We need to live in this world as equals. No one is better than anyone else. We are supposed to exist WITH each other, not against each other. Hate and negativity are constructs that evil men have perpetuated so they can benefit from our misery. They do nothing but destroy us.

I ask this, and dare any to come up with a sensible, logical answer to this. I will wait.

What is the point of hating?

What is the point of being negative?

If anything, all a person does is hurt the people who love them dearly. If hate and negativity are costing you your family and friends, you need to let them go, and you have to do it now. I cannot say anything fancy to convince you of this because it doesn't require any extra explanation. There isn't a single instance in recorded human history that can be used to justify hate and negativity. But there are infinite instances that can be used to prove categorically that the only real results of hate and negativity are regret, disproportionate loss, a life that could have been saved, ruined beyond repair.

I know it is a huge ask. The world is a nasty place, and life is a troubling journey for many of us. But this is where we can begin. We can begin by changing the way we look at life. Life is not going to go your way all of the time. That's life! If things went exactly my way, I would be filthy rich, lying somewhere on an exotic beach in one of the many exquisite locations scattered around the world, with no worries. I wouldn't even be writing this book. There would be no one homeless. People wouldn't be killing other people. There would be no wars. There would be no kidnappings or rapes. No one would be entangled with drugs, and everyone would have been happy. That's what I want, and that is exactly what I would have done if I could. But that is far from possible. Like I said, we can't always get everything we want.

Life does throw curveballs at everyone. We often believe that life, fate, or whatever you wish to call it, is being cruel solely to us and everyone else is happy. We are wrong. Life challenges us all just the same. Sometimes, we can do something about those challenges; sometimes, we can't. But there is one thing we can all do about it—we can all try not to let it get the better of us. We can all try not to let our circumstances make us mean and bitter. We have to accept things the way they are and keep moving forward. If we don't like it, we can and, in fact, must try to change our circumstances and fight for it. But there is no need to get mad.

Again! Why worry about something we can't change? And why cry over something that we can change?

Revenge should not have any place in your life. Learn to just let it go. I know people will push your buttons. Some people think they can get to you that way, and they will keep doing it. But the best response to such people is just to ignore them and let them go. They are not going anywhere, and they will distract you from your destination and goals with all these silly shenanigans.

I understand that emotions can run high. They are hard to control, especially when you're mad or sad. They can make you want to either kill someone or yourself. Neither is a favorable outcome. You have to find a way to control those emotions. If someone is mad, they need to surround themselves with positive things. I have shared with you some, told you things I do when I get mad. They are for you to find inspiration. I am sure you, too, would have something similar. If you don't, here is what I will suggest because I am hellbent on offering any suggestion that can help anyone save themselves from a lifetime of regret.

If you don't have anything at all, like a park or a water body near you to spend some time at, I am sure everyone today has access to music. One of the most calming things for me has been listening to old-school R&B love songs. Trust me, music has worked wonders for me and for many across the world. Those songs have actually calmed me down and helped me think more times than I can count. Love songs give me positive vibes. Not that I am fixated on them or reggae. You can choose a genre for yourself. Anything that you like, anything that influences your mood for the better and calms your nerves down would do.

Good humor is a nice antidote to anxiety and stress, too. When you feel your emotions overwhelmingly pressing, or maybe you feel a little blue, consider turning to humor. It is one of the best antidepressants I know, having next to no side effects.

When I'm sad, I watch a lot of comedy movies or specials. If media or TV is not your go-to, consider hanging out with people with positive vibes and elated spirits. When I don't feel like sitting in front of a screen, I surround myself with good, positive people who can make me laugh. People with a top-class sense of humor and, more importantly, people who have been through life's ups and downs and know that no problem is permanent. Such people can always help you lift your spirits.

Now, definitely, these two aren't the only two methods; there are just a few that I use and that work for me. You can try any other that suits you. But here I would like to raise an alarm. I might not know COMPLETELY what to do, but I do know what you SHOULDN'T—AT ANY COST! If you are sad, *DO NOT BE ALONE!* The worst thing you can do is be alone. When you are all by yourself, you do nothing but keep thinking about the situation that made you sad. Whatever foul thing happened that put you in that mood keeps playing in your mind on a loop. It only pisses you off more or makes you more sad.

If you're sad, keep yourself busy and hang around with positive people. They keep you distracted so you don't overthink. I understand that when we're sad, we want to be alone. It is natural. We think people might not understand what we are going through, but solitude is not a good thing, especially when you are not going through your best mood.

I so strongly discourage being alone when sad because things are prone to spiral in no time. When people get too sad, they might overthink to the point that they start thinking about killing themselves. I think every reader can relate to what I am saying because I am sure the thought might have crossed their mind at least once.

What does killing solve? Nothing. I believe, and I might sound harsh writing this, but killing yourself is the most selfish act you can do. If a person kills themselves, the only thing that tells me is that you don't care about your family, and maybe you never did. People claim they love nothing more than their families and then go on to end their lives because they *wrongly thought* they couldn't take it anymore. Why tell your family that you love them? Why tell your friends you love them? Why the lie? Surely, you don't care about them if you're going to kill yourself. When you kill yourself, you leave your family hurt; you leave them with grief because you were selfish; you leave them with scars that will never heal for their remaining life. If you care about them, why would you want to hurt them? That too irreparably. Think about how bad and soul-wrenching losing a loved one can make one feel. Why do you want to cause such pain? Nothing is worth killing yourself over. And I will repeat this. NOTHING. IS. WORTH. KILLING YOURSELF. OVER. Human beings are built to take all kinds of pain. Every time you endure something, your pain threshold goes up a notch. This simply means that you have an adaptability and resilience that you can leverage every time life throws something untoward at you. The simplest thing to do is to stay positive, keep healthy company, and believe in yourself to sail through every problem because you are built for that.

Another thing people do is the "Shoulda-Coulda-Woulda" thing. Yes, I touched on this subject in my first book. This time, I want to talk about the passing of someone you care about, especially someone who died in a tragedy, accident, or due to a lasting ailment. I have seen many times that people somehow blame themselves for the tragedy or accident. Then there are some who beat themselves up because they feel they didn't do enough when the person was alive. Not just that, they even regret saying things they wanted to or expressing themselves more wholeheartedly. I have heard countless times things like, "I should have told them I love them more," "I could have spent more time with them," "If I knew this was going to happen, I would have done things differently." This is that "Shoulda-Coulda-Woulda" mentality. This way of thinking is nothing but a curse. It only makes regret settle within you. What is done is done. You cannot reverse time and make amends. Hell, there are even times when things are inevitable; no one could have done anything to change whatever happened, yet people engage in such self-inflicting practices.

Don't get me wrong. I strongly believe in expressing wholeheartedly. Yes, we should say "I love you" more. Yes, you could have spent more time with them. Yes, you would have done things differently. But can you go back in time? No. Thus, there is no point wallowing and hurting yourself like that. I understand that it hurts when you lose someone you love. I know overwhelming grief tends to make you think a certain way.

But let me be real honest right now. I might sound harsh, but I say this only to save you from spiraling and losing yourself in an abyss of grief. You will never get over the death of someone you truly love. You just learn to live with it. That's just what it is. There is no magic wand to erase the hurt away. You just learn to live with it. When you start on the "Shoulda-Coulda-Wouldas," you start focusing on the things you didn't do for them. That is never going to heal you, and honestly, that is something even your loved one wouldn't have wanted for you—to wallow in grief, feeling helpless and sorry. Instead, they'd want you to accept and move on. They'd want you to be happy. If anything, for themselves, they would want you to celebrate their life if you can.

I am not asking you to just forget everything, dismiss your feelings, and just stomp ahead in life. No. I wouldn't suggest such a thing because that is not possible at all. This is what I suggest. When life throws such a tragedy at you—robbing you of someone you loved with all your heart—focus on the things that made you happy when you were with them. Live with that person in your heart. Some people will say, "Life goes on." But I say that it doesn't have to go on without the good memories your loved ones left you with. Never forget the good things. Never forget the good times you and your loved one had together. Some people will even tell you to get over it. Again! You will never get over the death of someone you care about. No one should ever tell someone to get over it after they have lost someone they care about. That is a cold thing to say to anyone who is already going through a lot. If someone tells you that, I am sorry, but that person is not your true friend or someone you should keep company with. He/she really doesn't care about you.

Believe it or not, but true love never dies. Just because the loved one is no longer with you, doesn't mean the love they had for you has died. Their love will always be with you. All I suggest is to let go of all the misleading "Shoulda-Coulda-Woulda" mentality, because it can hurt you irreparably and make you do something you regret for life. You are already suffering due to the passing of someone you loved; why inflict yourself more?

Moving on, since this book is about keeping yourself happy and peaceful and mellow and without worries, among many other things, I would delve into something troubling that I see many people engaging in.

I have observed that people have this negative bias where they want to cling to the very things that are dangerous and unhealthy for them in all aspects and manners. Things that destroy them in every way, yet they are unwilling to let it go. I know that it sounds unlikely—people clinging to something that is holistically destructive for them, but look around, and you will be surprised. In fact, you might discover that even you are one of such people.

It isn't wise to hold on to something that is destroying you from the inside and out without offering anything in return. Shed anything that destroys you mentally and physically. Let it go. Since I have observed this firsthand, I believe that you have to *choose* to be happy. More often than not, happiness is literally a choice. The world often tells us otherwise. It tells us that happiness is something that is offered by fate or destiny. The fact is that you can be happy if you want to be.

For starters, if you wish to be happy, among the first few things you can and must let go of is hate. Happiness and hate don't go together. I see that many people hold on to hate—towards people, towards culture, towards religions, towards nations, and whatnot—which is often ill-founded and almost always unnecessary. If being around someone doesn't make me happy, I simply just get up and get going. I don't wait around them and spend time on the same premises. I wouldn't look for beef with them, and no one will certainly see me spreading any kind of hate against them anywhere. I simply will not pay attention to them.

The same can go about things. If you don't like doing something, just find a way to do something else. If doing something doesn't make me happy, I'm not going to do it. For example, if I don't like a job, I'm going to find another one. You might accuse me here of oversimplifying things, but the truth is, most of the time, things are quite simple; it is we who, with overthinking, make them complex and then hateful. You might also say, "Then why aren't many people already doing that, D?"

To that, I will say something simple and plain: People do not believe. They don't believe in themselves. They don't think positively. They don't venture out to explore new things and stick to the comfort of things they are familiar with, even when they are inconvenient and unhealthy. Letting go is easy, no matter how difficult it seems. You just have to take the first few brave steps.

Everything else will align itself for you. It might sound unbelievable, and for that, I will not expect you to take my word for it. I invite you to just try it once. Let go of something you are currently doing that you hate and do something you enjoy. Then, write me back with the results.

Here, many of you might be waiting eagerly to ask me this daunting question: "Okay, D, what about if someone you love with all your heart is making you unhappy? Should we let them go too? Won't that be more hurtful?"

"Yes" to the first one, friend, and "no" to the second. Yes, letting go of anyone, even someone you love, will hurt you in the moment, but in the long run, it will be cathartic and healthy—always.

I know that it will be hard, but you have to love yourself enough to give yourself happiness. I also know it will take a lot of will and a heavy heart to do that, but I simultaneously know for a fact that this is the best and the only sensible thing to do. If someone you love genuinely is not acknowledging and appreciating that, if they are not changing their ways to reciprocate your love, they are not going to do that ever. Sad, I know, but also true. People only change when they want to. If they are not willing to change for the better in a positive way for you, they don't love you, even if they are pretending to (which might be the case with many people). Let such a person go. They are not worth holding on to.

Look at it like this. Would you eat something you don't like, something that is unhealthy? No, you wouldn't. You would throw it away. Then why hold on to things that are not making you happy and healthy? Why are you staying with someone day in and day out who is making you unhappy?

And while I am in the discussion of being with someone who doesn't make you happy, I'll surely delve into one puzzling arrangement. I have heard people say that they are in a healthy, loving relationship, but their partner doesn't seem to share their dreams and ambitions or doesn't seem to respect them. Red flag alert! I am sorry, but you are with the wrong person despite their confessions of love for you.

You should not stay in a relationship if the person doesn't respect your ambitions and doesn't support you. And I am only talking about the mental and emotional support. Being there for your partner is very important. If your partner has life goals, you should support them with eagerness and zeal. The two of you are supposed to be the better half of each other, remember, through thick and thin? What good is a partner if they are not there on the sidelines, cheering for you to take on life's challenges? There is no point in being with such a person, and honestly, your "romantic" arrangement is anything but. The only thing such an unsupportive person will do is bring you down. If you continue to be with a person like that, you won't be able to achieve much. And someday, you will look back and see that you have lost a great deal that you could have avoided. You will discover the many opportunities you would have lost. And before you know it, you will end up in the "Shoulda-Coulda-Woulda" rut. I don't think I need to explain again why you don't want that. Don't miss your opportunities in life because of your partner who claims to love you but doesn't do anything that might prove just that. Let them go so you can live your life.

I was with such a woman once. She never supported me in anything. Every time I did something for the better, something for us, she tried to knock me down. It seemed like she didn't want anything good for me. One time, I shared with her that I wanted to be a part of a marathon. I wanted to go on a five-kilometer run for a long time. Instead of encouraging me, she straight-up told me that I wouldn't be able to finish. She told me that I would pass out before I went across the finish line. Another time, I excitedly told her that I was considering doing stand-up comedy. She mockingly told me no one would show up to see me. Yet another time, I shared with her my ambition to run for county commissioner. And, as if she were maintaining a streak, she told me that I would never make it. Everything I wanted to do, she would knock the idea down before I would even take the first step. There wasn't a single thing she supported me in; now that I am writing this down, I don't think I can think of one thing where she might have had my back. I can assure you that I was very relieved when I ended things with her. No, I didn't become the stand-up comedian or the commissioner, but I certainly did many things that I wanted to later with her gone.

The gist of it all? If you're with someone who doesn't share your dreams, it's best for you to let them go. You don't need negativity in your life, especially from someone for whom you harbor emotional feelings. Go after your goals and dreams and look for a partner who is willing to at least respect them, even if they are not that eager for them themselves. In fact, this is an indicator to look for if you are looking for "the one."

I said a few paragraphs above that you're the only one who can make you happy. I haven't said or written a truer statement. And drawing from that, if you're hanging on to someone who is making you unhappy, that is entirely your fault. You're putting up with everything unpleasant and unsavory, even things that displease you, in a wishful hope that they might like you when, deep down inside, you know they won't.

Again, the same can be said about other things in your life. Your job, for example. If you are at a job and working hard simply because the salary you are drawing is a hefty amount, while everything else is toxic and unhealthy, the job is not as good as you think it is. If the supervisor is always fussing at you despite your efforts, there is no room to grow, and there is always a crushing workload, how is that good money? What amount of money can be good enough to rob you of your peace and your health? These are rhetorical questions. I know the answer. None. The pay is not worth the work you are doing. You need to let that job go.

You are in control of your own life. You are in control of your own happiness. You don't have to do anything you don't want to do. You don't have to put up with anything that doesn't make you happy. Just, simply let it go!

Chapter 5

Let God

I will begin this chapter by borrowing the words from The Book:

Let he who is without sin cast the first stone.

Get it? This single verse can be a counter to end most of the feuds we have today. *No one is perfect*—we all have paraded with this statement and shoved it in people's faces. I do not need a confirmation on this. But the one person we need to tell this more often than we do to others is our own self!

The truth is quite the contrary—we are busy judging others. Why, I do not have a clue. Before I delve into this further, I will give a disclaimer. Some of you are about to get mad at me with this chapter, but the truth is the truth. And I will say the truth even if it sounds like a tirade.

Right, don't wrong nobody! I have, in my immature days, questioned these golden words of my grandfather. They sounded like a responsibility—As if I have to be the one always doing the right thing. It was only later that I realized the many benefits of these valuable words.

I see today that people are throwing stones at others as if their slate is as clean as that of a newborn baby. They have demons in their closet, vicious, disgusting, and vile. Yet they have the audacity to act all saint. What gives you the right to throw stones at someone else? What gives you the right to judge people when you're not perfect? Nothing and no one. I am sure many of you believe that your sins are not as foul as others. Well, you can't decide that. I know many of you must have spat out a *"No one on this planet is perfect"* to someone at any opportunity you might have gotten. But many of us don't include our own selves in the "no one" of the statement.

What misplaced vanity or a stupid sense of "I am Mr./Mrs. Righteous" makes you think you're better than the next person? Why are you judging? In fact, judging, without context, without self-evaluating, without self-corrections, without a solid basis to back it up, is a sin—and a big one by my measures or any other measures of morality. What or who put you in that position to evaluate someone's character and pass judgments?

Here is a question that I am going to come back to later: *What is the only sin that is unforgivable?* I will let this one sit for a while before I carry further...

Figured it out yet? I know you probably have come up with the answer, but you might not want to say it out loud because you might be committing it and without remorse, too. Sorry to put it the way I am about to, but this is one sin—the sin of judging—maybe one that most "God-fearing" Christians might be committing. Hell, some might even be proud of doing it, believing that they are keeping themselves and others in check. They are doing anything but.

Some of these Christians want to be holier than other people. They might even be the ones who'd be hiding the most heinous demons, but they pander to their misplaced sense of self-righteousness by judging others. I know many of you might be offended because I took a jab directly at "Christians", but we cannot deny the fact that many "church-going", "righteous", and "God-fearing" Christians have scared away people from God.

Today, many young people don't want to go to church because church people judge them and put them down. The moment a young soul enters a church, the veterans will cross-check them with a whole list of merits: Do they have the appropriate attire on? Are they keeping their voices low? Do they have the right posture, and are they using the right language? Are they using a smartphone or something? Was he/she here last Sunday? I can go on, but you get the gist.

Since when did churches become interrogation rooms? You are supposed to welcome people to church. Love them no matter what. Encourage them to be a great person. Lead them to the Heavenly Father. Wasn't this the goal of churches? Since when did God only understand English, and that too of a particular type? Today, most of you "Christians" criticize them. You scare them by telling them they are going to hell just because they are dressed or carrying themselves a certain way. In actuality, you don't know where they are going. No one does.

I am not saying that the church doesn't deserve respect, or maybe that one can take a stroll through the church without having any reason. I respect the church by all means. It is a holy place and worth every ounce of respect. But its worth and respect doesn't lie in uniforms and talking in hushed whispers. It lies in abiding by its commandments. It is a sanctuary for all, without judgment, without critique, and with all the room for corrections. If we want people to welcome the place and respect it the way it should be respected, the best way is to welcome them as who they are and gradually let them understand the importance and merit of the rules, etiquette, principles, and commandments of the place.

You have these "holier than thou" Bible-holding people on the side of the road yelling at cars, telling people they're going to hell. They sit there and judge people. What kind of demented thing is that to do? They sit there and judge people all day, people they don't even know. Some of them sit there and hold signs with dead babies and fetuses on them. They are yelling at women, telling them they are going to hell for having an abortion. These people are judging women and don't even know them. They don't know how they got pregnant or what circumstances they are living in. The woman's body is a business that is solely between her and God. Not you, some church-goer who thinks they are doing their due just because they make a trip to the local church every Sunday, while hiding the most outrageous sins in their coffers. It is only between her and God.

What if she repents, gets saved, and then dies? Now what? Will she end up in heaven? I think the correct answer is a resounding yes, and Jesus' life has enough examples to make my case. This should raise the question: What will happen to you? Think about it. You've been judging this woman the whole time she has been on this earth. You've been sinning by judging her, believing as if you know all the rights from wrongs. When you die, are you going to heaven then? With a lifetime of sins of judgment in your balance? Something for you to think about.

What I would further want to highlight here is the irony (and hypocrisy) of what these "holier than thou" fanatics believe and do. Most people holding all these signs up talk and parade about being pro-life. They claim that a woman should have no abortion simply because they are killing a child. If that's the case, and you are so pro-life, why are you not holding up signs for feeding the starving kids? Where are the signs for the young ones starving and dying of malnutrition every day? Are those lives not worth saving? When I was a starving kid, I didn't see one person with a placard saying "Food for the starving!" I don't even remember anyone discussing it.

Some kids in this world are starving to death, and here you are, supposedly God-loving, God-fearing people, worried about what a woman is doing with her body. If you are so pro-life, where are you with your signs when someone takes someone else's life? I don't see a rally against murderers, child-rapists, and killers. Our correctional institutions are filled with murderers living in government-operated facilities, looking for an exit for good behavior, but I don't see people cursing and cussing outside penitentiaries.

The truth is that people are selectively pro-life. People are dying all over this world for nothing, and the same people who are at these abortion clinics and on the side of the road don't seem to have an ounce of care. According to some estimates, there are about 3.1 million kids who die from hunger each year. Google it, and you will come across the number. It might be even more than that. If you are pro-life, where are your signs? Where are your protests? Every day, about 37 people are killed by a drunk driver. Where are the signs to stop drinking and driving, or maybe to declare it a capital offense? You can't be selectively pro-life and not be hypocritical at the same time. Every life should matter to you.

If you're going to be pro-life, do it all the way. You should care that there is a little boy getting beaten to death by his parents. You should care about a little girl getting raped and left for dead. If you are truly pro-life and want a change, help make changes to real-world problems that are already present and in staggering numbers. Save the lives of those who are already living. Help feed the homeless. Help starving kids eat. Help raise awareness against child predators. Be an advocate to end child abuse. There are countless avenues to steer attention to. There are people living (or dying) in unspeakable conditions, and yet we have masses worried about what a woman does with her body.

Again! What a woman does with her body is between her and God. I know, to many, it sounds what is today called "woke," but it is not. It is logical. It is religious. People are going to be who they are, no matter what you say. In fact, yelling, cursing, cussing, and committing hate crimes is only going to make it do more of what these people are parading against. And from a Godly perspective, we have no reason to judge anyone. The Heavenly Father is the only one with that authority. The Heavenly Father doesn't need your help for judgment. The Heavenly Father is not hiring, and if he is, I need to put my application in. I'm just saying.

This might be one of the most unfair things people do—Judge others. And I say unfair because there is hardly anyone who holds themselves to the same standards as they do to others. Instead of focusing on loving people, showing them that they are great, letting them know that the Heavenly Father is the key to their life, and thus correcting them or allowing them some margin of error, people are always scrutinizing others. And even this scrutiny and judging seem to be done with an intent to infuriate rather than to correct.

I say this because all I hear people do is be critical and never offer a solution or another way of doing things. They point fingers, and that's that. When you only judge and point fingers, you do nothing but get people mad. When you get people mad, they no longer want to hear what you have to say. Consequently, even when you try to discuss a solution that includes a divine intervention from the Heavenly Father, people do not even try to hear anything you have to say. In fact, this drives them away not only from a *discussion* of God but also from places that might lead them to Him, such as church, sermons, Bible Studies, Sunday Schools, etc. The Heavenly Father says, "Go out in the world and preach to the people." Nowhere does it say, "Do it so aggressively that it scares them away from Him."

No matter who it is being done against, judging cannot be considered a pardonable or acceptable thing. For example, people judge other people because they are gay. Here is my view on that, and I know many people and readers won't like it: That's between the person and the Heavenly Father. Whatever a person's orientation is, it is an intimate affair that can and must only be judged by God. I'm pretty sure that they already know what the Bible says about being homosexual; The Bible is a very famous book and accessible to all. Why do you keep throwing it in their faces, judging or ridiculing them, and telling them they are going to hell? How do you know? Have you been to hell, or did God tell you Himself? Now I am not saying or encouraging others to disrespect the Bible or abandon or dismiss its teachings; all I am saying is for people not to be so vain as to decide who goes to heaven or hell because it is not their verdict. People change and repent and amend their ways, and they are given that luxury from God.

There was a guy named Richard Wayne Penniman, better known as Little Richard. In an interview, he shared his story about his orientation. He shared that at one point in his life, he was gay. He had spent a good part of his life believing and practicing that, but later down the line, thanks to a chain of events, he turned to God. He was able to make amends and fix himself up. Not only that, Richard was also able to serve himself in the way of the Lord. Little Richard preached all over the place. He talked about the Heavenly Father to anyone who would listen. Sadly, Little Richard passed away in May of 2020, but thankfully, he died a man of God.

To all the people who feel that God has hired them to judge, I want you to tell me something. I want to know what your answer to this question is. "Where do you think Little Richard ended up?" Heaven or hell? If you say heaven, and I hope you do, why are you judging other people for being gay? If Richard can find his way back to God after spending such a life, how do you know or maybe why do you think others can't?

Whether we like to admit it or not, the truth of the matter is that *you never know the path that the Heavenly Father has for people.* He is full of forgiveness and never closes the path back to Him on anyone. It is this judgment that sends people spiraling into sins, making them believe they can't repent. It is you with your untimely and misplaced judgment that scares them away from their loving God—you push them away and do not let them heal. If for anyone, you should be scared of being thrown into hell yourself.

God made all of us to love each other. The way some of you treat people for doing something *you* don't like is ridiculous. Yes, many people judge others for things simply because they are not a fan of what the others are doing. That's like saying, "Because I don't eat potato salad, I'm supposed to talk and treat people bad who make potato salad. I'm supposed to grab the bowl of potato salad, throw it in the trash and scream at you and scare you, and force you to not make potato salad but make mac and cheese instead."

Some of you reading this might be feeling guilty about mac and cheese while reading this. Maybe you love mac and cheese, and might even know how to make a good one, but since I used it in my example and talked about it badly, you might be hesitant. You might be second-guessing yourself for loving something that is being used as a bad example. Now, doesn't that sound ridiculous?

It is human psychology to be mad when people force things on you. If someone tries to force you to do something you are not ready for at the moment, and then, when you refuse to oblige and the same forceful people start talking bad about you, you will be mad. In fact, that is going to make you rebel against what they are trying to force you to do. That's exactly what happens when you try to force the Heavenly Father on people; it scares them away.

I know you're trying to do the right thing. And I can't appreciate you enough for that. But it is necessary to understand that there is always a right way and a wrong way to do something. And this right or wrong way makes all the difference. In fact, the method you choose to do the right thing is almost as important as the right thing.

The right way is to talk to them. Be patient with them and slowly lead them to the Heavenly Father. Let them see the value in God's way and understand why that is better. And you will have to do it more than once. Again and again, without exhausting and giving up.

The wrong way is yelling at them. Scaring them by telling them they are going to hell is never going to turn them to God, only away from him.

We don't have to look far and beyond to see what I am saying. Look around. Today, as aggressive as we have become, as much as we are trying to force God upon people, we see masses turning away. Just in case you didn't notice. It's not working with people anymore. You have more people turning away and not believing than you have people going towards the Heavenly Father.

There is nothing wrong with the people in the LGBTQ community. They are people, just like me and you. You are supposed to love everyone, no matter what they do or did. Remember these words?

"But I say unto you, love your enemy, bless them that curse you, do good to them that hate you, and pray for them that despitefully use you, and persecute you."

Isn't this from the same Bible that people shove against those whom they think are sinners?

You are supposed to pray for people. You are supposed to pray *with* people. You don't pray against people, at least not if you don't want to go against the book.

I could be wrong, and I dearly wish I were, but from what it seems, Christian people have a little hatred in their hearts for people they don't understand. They are quick to give out verdicts and show people the road to hell, even if the person is just a tad bit different from what they consider right. To all such Christian brothers and sisters, I say this, with a grieving heart, might I add, "You are no better than a grown person writing on a kid's Valentine's Day card, 'the KKK is coming.'"

Nowadays, more and more people don't want to go to church. "Why?" I'm glad you asked that question; it shows that you at least worry. From what I can see, and I am sure I am not the only one who does, it seems like going to some churches these days is like going to a fashion show. The last time I went to church, I observed that people were more worried about what someone was wearing than they were about what the preacher was preaching. I could observe people gauging and judging people's attire as if they were critiques in a fashion show. I bet many would have failed to recall and read me back a single line from that sermon if I had asked them immediately after the sermon.

That is not it. I have been to churches in modern times and found the congregation members to have the most appalling behavior, something that can never be expected from the regulars of a Jesus-abiding church. In there, I saw members talk down on people like they were better than them, like they had been given the glad tidings of going to heaven. And if you think this is all, allow me to prove you wrong. I have discovered, and I am embarrassed to even write this in my book about people of the church, that there are some churches that have congregation members, including the preacher, sleeping with each other. Can you imagine that? Regulars of a place that preaches not to sleep outside the precious covenant of marriage, doing just that?

I am not done. I have learned that there are some churches that collect money on the premise of outreach and charity and social work, but they never spend a single penny on helping anyone. Where does the money go? Well, it will sound sad and also infuriating if you are a true believer—*TO THE PASTOR AND THE OTHER RELATED CLERGY*. The pastor used the money to get a new car and a new house. If, by now, you are boiling with rage, wait till you hear this. There are some churches that have members who molest little kids. This one is something that boils my blood the most. How can you even spend your days in a holy place where the name of the Lord is called every morning, spend your time reading, analyzing, and preaching the Bible, and then go on to commit such an atrocity?

Are you not afraid of God's reckoning at all? Or are you not a believer?

The sins and misdoings related to the church are many and never-ending, and this, for me at least, is heart-wrenching. There are churches that have a pastor who preaches his whole life story but never shares about what's in the Bible in its truest sense. They only discuss the Bible to further their story. There are some churches with congregation members who fake devotion so earnestly, one would think they might not even know the spelling of a sin. But in reality and on the streets, these church-goers do bad, despicable businesses. And all these narrations, these listings of the kind of sins I have written, are not handed-down accounts. I have personally been to more than one church that might have one or another kind of sin running rampant behind walls and closed doors.

I know many of you might be furious with me for the love you might have for the church. I won't hold it against you. You might be thinking that D thinks of himself as too holy to go after the churches. I assure you, I don't hold any such belief. I am not perfect, but I know what love is and I know who the Heavenly Father is. And thus I can differentiate well enough what is right and what is wrong. I know what God will like and what He won't.

If these churches do the right things—treat people right, don't ridicule or talk badly about people—I can assure you that I will be the first one to appreciate them out loud by any means I can, even write a book if I have to.

There is a dire need to change our ways. We need a revamp, not just of the Christians in general, but even the church. Members of the church need to start welcoming everyone in their church without expecting anything from them, like money or even acknowledgment or praise. We need to make it a place that is drama-free, genuinely caring, healing, and without judgment. We need to make it a place where people feel safe, even when they are making choices that will alter their reality. Remember, Richard, Little Richard? I can assure you that he surely would have transformed himself because someone would have told him that it is okay to get lost as long as you are willing to come back. Someone would have told him the truth—that you can always find your way back to God because He is forgiving, always. We have to become the loving congregation we were known for. We make these changes, and I can assure you that people will come to church more.

While I have been mostly addressing my Christian folks, the readers might think it is only we who are at fault. I will take this moment to say it loud and clear that I am not just talking to Christian people. I am talking to all religions. Here I will turn to my grandfather's words: *Right, don't wrong nobody!* The "nobody" in those words isn't just for Christians. It is for everyone, for humanity itself.

Religious people often struggle with accepting, embracing, or understanding things that might not align with what their religion preaches. I get that. They define their lives in accordance with their religious teachings, and when something comes that lies beyond that realm, they become confused and ultimately angry.

To them, I'd say something that they might not want to subscribe but deep down in their heart, they'd know that it is true. *Some things in this world are not meant to be understood.* I am so sure of this because I know that all religions in the world ask for believing in things that defy all logic. No religion is an exception.

But I also say this because, from what I have observed by assessing people of different faiths, all religions, in the bigger picture, preach and promote love and healing. All religions preach that, as God's children, our most noble and paramount duty is to love. You might not want to agree with me, but I am open to discussion. Prove me wrong.

And after knowing that, I ask: *How hard is that?*

It might be one of the easiest things to do with the most return. If you ask me, that is the most lucrative trade I can think of.

Everything good starts with love—I don't have to claim a religion to understand that. *"Love thy neighbor"*—isn't that what the Book says? This is a question to the Christians, but I honestly believe there is a similar equivalent (or maybe even the same) in all other scriptures, holy books, tomes—whatever guidebook you follow. Which brings me to the same question: *How hard is that?* And this time it is rhetorical. I firmly believe that to love is the easiest action to undertake. There are so many ways one can opt that I don't think there is a single person who might be able to have an excuse not to offer love.

If someone is hungry, feed them. If someone needs clothes, clothe them; you can share yours, you don't have to buy new ones. If someone is sick, attend to them and assist them with their chores; even if that is too much for you—running errands—maybe spend some time with them, talk to them, enliven their mood a little. It's that simple. If I sit down to list examples like these, this book would be a million pages long, and that too would only be Volume 1.

And what confuses me more and throws me off is how skewed people are towards the idea of reciprocity of love. I see people turning their backs on people in need, avoiding anyone who they think might be even a slight inconvenience. But the same people are seen fuming mad when they get the same treatment from people. Isn't that ironic? Or better yet, dumb?

Why would you expect help from someone when you never help anyone else? That isn't how it works. Or should I say, that isn't how it *should* work. You send love out to the world, you get it back. It is that simple. And no, I am not being unrealistically optimistic, as many might think. I have experienced it firsthand; I have seen it work firsthand, so you can't convince me the world has run out of love to give.

If you are a little overwhelmed by the discussion so far, I apologize, but it is about to get worse. Another great vice that I see today is that in modern times, genuine help and assistance are acts instead of a wholesome, heartfelt service to humanity. It is motivated by a goal to merely *appear* charitable and garner attention. The only time I see people being helpful to someone is when cameras are around. Business owners and politicians are the most notorious ones in that. These people only appear to help those who can reciprocate their efforts. For a businessman, it is usually a fiscal return; for politicians, it is the vote bank and helping hands for their campaigns. The essence is lost on them. It is only publicity and fame, and a lucrative advantage that motivates them. "What is wrong with that, D?" You might ask. "Even if they are doing it for the showmanship, at least someone is getting helped, right?" Well, yes, right. But that kind of help is rarely a "help." It is a transaction. And to be honest, quite a non-profitable one for the people and only lucrative for the businessmen or the politicians. The people usually end up giving something far more valuable than they know.

When you do things for someone, it should always be from the heart and without an expectation of a return. "Well, that is asking a lot, man—giving without expecting anything in return, even the spotlight or acknowledgment…Do *you* even do that, D?" you might want to ask. Yes, I do. I am not the kind to preach something I don't follow. I am not, well, I am not a "politician."

And I will give you an example. Not many people know, but I have, on many occasions, done things to help people I found to be in some kind of financial constraints. There have been times when I came across someone at the cash register who needed things but couldn't afford them. I paid for them without a second's thought. And I will do it again every chance I get and my finances allow me.

I was out one day when I saw a woman trying to cross a four-lane highway in a wheelchair in the rain. It was troubling enough to see her struggle when something went wrong with her wheelchair or it got stuck. I could see people buzz past her, but no one helped her. I immediately got out in the middle of traffic and rain and pushed her to the bus stop that had shelter. I asked her if she needed a ride somewhere. She declined the ride because she saw the bus coming. I would have dropped her off if she wanted to, but I couldn't have forced her. I am sharing this not to paint myself as a hero. God knows I am not close to being one and don't intend to either. I am sharing this for two reasons. One—to remind myself that these acts gave me the most profound sense of satisfaction. And two—to remind the readers that spreading love and reaching out to people doesn't have to be a grand act with spotlights and cameras. You don't have to buy the entire grocery for someone, or maybe donate a million dollars to pay off someone's mortgage. Buying a loaf of bread and a carton of milk would do just fine. It doesn't have to be paying for someone's leg surgery to help them walk. It can be something as simple as pushing a wheelchair out of the rain to help them. These small acts are as valuable an act as any.

Whenever my budget allows me, I go to the store and buy a bunch of candy and toys. I leave it at the cash register and tell the cashier to give the stuff to all the kids who come into the store. They are not always the most expensive ones, but they are good enough to put a smile on a child's face. And no, I don't do it for the camera because I can assure you that I have been asked. Where I am a regular, I have been asked many times to at least let the children know who is paying for the candies, but I have always denied. I do things not for TV cameras, not because I'm expecting something in return, not even because I can write it off on taxes. I never wrote anything off that I have given to charity on taxes. I did it simply because I wanted to, and God has blessed me enough that I can. I do it because I want to do something nice for others, because I believe that if there is someone who is going to make this world a livable and a happy place, it is us—the common people. You and me. Not these politicians, not these businessmen, not these so-called leaders of the world and peace ambassadors, but us, the people.

A lot of these politicians only make a move when the TV cameras move. I know I might be sounding bitter, but I'm being real honest. Most of these politicians are in office only for the money. And I am not hating. I know people have good in them. Some of these politicians probably did start off wanting to do the right thing, but somewhere along the line, they lost their way. Either they got corrupted, or they were so cornered off, they ran out of options to comply with the corrupt system. Not all politicians are bad, but when the good ones try and do something good for the people, the bad ones knock them down.

There is a systematic corruption that governs us. There are a lot of laws that I don't agree with. And not because I have an ego problem or I am a rebel. It is because this systematic corruption designs and imposes rules over us that it either punishes us unnecessarily or limits us. And these corrupt politicians peddle these rules as if their lives depend on them. They play holy and innocent, as if they, too, are cornered off. Some of these politicians will try and tell you it's hard for them to make a decision because of the budget. The truth is, it's not hard. We have enough resources to go on. And enough intelligent people to come up with smart plans to use these resources efficiently.

If people need help, you help them. It's that simple. That should be the first point of attention (which is not the case), instead of devising elaborate rules and sanctions and charades to appear holy. For example, I don't think there should be such a thing as a homeless veteran. Those people fought for a country. And what did the country do for them? It left them hung out to dry. Some people lost limbs, lost loved ones, lost their sanity for this country, and they are living their lives under a bridge in the most deplorable conditions. There is no rule, ordinance, or constitutional clause that can convince me that it is right. No sir!

Another thing! The people who wagered with their lives on the battlefronts for this country, for its freedom, for its success, shouldn't have to jump through hoops to see a doctor. It's simple. If you serve in the military, health care should be free and easy. It should be a seamless process. There shouldn't be co-pays, waiting lines, or gaps in coverage for veterans. Veterans should be able to see any doctor they want without having to pay a penny. And any system catering to the vets should be designed with convenience in mind. Many of these people are not very good with technology and similar "smart" systems. Whether it's at the VA hospital or at a civilian doctor's office, a veteran should have more access to easy health care.

And it shouldn't be limited to medical assistance or hospital visits. That is only half the plight. Or maybe half of half. In fact, there are crises that can be addressed beforehand, which might save our veterans from turning to hospitals in the first place. For example, the crisis of housing. There is an alarming number of our veterans who are living in the worst of the worst conditions. They should have easier access to housing. The government spends more money on wars (some even not our own) rather than helping the people and rehabilitating those who have already served with their lives. They send billions of dollars to help another country that is at war, but some people who fought our wars can't get decent housing, food, or health care.

Need I remind you that these veterans didn't go to war just to protect their own families? They didn't battle it out on the front to protect their own neighborhood. No! They went to war for every American. They went out for us—for me and you. Why is it that we can't protect our veterans who protect us? Why is it that when it comes to rehabilitating and looking after our protectors, things become "difficult?" Why can't we speak up for them?

I hear politicians claim just that, producing botched-up, manufactured, and exaggerated statistics to substantiate their claims. It is as easy as anything. It is easier than spending billions of dollars and sending thousands of troops to foreign lands for foreign wars we don't need. The government wastes millions to blow up rockets for mere experimentation and to make weapons of mass destruction. You can't tell me the government doesn't have enough money to help veterans. The government shouldn't be asking people to step in for help. We shouldn't have commercials saying "Help the veterans." It is supposed to be a job governments should endorse proudly and responsibly.

The veteran must have everything—housing, welfare, medical. And governments should do it without politics. Politicians should never play politics with the well-being of veterans. Very often, we see politicians using veterans' welfare to win votes. I cannot think of anything more despicable than that. It shouldn't be brandished as a service. It should be considered a duty. You don't see a doctor preening and campaigning as holy for prescribing medicine. They do it because it is their duty. Our veterans served with honor, and they deserve nothing less. They served us with their lives, and it is only decent that we dutifully ensure their lives are honored and respected and taken care of with utmost diligence.

I had a friend who fought for this country. And if I had asked him, I am certain he would say he would do it again if he had to. He got cancer. He went to a VA hospital, but he was told they couldn't help him. He went to another. There, too, he got a similar response. They kept screwing him around with the paperwork. A form after another was served, collecting information I am sure they already have. After a library full of paperwork was squared away, he was granted all the co-pay options. No, it wasn't much, but here is the point: VETERAN HEALTHCARE SHOULD BE 100% FREE. This isn't an emotional suggestion; it is a practical one. If he hadn't fought for this country, he would have never gotten sick with that dangerous disease. We used him in his prime days, days he could have used to make a strong financial foundation for his rainy days.

But instead, he served those days for us. Now he needed help. The only logical and moral thing to do here is to help him. No questions, no tomes of forms and paperwork—help. Plain and simple.

I can go on this one atrocity alone, but I have some more things to highlight. It is not just our veterans who are getting the short end of the stick. It is every one of us. At least, most of America. I have been a patriot, always will be. I might have rooted for some politician or other, but, with age, I have woken up to a truth that we all have to understand before it is too late (it almost is).

I can say with certainty that most of the laws that are passed are not for the middle class. Most of them are not for the working men or women. In fact, they are to *exploit* the working men and women. The laws serve and benefit the rich. Everyone else who is in the middle has to fight it out. If we look closely, we will discover that most of these politicians are really rich. Those who aren't, become rich over time, serving these offices they hold. So it is foolish to think they want to serve the middle class or other classes. Do you really think they care about the middle class when they stay rich by exploiting them?

And this isn't a jab at the Grand Old Party or the Democrats. I'm talking about all of them. Most of these politicians own businesses. They want you to be consumers only. They'll never want you to be so independent and will never care about your welfare. In fact, as long as you buy their products, they couldn't care less about whether you have a place to live, whether you own a car, or have healthcare. They only care about how to ensure you stay in the position you are in and keep buying their addictive products.

Before I start talking about the next thing, I want you to understand that my preference and inclination are always towards resorting to forgiveness when faced with an option. I think you should always forgive someone, no matter what they have done. I know it is an expectation too big. Sometimes the crime isn't pardonable. But that is also when forgiving is most valuable.

Now, I am not saying that any wrongdoer must not be punished for what they might have done. All I am saying is that forgiveness is far more relieving, healing, and liberating in the long run, and if you can find it in yourself to forgive someone who has wronged you, I will always encourage you to choose that option.

With that being said, I would steer you toward the law on murder. Murder is categorized into individual groups—you have first-degree murder, second-degree murder, capital murder, manslaughter, and so on. I have never understood this law. It doesn't seem quite well thought out. I believe the law needs grand amendments. Here is why.

Let's just say someone kills someone you care about, God forbid. Let's just say the killer/murderer is about 35 years old at the time of the crime. When the killer/murderer goes to court, goes through the whole process, and finally pleads guilty to manslaughter, he might get up to 20 years. That is an average sentencing. By the time he would have served his sentence, he would be about 55 years old. That doesn't seem right to me. According to the law governing manslaughter, it goes something like if you pull a gun on someone and shoot them, and if you somehow prove that you really didn't intend to kill that person, you get 20 years or so.

That seems a bit absurd. I believe that if you pull a gun, that is already enough to conclude that you *wanted* to kill that person. How can one maintain that they had a gun, they pointed it at someone, they fired a shot, and yet they didn't *intend* to kill them? What?

Everyone knows what guns are capable of. Is it justified that someone who did that be out at 55? What about you? You lost someone who you can't wake up, get them out of the grave and hug them and go back to the happy life you might have been living with them again. They can't get up and go home with you. If they are not returning, how and why exactly is the killer/murderer getting the same opportunity? They made a choice. Between drawing the weapon and shooting it, they might have a hundred chances to not use the weapon, but they did. Why shouldn't they bear the complete consequences when they took complete action?

I might sound cold here, but I strongly feel it should be a "life for a life" law. If you kill someone, you do life. And this doesn't just include reckless shooters; it includes everyone reckless and irresponsible enough to do anything that mortally jeopardizes a human life. For example, if you drink and drive and you end up killing someone, you should get life. You might argue that you *never wanted* to, but you did. You ended a life. You incurred irreversible damage. You robbed someone of a loved one. You disrupted a family. You robbed a soul of a life they could have enjoyed. That all amounts to a consequence of a commensurate proportion, which, of course, translates to a life sentencing. I cannot think of another befitting punishment.

Now, if you are thinking that I am going for an eye-for-an-eye approach blindly (no pun intended), wait. I am proposing no such thing. I know accidents happen. And that is why I am open to scrutinizing the intent of actions. Not everyone who killed someone should see the noose. If someone dies because of an accident, there should be no charges. If someone killed in self-defense because they were being threatened physically, they should have the right to defend themselves. The justice apparatus should reinforce the system to gauge the intent of actions as accurately as possible.

The system should be strictly rigorous and must not have any loopholes to exploit. If someone dies because you were negligent with something that you knew one day might hurt or kill someone, you shouldn't have any respite. You should do some jail time. You shouldn't have leverage, loopholes, or gaps in the legal system to exploit. Many times, we see someone who clearly deserves the death penalty but goes away free with almost no jail time. Loopholes are churned based on critical reasons such as lack of intent, diminished capacity, insanity pleas, etc. The system should be fortified so that no one can exploit any reason to get away with vile crimes.

And the focus is not merely on someone killing someone. It includes everything that inflicts irreversible harm on people. Things such as someone selling illegal drugs, firearms, fake passports and money, human trafficking, etc., anything that can lead to one soul killing another.

Like I said already, if I'm 25 years old and you are 25 years old and you kill someone that I care about, God forbid, I don't want to see you out on the street when we turn 55 years old. That would be a kick in the stomach—gut-wrenching and heartbreaking.

Why am I emphasizing fixing the system "rigorously" and "strictly"? Let me explain. I'm about to show you the great divide in the justice system and show you how the law works for the rich and politicians as opposed to the common man.

Let's say a 25-year-old someone critically injured a loved one of an influential politician—someone the politician really cared about deeply. Now the emphasis is on "not kill but critically injured." The person injured, the politician's loved one, survives—wounded and all but alive. The way our justice system works (unjustly), it will give 40 years to the person who injured the politician's loved one. Ask yourself this: Will the same punishment be given if the injured person were not a politician's loved one? If the person injured were a common man, someone with no influential ties, the perpetrator would have been given 20 years max. That isn't fair by any measure, is it? But the sad part is that this is an actual reality of our justice system.

The law should be across the board—universal and just. A life for a life makes more sense to me. You might want to disagree, but before that, I would want you to think once and imagine yourself in a position where you are being hung for an accident or your loved one being injured by an influential person who gets away easy. Get back to me once you do that...

I believe our system is a bit lenient towards many heinous crimes. For example, I think all rapists, child molesters, traffickers and abductors shouldn't get less than 60 years in prison. And trust me, that is me being lenient. These aren't crimes that should be dealt with any respite or leniency, but we live in a world that believes everyone deserves a 2nd chance, so I'll just conform. But at least 60 years is enough time to make such criminals regret destroying a life.

The justice system should be deterrent before it offers opportunities for moral amendments or second chances. The idea is simple—We make the laws tougher so criminals would think twice before they do it. We should focus on stopping the crime before it happens, more than we focus on deciding what to do if it happens. I feel—quite strongly and with visible evidence—that tougher laws will reduce criminal activity. Lawmakers should always think about keeping people safe, and one of the best ways to do that is to enforce a system that deals out the harshest punishments to criminals. People are dying every day because lots of people don't fear prison. Criminal minded people know that at some point in their lives, they will be walking the streets again. Add to that good behavior and other leverage, and they might even be back out killing and committing crimes before even serving a just length of time. I think I am starting to drive my point home—let's make laws to make people think otherwise.

But here, I would like to take a step back. Before I go on about suggesting changes in the system, I'd say this: Hate for criminal activities starts at home. I strongly believe that it is our duty to endorse the responsibility of bringing up our children right, with the correct values and morals. We must raise our children with a natural disgust for crime and wayward ways. We have to do better in our homes. We have to do better at the schools. We need to keep our children out of jail. Childhood is where it all begins. Often, we let go of or ignore habits that culminate in criminal behaviors at a later age. Parents are letting their children go by with things that should be concerning. The responsibility to make our country a peaceful one isn't supposed to be endorsed only by governments or politicians.

All I hear is people fighting for more money for prison reforms. We want governments to take reformative measures and spend millions on fixing criminals. How about if we spend those millions to keep our kids from going to prison in the first place? The rapper/actor Ice Cube is big on prison reform. He has been fighting that fight for a while now. I always had great respect for Ice Cube. He has done a lot of good, and he deserves to be commended for that. In fact, I support what he is doing on prison reform with all my heart. But I believe more attention and money should be steered toward saving them from going to jail/prison in the first place.

Here is how I see it. If someone goes to prison, they will get a record. Once they get a record, their life becomes more challenging than it already is. Finding a job becomes hard; finding a home to rent becomes hard. Subsequently, they will find it difficult to make traction in life, which will take a toll on their minds. In no time, such people are likely to spiral into a life of crime, and in the long run, they will likely be back in jail or prison.

If we prevent it before it starts, we can stop the vicious loop of people going to prison more exhaustively. Of course, this will take all of us to work together. As the saying goes, "It takes a village to raise a child."

The first link in this effort, and the most important, must I add, is parents. Parents need to be more wary and corrective about what their kids are doing. They should instill a hatred for crime and foul behavior in the children from an early age. Then, the next link is the teachers. Teachers can be the most effective helping hands in this effort. They are almost as valuable as parents in *teaching* things to kids, and kids bond well with their teachers. Both these links are emotionally useful as children are very receptive to them.

Then comes the law-enforcement apparatus, such as the police. They can also play a big part in help prevent kids from going to jail. You must be wondering, "Police? That doesn't seem like a very effective group to engage in child rearing." Hear me out. Throughout our communities, police officers are one of the most effective channels that can be leveraged to spread positive vibes. Police officers are people who are often seen to be structured and disciplined. They have an authority that is often feared. Fear has the capability to turn into hate really quickly. On top of that, fear invites unwanted resistance. And thus, many times we see people not liking police officers for no particular reason.

I believe police can actually build trust and a bond with the community better than other public entities. People get to see police officers daily. They are patrolling around the neighborhood and are familiar faces to the public. But they are also seen as people of sheer authority and power rather than normal people trying to maintain peace and order (something that we all want). That image needs to change.

I recommend that police officers wear a more amicable profile in their day-to-day routine. If you are a police officer, patrolling or maybe just sitting in the car, and you see kids playing or passing by, give them a high-five or interact and play with them a bit. If you are at a park or driving by a park, and you see some kids playing basketball, throw a few hoops with them. If you see an elderly person sitting on their porch or on a park bench, have a small chat with them, maybe ask them how they are doing. These small acts can go a long way in establishing cordial relations between the people and the authorities and subsequently dissolve the fear and the resistance.

Police are more like ambassadors of the justice system and should focus on building strong relationships with the community. They are the ones who can convince people that the laws and regulations are for people's own safety and protection, not to limit them or maybe rob them of their freedom. Many times, I see police officers spending more time sitting in the car talking to each other.

Now I know the job demands some boundaries, and I respect them. But those boundaries shouldn't be walls and barriers. To any police officer reading this (and to the rest), I urge that instead of creating barriers between them and people, they should get out of the car and maybe just say a little hello. Let your community know you care about them. Little kids will start noticing you, and you never know which kid you are influencing to do the right thing. You leave a good impression on even one kid, and you might be saving a generation from bad decisions. Save the children before they turn bad by giving them something that builds their trust in the justice system.

Kids are not bad. They just have bad influences in their life. We often sell misplaced notions to them and sell them fears. Notions like "Guns kill people." No! People with guns kill people. These are the kind of correct lessons we have to teach our kids, and I don't think there is a better candidate to teach this than the police.

With your courteous and amiable approach, you can tell the kids and the community that instead of taking matters into their own hands when a scuffle or a feud or an argument goes south, they should reach out to the police and the law-enforcement authorities. This can save many kids and people from making one wrong decision and save them from years of regret. Know that kids are easy to influence, and healthy, friendly, positive vibes leave far more lasting impressions than aggression and authority do.

I know not all police officers are bad and just slacking off in their cars. I know many officers focus on what I have laid out here. They interact with people to build trust and respect in the community. It's just that the bad ones make it bad for the good ones, which leads to the community, especially young ones (the more emotional and erratic ones), regarding the police with suspicion, which can obviously lead to dangerous actions and decisions.

I say this not out of a place of disdain for police, but I have lived experiences to back what I say. I have had a lot of bad run-ins with the police. Many times it was the usual: me being wrongly profiled.

Once, I was driving on a road when a police officer pulled me over. When I asked the reason, he said he pulled me over because he saw my passenger reach under the seat. I found the reason a little irksome. In a sarcastic way, I said, "Really."

"Yes," came the reply, short and to the point. He then asked me, "Do you mind if I search your car?"

Of course, I said, "Yes, you can." My passenger wasn't quite convinced of the idea, though, and he exhibited his ire quite clearly to me. He said, "You don't have to let them search your car." I know better than to provoke a police officer, and I had no problem agreeing; I wasn't hiding anything.

I tried calming him down and said, "I know, but this is going to be fun. We did nothing wrong, so let's do this."

Without wasting much time (because we know what that could have escalated into), we got out of the car. The officer told us to lie on the ground while they searched my car. Now that was pushing some buttons. Still, I maintained my calm. My passenger wasn't as stoic as I, though. He got mad. He didn't want to lie on the ground and be treated like a criminal without even an ounce of reason. That is where I knew I had to step in. I calmed him down and convinced him to just comply. We didn't want to give them a reason. With ire and disdain, he agreed, and there we were, two guys without any reason, lying on the ground like worms.

While we were on the ground, the officers searched the car thoroughly, extensively, and entirely. They rummaged through the car for a good two hours. Obviously, they didn't find anything. Almost dejected and disappointed, and obviously tired, they asked us to get up. I didn't say anything and simply complied. They told us that we could get up.

One of the officers pointed at the street I passed and said, "It's a lot of drug activity that goes on down that road."

"So what does that have to do with us?" I asked. I was irritated too by the behavior, but it wasn't something I wanted to go to jail for. Plus, throwing a tantrum would have been futile.

He knew he had made an epic blunder and made a fool of himself. He didn't have any other explanation. He just looked at me and said, "Have a nice day." The dumb expression on his face was enough satisfaction for me.

Most of you might be wanting to tell me that I should have complained about the officers. While that would have been an excellent step to take, that is not how I do things. For me, the punishment lay in highlighting the incompetence of such police officers. Because while we were down on the ground and the officers were scanning through every crevice of my car, I saw about twenty-five to thirty cars whiz past the very road the officer had pointed out. People of all races, in all kinds of shady vehicles, just passed by while they were busy searching our car without any legitimate reason or anything suspicious we might have done.

The result? They missed out on a potential bust that might have looked good on their resume. The officers probably could have easily landed an actual drug runner if they weren't *profiling* me. They came up with an excuse that I know was bogus just to pull me over. What they should have done was just sit there on the very road they told me had a lot of drug activity, keep an eye out for any vehicle that kept going back and forth, mark that vehicle down, and then pull it over after running some basic checks. They might have had better odds of actually catching some drug runner, but they were too busy profiling and ended up empty-handed.

Another bad incident I had with police officers was when I had a neighbor who—multiple times—harassed me and the people I lived with. Let me go ahead and point this particular detail out (and no, I am not being a racist at all): This neighbor of mine was a Caucasian man. Let's just call him "Good Guy." The reason I picked that name is that, to the police officers, he was just that, the good guy. When we first moved into the trailer park, everything was cordial. Out of seven trailers, only three were occupied. I lived in the second trailer. The other families lived behind me, and there was an empty trailer in front of me. About a year after I moved in, a family moved into the empty trailer in front of us.

A month in, my girlfriend's brother decided he wanted to be friends with the Good Guy. It was cool. I didn't see anything wrong with it. I didn't see it as anything more than a neighbor befriending a neighbor. Who sees the color of the skin anyway, right? We all got to know each other, and the place was turning into a warm neighborhood. Until… one month later, everything started to go downhill.

The Caucasian man, the Mr. Good Guy, started to get drunk and would scream racial slurs at us. It wasn't very frequent at first, but soon that changed. Every other day, we would have a white man standing right in the middle of the road, spewing words that were laced with hate and rage. In the beginning, we tried to ignore him. We brushed it under the carpet on the notion that alcohol can do that to you... *Never mind, the man's just drunk...* But soon things started to spiral out of hand.

One day, he came over and started bashing at our window. At first, we tried to talk him out of it, but he wouldn't listen. The racial slurs, the curse words, only got more vile, vulgar, and abundant. We were left with no option but to call the police, and we just did that. Two police officers pulled up. They came and asked me what was going on. I told them exactly what had happened. Then it was Mr. Good Guy's turn.

We were hoping for some swift action, something that would knock some sense into our unruly neighbor. Nothing of the sort happened. On the contrary, the two officers came back to our trailer and started hassling us instead. They told us that they couldn't do much about anything because no serious crime had taken place. I thought this was as far as this goes. It was infuriating, but more was yet to come. Then, without any sound reasoning, they asked me, my girlfriend, and her brother for our ID cards. I don't know what they were told, but whatever it was, I know it was a lie, and any sound man with judgment could have seen after interacting with our mad neighbor who would've been at fault.

Regardless, we showed them to the officers. When I inquired what it was about, they said they wanted to check to see if we had warrants. Despite the rage simmering within me, I didn't react. I knew better than to give them a reason to harangue us. Plus, we were almost used to it. They ran our names, and nothing came up. The police officers quietly left without Good Guy receiving any punishment. Honestly, at this point, I would have been satisfied if they had run his ID, too.

Things quieted down for a couple of days, but that was short-lived. Three days later, we were having a cookout in the back of our trailer. My girlfriend's dad was among the attendees. Before we knew it, Good Guy was at it again. My girlfriend's ten-year-old daughter was in the front yard playing, and my girlfriend's brother was right on the side of the house.

Good Guy came out of his trailer and started spouting racial slurs with the kid around. Can you sit still while reading this? I don't think you can. When the vile man saw he wasn't getting any reaction out of us, he upped the ante. He brandished a knife out of nowhere and started flailing and waving it in front of the kid. Not just that, he threatened her and said he was going to kill everyone who was in her house.

My girlfriend's brother heard that and came. Not acting rashly, he quickly whipped out his phone from his pocket and put it on record. He didn't get everything Good Guy was saying, but he got most of it and took the child back into the house.

I called the police again. We had evidence this time, and thought, at least this time, the lunatic would get something he deserved. The same police officers came. We showed them the video. Everything could be clearly seen and heard in the video. They saw him with the knife, waving it carelessly, and heard him give a death threat to all of us. The police officers went over, and we were expecting a rumpus. *He isn't going to comply; he would surely have to be dragged out of here by the officers.* Nothing happened.

They simply went over, had a conversation with him, and then came back over to my trailer. Again, they said they could do nothing. What's worse is that they instead ran our IDs—again. Even my girlfriend's dad was asked to surrender his ID for a cross-check. They ran all of our names, and obviously, everything came back clean once again.

By this time, I had had enough. I knew that if the police weren't going to provide protection, I would have to take matters into my own hands. And trust me, it would have been easy for me to take the madman down. As the police officers were about to leave, I stopped him midway and told him that if Good Guy came over here with that knife again, I would have to defend this house, and I would do it—my way. The police officer looked me right in the eyes and told me that if I did anything to him, they were going to put me in jail. I asked, "Even if I was defending myself and my family?" The officer coldly said, "Yes."

The officer then ordered me to go to the house, and with that, they left. About two hours later, Good Guy was back at it again. He started hurling things at our trailer and yelling the most vile racial slurs he had in his notebook. Now, my family and I believe in the justice system—despite us having all the reasons not to. We knew that no matter what we did, we'd get the short end of the stick. We decided not to respond to him.

I called the police again. I wanted the police officers to see him in the act, not that they already hadn't in the video. The same officers came, and the same routine played out. They left without doing a single thing—not even a few words of warning were spared. Before the officers could leave, I went to one of them and asked if I could speak to their supervisor. They said they were going to call their supervisor, and he'd get in touch. The officers left.

An hour went by, but I didn't hear anything. I noticed that everything outside seemed too quiet. I expected another alcohol-induced rage episode from Good Guy—as was the routine after a police visit—but nothing happened. I looked out the window and saw four police cars outside, in front of Good Guy's yard. I went outside to see what was going on.

After about five minutes, one of the usual officers who would come and do nothing whenever we used to call, came up to me and asked if I had seen anything that had taken place next door. I hadn't, and told him the same. We hadn't seen or heard anything.

I saw that they had the supervisor in tow and immediately asked for a conversation with him. The officers told me to wait and went to the supervisor. When the officer opened the car door, I saw Good Guy in the back seat. They had arrested Good Guy for some reason—surely not for one of my complaints. But I was glad just the same.

Five minutes later, the supervisor pulled up. I was already standing in the yard. The supervisor asked me about the problem I had been facing, and I told him everything—from the first call to the last. I told him what his officers did and that they didn't do anything despite us showing them the video. The supervisor surely was a sensible man. He apologized. He then told us that Good Guy was actually arrested for punching his stepdaughter in the face. He told me that Good Guy was trying to get into his truck and planning to ram it into our trailer. The stepdaughter had tried stopping him. She had taken the keys and wouldn't give them to him, even after his insistence and curses. For that, Good Guy had punched her in the face.

The news was terrible, and I was glad that the frantic man was finally in cuffs. The supervisor then proceeded to tell me that they had run Good Guy's name and discovered that he had a long list of violence and kidnapping charges. He also had a warrant for arrest.

I knew this was the opportunity to raise the concern and drive the point home. I said, "So you're telling me that when your officers ran out names for warrants, they didn't run Good Guy's name."

He embarrassingly said, "No."

The supervisor again apologized for everything I went through and took the Good Guy away. This story is the point I have been trying to make. It showcases both the good policemen and the bad ones. It also shows the grave danger that the bad ones pose, and the need for the good ones. The two police officers had constantly ignored my complaints, wrongfully IDed me. On top of that, they DIDN'T ID a potential criminal and let him go free despite evidence against him. Imagine what he could have done. He could have rammed my trailer while we were all in there. He could even have killed or irreversibly hurt his own stepdaughter. What would the two reckless cops have done then? Who would have taken the responsibility? Could their apology undo the damage the madman might have incurred? Food for thought...

I'll repeat again—a thousand times if I have to! *Not all police officers are bad.* I have had officers treat me with respect—the supervisor being an obvious example. That is maybe one of the reasons that I still believe in the potential for good in our law-enforcement apparatus. I only press for the correctness of officers because the critical nature of police work doesn't leave any room for error, negligence, or bias.

And I am all up for offering a fair trade. I know that it is a two-way interaction. People too need to embrace the responsibility of making amicable relations with the police. I am well aware that sometimes people do wrong things to the officers. The people of the community can do many things to make a strong, friendly bond with the police officers.

To the people, I say this. There is nothing wrong with seeing a police officer at the store, at an event, or just sitting in their car. Just walk up and tell them thank you for their service. A few words of gratitude go a long way. Thank them for the things they do to protect the community. Show them some appreciation. We all need to come together and do our part to make the community better. Police officers are human as well. Being a police officer is a very dangerous and stressful job, whether we like to admit it or not. They too often face life-threatening ordeals. Sometimes they have to go against mad shooters, sometimes they have to go against drug lords. Some of our streets offer the most dangerous experience to the police force, and we all know what I am talking about.

All in all, our policemen deserve all the respect for the fine work they do. They keep the streets clean, so our children can play around and grow up in a safe environment. They keep our neighborhoods clean and lend a great deal of help to keep them drug-free. We can do things to make it easier on them as well, and give back to them.

Everyone messes up now and then. Judges, lawyers—everyone makes mistakes. Just like police officers, some judges profile as well. You can believe it or not. Of course, there are fair and honest judges. But again, the bad ones make it look bad for the good ones.

Here, let me share an example. I was in a courtroom one day. I was there to be a witness for the brother of a friend of mine. After a while of sitting in court, a Black lady went in front of the judge. She was in a work release program. If you don't know what a work release program is, it's a program where, if you don't have that much time left in prison, you get out of prison early and go to a work release housing facility. There you will stay for the remainder of your sentence and take up a job. Some people who qualify can actually go home on the weekend and return for the weekdays. Of course, there is a certain time limit to observe and return to the facilities. If you violate it, you obviously could be sent back to prison.

Now, coming back to the story... The lady was being questioned by the judge and was asked why she was late returning to the facilities. The lady told the judge that she was at a job interview and the interview ran late. The public defender said that she was telling the truth. The interviewer was also there in the court and testified the same—that the interview was running late. Not only that, the supervisor in charge of the work release facilities also testified that the lady was never late before that. She further added that the lady was always on time, never caused trouble, and that she feels that the defendant deserves a second chance.

Even the defense attorney agreed with them. The judge, however, discounted all testimony. He looked at her and said that he didn't think she was going to do good at the facilities. He simply sent her back to prison.

Soon after that case was a hearing of a White lady. Coincidently, the White lady was also from the same work release facility, and her record said that she had run away from the facility multiple times. The judge asked the defendant for the details and explanation, to which the defense attorney said that her client didn't like the facilities and she didn't want to be there. At this admission, the supervisor of the work release facilities intervened and protested that she, too, didn't want the white lady in her facility because all she did was start trouble, get into fights, and keep running away.

Now, with such testimony mounted against a person and such vague reasons presented to the judge for running away from the work-release facility, one would assume the judge would deal out a corrective and swift punishment, right? Wrong—the judge simply looked at the defendant and figured she needed another chance. He told the defendant that if she ran away again, he would have to put her in prison. Downright outrageous! I couldn't believe what I had heard. Everyone in the courtroom was whispering under their breath. Surely, the verdict was an absolute transgression.

Even after the court was over, people were in the hallway talking about the decisions for those two women, and the sweeping majority had the same thing to say—*THE DECISION WAS NOT RIGHT!* The entire courtroom and its premises were abuzz with the controversial decision. Every which way I turned, people were saying the same thing.

I feel that everyone who turns to the court must be treated according to the grievance and crime, irrespective of the color of their skin. One should absolutely not be profiled. If you commit any major or minor crime and feel no remorse, you must be sent to jail, but if you are doing the right thing and you're trying your best, you obviously deserve some leniency. This isn't an emotional notion; it is a logical one.

It shouldn't matter what race you are. It shouldn't matter if you are poor or rich. It shouldn't matter what profession you are in or what office you hold. Politician, judge, police officer—anyone and everyone should face the same consequences for their transgression. In fact, the way I see it, professionals who are part of the justice and legal systems should be more careful about the way they do things. They should focus more on always doing the right thing. People naturally respect and trust those who hold an office and respect its obligations and consequences, even if the office holder themselves are being punished. These office holders are held to a higher standard and should act like it.

The situation is so bad that even some lawyers and doctors are not always on the people's side. These are people who *must be* pro-people. It is more like their job description. Not without logic and reasoning, yes, I agree, but for the most part, they should prioritize the well-being of those who deserve it. Some lawyers and doctors are just in it for the money. And, again, not all lawyers, but an alarming number nonetheless.

Such lawyers are more concerned with their track records than with their clients' well-being. They will have you plead out or settle a case for less than it is worth just so they can have a win. Lots of people have settled a lawsuit for way lower than it should have been, just because the lawyer told them that it's all they can get. The lawyer gets the win that makes him or her look good for advertisement, and you get a lifetime of injuries. And I don't make these claims just merely out of bias. I have seen many cases where that has actually happened.

And building on that, I will say something that many will say is a controversial claim. But I shouldn't shy away from the truth. Just to let you know. Workmans' Comp is not on your side. The labor force of our country is at the mercy of people who don't really care about you, or at least that is what it appears to be.

If you get injured on a job, it is likely that the doctor they send you to is on their side and not yours. These doctors—while their Hippocratic Oath must make them—are not worried about your health. Some of these doctors will tell you that there is no serious damage and send you back to work. Later on, as time goes on, your injuries will start taking their toll. The pain, which the doctor would have brushed away as "that's just normal, it will go away with time," will go from mild to worse. Before you know it, the pain will start interfering with your mobility and daily tasks and, obviously, with work. Now you can't work with the same dexterity and ease, and forcing yourself to work only aggravates the pain.

And maybe now you might think that the injury is now grave enough, and the doctor might treat it with concern, and Workman's Comp, too, might pay attention. WRONG. When you go back to try and get compensated for that injury—an injury that has aggravated and is more than before—Workman's Comp will tell you that you could have reinjured yourself, and they are not responsible. Great, right? Suddenly, you, who were supposedly the victim of neglect and malpractice, are now your own culprit.

And that is just a secondary concern. The first one obviously is that you are not able to work due to your injury. Consequently, you will get fired and end up losing everything you worked for. Why? Because the Workman's Comp doctor didn't treat your injuries properly.

It is important to take any work-related injury seriously. If you get hurt on the job, ensure that the doctor treats your injury accordingly. Don't settle unless the pain is gone for good. If, after a visit or two to the doctor, you are still hurting, and you feel that the doctor is not doing their job, do not hesitate to request another doctor. Usually, the first thing the doctor's office will do is give you an X-ray. An X-ray only tells you if you have broken bones. Then the doctor might tell you that everything is okay and send you back to full duty while your injury is still not healed and you are still in pain. Don't buy that. If you are hurting, request an MRI. The MRI gives you a more in-depth analysis and picture of the affected area. My suggestion is to find out how bad your injury is, not just at the moment, but how dangerous it can be in the long run. Injuries, especially internal ones, can have lasting effects. Some might even manifest as a problem later in life, even if they are not showing any signs or causing any pain at the moment. You have to know, as best as you can, if you are injured to the point that you might or might not be able to work in the future.

The 5Ls

Let me share my experience with you. I once got hurt on a job some years back. I went to the doctor's office to get it checked. The first day in the doctor's office, the doctor asked me what had happened. I told him how I got injured and the extent of pain. I also told him that I wasn't big on taking medicine because I am not. I just wanted to stop hurting.

Like I mentioned a few paragraphs above, the doctor told me to get my X-rays done. I did. When the X-ray came back, it showed that I didn't have any broken or displaced bones. After reviewing the X-ray, the doctor manually inspected the injured part. He pressed on the spot. Immediately, I jumped and told him it hurt a great deal. Funnily enough, and to my surprise, the doctor told me I was exaggerating. I was a bit confused and a little alarmed, but I gave him the benefit of the doubt. After all, he was the learned expert here.

The doctor wrote me a prescription and told me he would see me in two weeks. In my head, I was thinking, *I just told him that I'm not big on medication, and still, he wrote me an anti-inflammatory prescription.* Still, I just did exactly what he told me to do. Two weeks went by, but the pain was as persistent as before. I wasn't feeling any better. The next visit to the doctor's office came and went by with the same routine. He inspected the injured area, pushing the same spot or two. This time, too, the inspection buzzed a jolt of pain through me. This time, too, I jumped and told him that it was excruciating. And just like before, he tells me the same thing—that I was exaggerating.

This time, I got a little vexed at the comment. I told the doctor that I really needed him to help me because the pain hadn't subsided one bit. But he didn't seem to take any notice of my pain. Instead, he told me that there was nothing wrong with me and that I was faking.

That kind of got to me. I instantly replied, "No, I am not! I'm really hurting bad."

That's when the doctor's voice got louder. He told me the same offensive thing, that I was faking it and claimed that I just wanted pills or money. Mockingly, he added that he was aware of this so-called scam because *that's what everyone who comes to his doctor's office wants—either pills or money.*

I replied, "I don't want neither. I just want you to fix me."

At this point, the conversation was turning into a heated exchange. I told him that I would like an MRI. He told me that it wasn't up to him to make that decision; it was up to Workmans' Comp. I asked him if he could put in a request. He said yes, but he wasn't up to it because *there was nothing wrong with me.* I told him to just put in the request and let's find out. After much to and fro, he agreed. "I bet there is nothing wrong with you," he said.

288

By now, I was locked in too. I instantly replied, "Bet!"

A week later, I got the MRI done, but never got the results. I was waiting for the result when I got an email from the doctor's office saying they had discharged me as a patient. I was never told what the results of the MRI were. I contacted the people at Workman's Comp and told them what happened between me and the doctor. They said they would get me another doctor.

Two weeks later, I was still in pain. I called Workman's Comp again. They told me they were still trying to find me a doctor. Another week passed, and now my pain was getting worse. At this point, I was livid. I called Workman's Comp again, and again, they said the same thing. I was done talking. Immediately, I called a lawyer, told him everything about my plight and asked him to take legal action. I couldn't take it anymore. My lawyer got on the job real quick. Two weeks, all of a sudden, I got contacted by the Workman's Comp, and they now wanted to do everything they could to help me.

In no time, I got another doctor's appointment. I went to the doctor and told him the same thing I told the first doctor—that I'm not big on pills and I just wanted to be fixed. He told me he will do his best. I had gotten a disc of the MRI from the last MRI place, which I shared with the doctor. He looked at it and told me that the MRI showed that the injury I sustained was really bad. He

289

immediately started the treatment, and thankfully, I was finally able to get myself the attention I deserved. It had taken two months, a lot of hassle, a lot of pain, and finally a lawyer for me to get some help.

The lawyer, fortunately for me, was a good man. He was someone who genuinely helped the people, as opposed to someone who was looking to maintain a winning streak. I really appreciate him for everything he did for me and can truly vouch for his intent for the good of people. He is one of those people who can help you restore your belief in the legal system if you have suffered injustice at the hands of some ill-practicing law enforcers. If he ever reads this book, I would like to say thank you—with all my heart. You are truly an awesome guy.

Coming back to the discussion at hand, I cannot assert enough how important it is for doctors to have a mindset of helping people in need. Preferring money over people's well-being is wrong. I will repeat again (because I believe it is my sworn duty to do justice to the professionals who are truly helping save lives), *NOT ALL DOCTORS ARE BAD*. I would like to mention here that I am including all the dentists, too. They are an equal and integral part of our medical fraternity. If you hear an emphasis on doctors, that is because these professionals are the best equipped to help a person in pain—it is literally their job description. There is nothing more noble than helping others. And I am not saying that doctors should just start treating people for free. That isn't quite practical. All I am saying is one, what my grandpa would say, *"Right, don't wrong nobody."* Don't misuse your station and your profession, and don't exploit people. And two, at least help when you can.

There are people who are extremely ill or suffering from enduring and excruciating pain simply because they can't afford to go to the doctors. What do they do? They stay sick and in pain. How is that just? How is that humane? When will the world at large and our nation in specific realize that *"Money isn't everything"*—at least when it comes to someone who is sick or in lifelong or life-threatening pain?

You might notice I am specifically mentioning not just "sickness" but "pain" too. Also, I mentioned the profession of dentistry a few lines back. Let me share this story, so you can understand why exactly. I had a toothache once—a bit too severe, might I add. I went to one dentist's office and was told I didn't have insurance coverage for a dental treatment. Note that this wasn't for aesthetic dental enhancements of any kind. I was in excruciating pain and just wanted to get that looked at. The same happened with three other dentists, which makes a total of four different dental offices refusing to treat a patient in severe agony. I couldn't get any help simply because I didn't have any insurance, and I couldn't afford to get my tooth pulled. And yes, it was just that—a mere tooth extraction. That's all. It wouldn't have been a cost-incurring treatment, but again, I was at the mercy of the almighty dollar—or lack thereof.

At the time, I was working at a lawn care company. One day, we went to cut the grass at this dentist's office. I was in so much pain that I would hold my jaw every now and then. If it were something less severe, I would have ignored it, but the pain was tormenting. Those who have gone through this kind of pain would know what I am talking about. I guess the dentist saw me caressing my jaw again and again and grimacing. She noticed that I was in severe pain. After we were finished cutting the grass, we were loading the equipment back in the truck—we had another lawn trimming place scheduled. We were about done when the dentist walked out of the office and asked me what was wrong. I told her I was hurting really bad. Immediately, she invited me into the office. She said, "Come in the back so I can take a look at that tooth."

Now, due to my past experiences, I thought it was necessary that I mention the main issue. I told her that I didn't have any insurance or any money to cover any of the costs.

She simply said, "I didn't ask for that. Now come on back."

I even protested a little and told her, "But I'm at work."

She emphatically and demandingly said, "Don't worry about that. I will talk to your boss. Just come to the back so we can see what's going on."

It was like a dental messiah had appeared out of nowhere. I was in so much pain, and didn't want to miss this opportunity (or my other teeth). I just went back there. She examined the hurting tooth and gave me a prescription for some antibiotics and something to take away the pain. Again! I'm not big on these medications, but I was hurting so bad I didn't have a choice. Trust me, those medicines were some relief.

The doctor told me that, for some medical reason I can't quite place, the extraction of the tooth wasn't possible at the moment. She gave me an appointment for next week. I simply complied and went back the next week. This time, she checked and concluded the tooth needed to be extracted. And without any charges, she went on with it. I reminded her about my financial situation and the limitations of my insurance coverage, but she didn't listen. She said that she would do it because I was hurting, and that was reason enough—she wasn't in it just for the money. I am and forever will be grateful to her.

This story of mine has an example of everything I have been trying to highlight. It highlights the four dentists who wouldn't operate on a patient because he didn't have money. I will highlight again that this wasn't an aesthetic procedure. I was simply a patient in extreme suffering. This highlights that money wins against all suffering. And, this also highlights that there are good people, too. A notion that is a parallel part of my discussion...

Helping people when they are in need should be a natural instinct for humankind. But sadly, most people only think about the money, even when they are helping someone. Even good people, such as my dentist up there, don't seem to influence the people who are chasing the bag, even in such noble professions. I understand that money is a prerequisite for a stable, good life. And I never say that such professionals must lend their services for free. Of course, they have mouths to feed, too. All I say is that money shouldn't be the first thing (and the only thing) you think about when you help someone. Helping other people, no matter how much money they might have or not have or what they look like, should be a primary job for each of us. We shouldn't wait to help someone by first questioning if they can afford it or not. Help should be universal and immediate.

The sad truth of our lives is that such is not the case. Help, too, has to be earned. In fact, in most cases, it has to be fought for. Now, I am an advocate of the notion that one should earn what they want and need. Don't think I am asking for freebies and free lunches. No! All I am saying is that compassion shouldn't be out the window, and at least basic humanity should prevail.

And when I say "Help should be universal," I mean every kind of help, not just a medical one. Even the legal system that works in tandem with the healthcare system should be helpful and at least focused on serving, not just making big bucks. That brings us to something I touched upon in my discussion earlier—lawyers. Since we often have to fight for even the basics, I urge people to be careful and vigilant with the lawyers, too. Your lawyer might force you to settle for less. Don't. If you do, the money won in the case won't last long. A few doctor visits, and it is long gone. Now you're stuck with doctor bills and an injury that you never got treated for completely. You can't work because of your injuries, and thus, now you have even less money. It is a vicious trap. Don't fall for it.

Don't just settle for anything. Make sure that the lawyer puts your best interest as a priority, not his/her winning streak. Yes, I understand that sometimes it will take years, but keep pushing until you feel like you're compensated fairly, getting something you deserve—not something that is gone in a visit or two to the ER.

Some people have settled for way less than what their injuries cost. In fact, in the long run, the cost incurred grew exponentially. Why? Because the lawyer wanted the win. Save yourself from such lawyers, or you'll regret a lifetime.

Here, I will circle back to what the discussion started with— the abhorrent problem of profiling, which plagues the system and sends people in loops of misery. Profiling someone is wrong, no matter who is doing the profiling. You can't assume who the person actually is by just looking at them. Get to know that person and find out the kind of circumstances they are in.

Make your judgments on a thorough analysis of the past and present. Don't make the grave mistake of judging people only based on their past. It is a common problem, even in this day and age. Not one of us leads a perfect life. All of us have done something we wished we hadn't done.

I would like to lay myself bare because I have realized that correction begins with self. I will not act as a saint. I did things in my past that I am not proud of. I have sold drugs in my past. I have hit a woman before. I have cheated on a woman before. I have even cheated on a test in school. And it goes back as far as I can remember. Back when I was seven years old. I tried to steal. My third to the oldest brother caught me trying to steal something. He made me put it back and told me it was not worth it. I told him I was hungry. He said, "No matter what, stealing ain't worth it." *Right don't wrong nobody.*

I looked at him and said, "I understand." I put it back, and we walked out of the store.

So, yes, I tried stealing and did many worrisome things. But do I try to justify them? No, I don't, and I won't.

I have done things that I wish I never had. And I would let you judge me for a while because I want to show you how futile that is. In fact, I ask this: If you were to judge me by the things that I did in my past, what would you say about me? Would you say I was hateful and heartless? Would you say I was a coward and spineless because I hit a woman, or would you say I was correct to steal because I was hungry? Or maybe, based on some nice things you might have read until now in this book, would you conclude that I am nice and selfless? What then about the woman-beating or stealing? See, it can be a conundrum that doesn't quite have a fair answer.

No matter what you think of me, it won't change me or my reality. I know who I am, and more importantly, who I am now—a changed and evolved man who has learned his lessons, some even the hard way. Just because someone had a bad past doesn't make them a bad person.

I have met prisoners who were some of the nicest people you would want to meet. I have also met people who have never been to jail but were the most hurtful people you would ever meet. So you cannot make an assumption of what the entire person is based on their history. The wise thing to do is to ensure you get to know a person and not just their past. The experience is usually always bad for both you and the person.

I have had people treat me a certain way because of who they thought I was. I have had people treat me badly because of the way I look. They never once tried to find out who I really am. Just because a person is black, does that mean they're lazy or dangerous or drug sellers? Just because a person is white, does that mean they are selfish, prejudiced, and on drugs? If a person is Latino, does that make them a gangster, a coke runner, or maybe someone who is always wanting to fight anybody? No, it doesn't. People are who they are because of their individuality, not because of their race, nation, or ethnicity. For some inexplicable reason, people don't seem to grasp this simple idea. They are always judging and stereotyping. In fact, it is so rooted in our habits and daily lives that some people might be doing it without knowing. Some people might not even know what stereotyping means. Let me get that out of the way.

Stereotyping, in simple words, is assuming things about people based on their caste, culture, creed, color, etc. It is when someone forms a mental image about a person without understanding the person or what their life has been about. And that poses are grave problem. When you don't understand the next person, it's easier to hate them instead of trying to understand them. It is almost human nature to hate something we don't understand, especially if it becomes even slightly overwhelming.

This often occurs because we seem to be in kind of a rush in judging people and making assumptions. It is like we are hardwired to do that, when in fact, we are not. The truth is that we are all allowed to form our opinions based on our observations; we simply don't do that because we are a bit lazy and want to play it safe. We buy what society is telling us, which is, in most cases, a botched-up, short-sighted analysis.

That is why I always urge people to be patient. Take your time to get to know someone. Don't just buy what you hear. Make your own judgments based on real experience and observation. Learn before you conclude. I don't just say it out of some misplaced liberalism or maybe because I want to sound pacific. No. I say this because it is smart and can be very beneficial.

You never know who will become your partner or your best friend. You should always love everyone, no matter the race. If you make assumptions and impose unnecessary walls and barriers, you might miss out on someone who can be the most valuable thing to happen in your life. Go out there and just look around. You will see a world of people from the most unlikely backgrounds and settings being the truest and most wholesome friends, business partners, spouses, neighbors, etc. Diversity truly is rewarding if you look at it through a lens of acceptance.

Some people think it's wrong to mix races. They say it is wrong to date outside of your race. Is that really true? Are you one of those who think that way? Allow me to let you in on a little secret:

My kids are mixed.

What!!!! Does that make me a bad person? Does that make my kids bad people? Before you answer that question, I would like to ask you another question. Do you think Moses is a bad person, and do you think God is a bad God? Again, before you answer that question, I would like you to consider this story right out of the Bible. In the Bible, there is a story of Moses and his wife. What about it? Well, Moses's wife wasn't a local. He married an Ethiopian woman. Imagine that!! Moses himself was from Egypt, born and raised in the house of the rulers of the nation. Yet he married an Ethiopian woman. Just like many of us today, who make judgments on appearance and ethnicity, Moses's brother and sister resisted him. They didn't like her simply because she was an Ethiopian woman. They didn't accept her and used to talk down to her. Do you know the end of the brother and sister? God punished them both. That's the short version. I can give you the whole account, but I would love for you to go and read it yourself. You will get a better understanding, and it will be eye-opening. And this is an invitation to everyone, not just Christians, because the lesson is invaluable—something all mankind should understand.

What I got out of the story is that the Heavenly Father doesn't want us bickering and hating each other because of who we are and where we came from. It also shows me that the Heavenly Father wanted us to love each other, no matter the race or culture or creed or language.

Think about this. The Heavenly Father has created all the different types of species on this Earth. Let's take the Equidae family, for example. For those who don't know, Equidae is a family of the horse species. There are many types of Equidae that are in the horse family. That includes all types of domestic horses, mules, donkeys, and zebras. If you take a mule and a zebra and raise them on the same farm together, a mule won't dislike the zebra because it's a zebra, and that zebra will not look at that mule with disgust simply because it's a mule. If those animals go into heat, and they are of different sexes, they will even breed together. That is the same for all the horse families, no matter the horse. This is the same with every animal species on this earth except for humans—dogs, cats, bears and so on.

Yes, I know, some of you might say a horse cannot breed with a cow or that birds or fish don't breed like that, and yes, you are right. But they do breed among the same species.

I know a duck and a chicken can't breed. They are two different types of species. Their organs are different, but a chicken can breed with all different types of chickens, no matter what color or what breed. It's the same with ducks and every other bird species. Fish, too, are the same way. The idea is that if the species are the same, coexistence and procreation are possible. All creation exhibits this practice. Why then, when it comes to humans, are we so caustic and against our fellow humans simply because they speak a different language or look a little different?

We as the human species have to share this planet, but for some reason, we do not like each other just because of the color of our skin. That is the most ridiculous thing I have ever heard people say. If you love someone, be with them. Don't let people or the world tell you who to love and who not to love. And if you are someone who opposes the notion I am trying to establish through my discussion here, I ask this: If two people from two different races love each other, what does that matter to you? How does that hurt you? If someone from Japan falls in love with someone from Italy, why should that matter? Or maybe if somebody from China falls in love with somebody from Jamaica, why should that matter to anyone? If someone from Africa falls in love with somebody who is Dominican, why should that matter to the whole African or Dominican world? If someone from Israel loves someone from Gaza, why should that matter? It shouldn't, and no one can convince me otherwise!

This is the problem with the world today. People are so worried about what the next person is doing that they miss out on the blessings in their lives. People are always complaining about life—about it being a torment, about it not going their way. Simultaneously, we are neck deep in other people's business. We are always ready to hand out judgments and verdicts to people without either thinking about the repercussions or the fact that it doesn't affect us. If we all focus more on our own lives and less on someone else's, it would be a better world. Focus on yourself, on your family. I can't worry about what goes on next door and miss out on my own family, and then expect to have a happy life. It just doesn't work like that...

Imagine this. If your house catches on fire and you and your family are in the house asleep. You wake up and see your house on fire. You don't wake your family up and ensure they get out safely. Instead, you jump out the bed, run next door to each neighbor next to your house, wake them up, and help them get them out of their house safely, just in case the fire spreads. Once your neighbors are safe, then only you run back into your burning house to get your family. How does that sound? Dumb, right? Is that something you would do? Obviously not!

I cannot quite understand why we can't worry about ourselves, count our blessings, and focus on adding to them. A woman choosing what she wants to do with her body, a person liking someone from the same sex, or someone from a different race, or maybe even choosing to be in an interracial relationship, is no one's business but their own. Worry about your own business.

Countless times, I have seen people lose a great many blessings because they were too busy poking their noses into the lives of others. People lose their family, their job, their whole lives worrying about the next person. The Heavenly Father didn't put us here to hate each other. We should all love each other and do right by each other—or at least NOT do wrong by each other without a reason. Again! *Right, don't wrong nobody.*

Most people think we all can't get along. They believe we don't have enough in common to bring us together as a species. Well, I say to those people, *"You breathin', ain't you?!"* As long as you are alive, you have the opportunity to at least try and bring people together. All you need to do is believe that such a thing is possible. We are all great people, and we all have the capacity to come together—only if we see the world without a lens of bias and misplaced judgments.

But I know this bias is difficult to deal with because our world is plagued with people who do bad because they WANT TO do bad—Not because of circumstance, not because they are cornered off or maybe hurt, but for the simple love of it. My grandfather used to tell me, the only thing that locks do is keep an innocent person innocent. In other words, the only people who will break that lock are the people who are going to do wrong anyway. It is a universal metaphor. The meaning of this whole bit is something like this. To explain, I'll use the example from the discussion we were having earlier in the book: people going through health problems and the challenges they face at the hands of doctors and medical institutions. The good people, who are actually in a lot of pain and need the required drugs or pain medication, can't get them because of those who abuse them. Laws, regulations, and punishments do not deter those who are abusing the drugs. They only rob the genuine people who actually need the drugs of an avenue to get the much-needed medication. The people who abuse those drugs still get them illegally, or they up the ante and start using a much worse drug. Only the people doing the right thing suffer. They have to wait for longer periods to get the desired medication, as they have to go through many legal and other checks and procedures to prove they are not abusers.

If the drug abusers are getting the pain medication illegally anyway, why should a good person, a person who actually needs it, suffer? The good people have to jump through hoops to get their hands on something to ease their pain.

And this is just one example. The problem is an omnipresent one and affects good people everywhere. There are good people who want to get a handgun for protection, but they can't. The bad ones have used guns recklessly, and now regulations are imposed that the good people have to go through to get a much-needed firearm. A normal person might have an actual need for it. Maybe they have a business or their house in a rowdy neighborhood. Maybe they have to travel late into the night for their job or something.

Don't get me wrong. I am not asking to arm the whole nation of America. I completely agree that there should be background checks before one can buy a firearm. But I would still highlight that while the good people are doing the right thing by going through the right steps to get a firearm, the bad people are getting them illegally and more quickly. That should be a concern for us. It should make the policy-makers wonder if their policies are actually worth it or not.

It is a whole mess out there. There are people doing the right things, going and buying houses with all the legal paperwork and hard-earned money. Next you know, their houses are being usurped by squatters who claim the house for themselves, as if the place is theirs by right. It's not fair for the homeowner who purchased the house the right way, and then the squatters just come along out of nowhere and take it over.

Good people are even being exploited at the hands of the systems the government wants them to abide by—yes, I am talking about the insurance companies. Good people are doing the right thing and still getting screwed over by the insurance companies. Whenever they make a righteous claim, they have to navigate through a maze of formalities and meaningless documentation, each a hindrance to getting what they are due. On the other hand, bad people are doing all kinds of illegal things to get money for an illegal claim from the insurance companies, and the insurance companies happily oblige. Good people have to pay for what bad people do to them, but the bad ones get anything they want illegally anyway. Like my wise grandpa used to say, the only thing locks do is keep an innocent person innocent.

I am going to give a disclaimer here, as authorities might claim I am inciting my readers. I am doing no such things. I'm not saying to start doing bad things and acquiring the things you want or need illegally. In fact, I am doing quite the contrary. As I have always been an advocate for it, I'm saying you should always do the right thing, no matter what. Many people, in fact, start doing the wrong things simply because they have been hurt by the system and don't trust it anymore. Through this book, I am addressing all of them.

Yes, I know, it is harder to do the right thing at times, but the reward for doing the right thing is greater than doing the wrong thing. It might come late, but it does show up, and it is abundantly rewarding. Moreover, I'd also like to remind people, especially the good ones on the verge of going to the other side, that eventually, the wrong ones do get caught and end up in jail. It might not seem like it, but justice does catch up with them (or karma does).

One of the reasons why people easily resort to bad things is that they listen to what people tell them without an ounce of verification. There is a lot going around in this world. Many things you hear are true, but most of them are not. It is easier to believe a lie than the truth, yes. Most people do not research things for themselves. They just go by what people tell them. If I tell you that the sun is going to turn plaid next week, would you believe me? Logically, you shouldn't. But the sad truth is that many people will. I might have to act as if I know what I am talking about, but people will. The crazy part is, I won't even have any proof that it will happen, but some people will believe it without much convincing required.

It is about time we fix this. We need to find out our own truth for ourselves, rather than just buying what people are telling us. Misinformation is rampant, and it is dangerous to take anything at face value.

In today's world, there are more followers than leaders. And the sad bit is that many of those so-called leaders aren't as wise as they are supposed to be. They are just wearing a façade of being a leader to fool and exploit the masses. Leadership has become an act. If a homeless man, sitting on a bucket under a bridge, shares some great knowledge about something, he will be dismissed. Just because he is homeless, most people won't even listen to him. Some people won't even acknowledge his existence. On the other hand, if a celebrity says the same thing the homeless man said, everyone would listen and say how intelligent the celebrity is. What is the difference between the homeless man giving you good knowledge and the celebrity giving you good knowledge? Let me answer that for you. Nothing! There is no difference. The only difference there might be would be in how they delivered the knowledge, but the message will still be the same. Still, the celebrity will get more credence simply because they might be acting intelligent. The celebrity might even have borrowed that knowledge from somewhere, but they will be applauded for it. Whereas the homeless man's word might have been learned through lived experience, but he would still be discounted and ignored.

We have to stop believing anything someone says. We need to start looking for the truth for ourselves. A celebrity will tell a lie, and lots of people will believe it because they are a celebrity. That goes for the politicians too. They openly tell a lie, and they know they are lying, but people also know that people will believe it. A politician's job is to scare you into voting for them. Again, not all politicians, but most of them. No matter the party, when a politician says something, especially when it sounds a wee bit odd or unlikely, we need to look into it ourselves before we go on about believing it.

Another thing we must rid ourselves of in this age of deceit is believing someone is true because they have been truthful in the past. Now I know this is a tricky one. How will we ever trust anyone, right? Well, at least with politicians and people who appear to be leaders or thought leaders or teachers in the mainstream media, we have to adopt this practice, because in politics, priorities and goals change, and thus alliances change too. Another example is that of the pundits and the soothsayers we see on the internet. If we were to believe them, the Earth should have been destroyed a long time ago. Every year, someone comes along with a twisted theory saying the world will end that year, and people will believe them without even once asking for proof. Now I won't say that all of these people are fraudsters. Some people really do believe they are telling the truth. They make some misplaced calculations, which convince them they have figured it out. Then there is the wishful bunch who thinks that if they keep saying it, maybe one day they might be right.

We live in a world of "Influencers"—people who listen to anything and start preaching and promoting it without getting the facts right in the first place. Thus, it becomes incumbent upon us to verify what we hear, even if it is coming from our favorite celebrity. I know sometimes the truth is hard to believe, so we go with the lie because it's easier to believe. But that ease isn't going to do us any favors. Especially in the long run, that lie is going to hurt us far more than the truth would have.

If I said there was a man who was born around 280 AD in Patara, Lycia, and his name was Nicholas, his parents died and left him a fortune, and he mostly helped the poor and kids and everyone he could, gave out presents and spread joy and cheer to everyone, served as a bishop of Myra, would you believe me or would you say that I don't know what I am talking about? Well, that is a true story, but I won't say you take my word for it. Look it up for yourself. That guy that I just mentioned is best known as Saint Nick or Santa Claus or whatever you want to call him these days.

Most people tell their kids there is no such thing as Santa Claus, but technically, that's not true. Like I said, it's easier to believe a lie than to look up the truth for yourself. If a kid asks me if I believe in Santa, I say yes. Saint Nick is a real person, and his story is fascinating. If you look things up for yourself, you will always find some explanation. You will know for yourself if it's true or not. I'm not saying what you should believe in or what you shouldn't believe in. All I am saying is to look it up for yourself before you believe anything. If a politician tells you something, look it up for yourself. If a celebrity tells you something, get it verified from as many trusted sources as you can.

There are many examples we can see where people are just selling stuff without any merit. People try to sell products, making you feel insecure about your body. *If you want to lose weight, you have to buy this product. If you want to gain weight, buy this!*

311

Feeling sluggish? This might just be the energizing drink you need! They claim magical benefits and promise results that are almost impossible.

In reality, it's all mathematical; nothing you can't do yourself without requiring any medicine or an elixir. Just lose more calories than you eat. It takes hard work and dedication, yes. But for anything worthwhile, there is no easy way. There is no pill to help you lose weight. Even if a pill does that, it might also be doing some damage that might be irreversible. Those meals that a company tricks you into buying, you can buy and cook those meals at a cheaper price for yourself at home. Also, it's not what you eat but how you eat. It's not what you do, it's how you do things. Managing your body is easy. In order to lose weight or build your energy, the first thing you have to do is learn about your body. How can someone *else* tell *you* about your body? It just doesn't make any sense. If certain things you eat or drink make you gain weight faster, then eat or drink less of that. If certain things that you eat or drink make you feel sluggish, stop consuming them. Yes, it's true that vegetables have certain things in them for a healthy body, as these products claim. But you don't have to use their synthetic products that claim the benefits of a vegetable. All you have to do is find out what your body is lacking and eat more of that. The best thing for my body is that I buy fresh fruits and vegetables rather than processed fruits and vegetables in ready-to-eat meals. You might say, "How am I supposed to know?"

Well, your body tells you everything. You can easily learn about the symptoms of the deficiency for each necessary nutrient. What I'm saying is that it's best to learn about your body before you spend all your money on someone's product, making them rich from something you can do for yourself. Love yourself enough to know what's best for you.

Returning to our discussion, I would stress again that it is essential to support what is right. I know it can be hard sometimes, but we should always do the right thing no matter what. I am not saying that you should accept as right or wrong what the world is telling you. You have that choice to figure it out on your own. And I preach to you to exercise this choice because I do it too, even if, at times, it puts me at odds with my own people.

This is why I say this. I think the way people support "Black Lives Matter" is wrong. I believe that if people support this movement, then they should do it holistically—black lives should matter across the board. Black Lives Matter shouldn't only care when another race kills a black American. Black lives should matter if anyone kills a black American, even if it is a black American doing the killing. Where is the outrage and the signs when black people kill their own people? Black lives shouldn't just matter if we can make a profit off of them. Black lives should matter no matter what. Every time I turn on the news, I see young black men and women who have killed another brother for some outrageous reason or a petty feud. That leads to two lives being taken away from the black community—The person who is dead and the person who killed and is now going to spend a great length of time in jail. Where is the outrage when that happens? We have to end that violence. Why aren't black people calling it out? We have to stand up to the violence in our own communities, for our communities.

In fact, this statement also goes out to all other races. It shouldn't be for one singular race. The Heavenly Father didn't put us here to kill each other. He didn't put you here to be hurt, sad, mad, hateful, or envious all the time. We need to be there for each other and care for each other. Care and love shouldn't be reserved for a mere race or two, and neither should be the judgment we often have for races that aren't ours. If someone from our race wrongs us, we should call them out as boldly as we do others.

And how do we go about doing it, you might wonder. The answer is simple. We let the Heavenly Father be our leader as opposed to our fake leaders. We need to let the Heavenly Father lead us. Let the Heavenly Father be there for you. He is the only influence that you and I need. He leads, and we follow. We all go through or have been through something. There is always someone who is going through things worse than you. People go through that no one else knows about. They don't tell everything to people. Some do it because they fear someone will judge them, while some do it because they don't have anyone to share with. There are also some who are ashamed to say things out loud.

Ideally, you should never have those feelings, as long as you are ready to right the wrongs. People should create a safe place around them so others can vent out anything. Those who are carrying burdens should know that talking always helps. There are people who will listen to what you have to say without judgment. You never know who has gone through the same as you, and they probably have answers for you. They might have just the thing to say that you need to hear in your situation.

I have been through this, very early on, might I add. Let me share one incident that happened when I was a kid. I didn't tell this to anyone for a long time. I had just turned 5 years old, and I got messed up by an older woman. I ended up with a venereal disease. She gave me gonorrhea. It was curable, so that wasn't much of a scare, but as a child, I was terrified. No 5-year-old should have to deal with an STI. One day, my mom was changing my clothes and noticed something wrong.

She called and made her inquiry, "Does it hurt when you go to pee?"

I said, "Yes, ma'am."

She and my dad immediately took me to the clinic. When they discovered that it was gonorrhea, they asked who had messed with me. I never did say anything. They insisted, even got a little angry, to intimidate me and make me speak, but I said nothing. For years, I kept it to myself. But I knew I had to let it out. Over the years, I told a couple of people. The problem was not that I was scared or something—I wanted to tell someone, but I was ashamed.

This is a common issue and precisely why we should create spaces for people to talk openly. You never know who is holding on to something they're scared or ashamed to tell someone. We need more compassion in the world so that people who are holding on to something that makes them feel ashamed and scared can spill it out before something dangerous happens.

This compassion and the space we will create will help them feel comfortable talking to someone. Everyone needs someone to talk to. Even the most introverted, solitude-loving people need someone they can talk candidly with. When I caught that disease— the embarrassing gonorrhea—even though I didn't tell my family how I got it, they knew about it. But luckily, it was only them who knew and no one else. Now, this could have been an embarrassing situation for me. They could have mocked me, insulted and reprimanded me in different ways. They could have taken strict actions like grounding me. But they did no such thing. They dealt with it with compassion and mercy. Had they thrown a fit and taken some aggressive action, I surely would have never trusted them in my life. I would have been scarred mentally and would have never bonded with them like I have. That is how stigmas and problems must be dealt with—with patience, mercy, and compassion. My family supported me through it without once making me feel any guilt about it. That's what good families, good communities, and good people should do.

Yes, the things we do in life reflect on our future. What we might do or not do today, or what we might have done yesterday, will surely come back to reward or haunt us tomorrow. Some people use that past as an excuse. They blame their history and use it as an explanation for why they act the way they do. For example, many people will behave a certain way, and when asked or confronted, they would tell you the way they grew up makes them act like that. And that mostly happens when the behaviors are unruly or hurtful, or downright wrong. But I don't think that is a good reason to hurt people or be a menace to society. Everyone goes through something. People are able to send forward love and smiles after living through the worst life imaginable. There are kids out in the world who are starving. There are kids out in the world who face domestic torture—beating, berating, and bashing—at the hands of their parents. Worse, there are kids getting molested by the very parents who should have been their safest sanctuaries. There are kids who are being tortured and massacred. There are kids who were forced to kill their own siblings. There are people being driven out of their cities and homes. There are people who are living in the worst living conditions because of their government's neglect. Those are just some of the horrible things that some kids and people go through. So when you make excuses about why you act the way you do, just remember: there is always someone out there going through something worse than you.

I am not being dismissive of your history or pains. I know sometimes it's hard to get your life back on track after going through a hard life as a kid. But I also know that old wounds can be alleviated a great deal just by talking through them. In fact, sometimes all one needs is to just have a conversation with someone with a sympathetic ear.

And trust me when I say this. It is help that you can get in great abundance. All you have to do is turn towards the right people. But wait. I will correct myself here. Before you go looking for someone who will lend you an ear and a heart full of love and compassion, there is one tiny thing you have to do. You'll have to be a little merciful on your own self. You might think that you don't need help. Many people tell themselves this lie and keep living in buried pain. They carry traumas and let those traumas ruin their lives. But I ask those people an honest question—a question from someone who cares and is willing to hear all your sorrows, only if you are willing to share. And the question is this: *"How do you know you don't need help if you haven't ever given it a try?"*

I know it might be difficult for you to let go and ask for help. I know this because I know the world lies to us. It tells us that strength lies in not showing weakness and carrying our burdens alone. That is a blatant and ugly lie. The truth is that you don't have to hold everything in. You don't have to do it alone. Some of you have let that buried pain turn you into a foul person, someone who the world sees as unruly, aggressive, unyielding, foul-mouthed, and many other derogatory words the world hurls. But through this book of mine, I say it hands on the heart that you are a great person. You have greatness and love within you that the world might not be able to see in you. But you can show it to them and prove them wrong. And you do it by beginning with yourself. Love yourself enough to help yourself.

I know life throws curveballs at all of us. That is life's way of making us tougher. So in some manner, all the hardships that were dealt to us were supposed to make us tougher. Sometimes, we all need to make better judgement on our lives. And when on that threshold, we have to believe that the Heavenly Father has given us the power of free will. We all have a choice to choose between good, bad, and evil. Not only that, He has given us the intellect to discern between them, too. The only problem is that we don't use that power of discernment and let the world tell us what to choose. But at the end of the day, we cannot even blame the world. It's up to us to make the choices we make in life.

There are good choices and bad choices, and we all know what's good and what's bad. We all know what would put us in jail, what would damage our health, what would bring shame on us and our families, what would dishonor us. And simultaneously, we know what will save us from it all. The choice, whether many of us like it or not, is on us—always. I know sometimes, we do make a wrong choice because the wrong choice can often seem tempting and more rewarding than it is. But as long as we are breathing, we have a chance to make amends for that bad choice. We have the opportunity to apologize. We have the opportunity to repent. We have the opportunity to start anew. We have the opportunity to do what is right, no matter how much wrong we might have already done. And no one can take that opportunity from us.

I know that your life is yours to do whatever you want to do. But why would you want to spend the rest of your life behind bars? Life is best lived when you are free. Of course, the right choices will be sometimes hard—no one ever said life is going to be easy. But we have to stay strong and keep pushing forward because we can. Look within yourself for that strength and stand strong. It might seem that you don't have it in you. You might have lost many uphill battles with life. But I can assure you that you are wrong—dead-set wrong.

Be that person who keeps breathing and keeps moving forward. Be that person who knows they are great and will accomplish that greatness despite all the barriers the world throws at them. *"You are great,"* and I believe in every word of this statement. The only question is: Do you? Because greatness can only be achieved when you believe in yourself. That's step numero uno—sometimes the most difficult one, but I can also assure you it's also the most rewarding one, too.

Yes, I know it feels good when someone else believes in you, but that is only a bonus. And a futile bonus if you are not willing to believe in yourself. Moreover, if you believe in yourself, whether someone else does or does not becomes pointless. You're the only one who can make you happy. Genuinely, exhaustively, completely happy. Your happiness is not in someone else. Your happiness is in you. All you have to do is look within.

The Heavenly Father didn't put you here to be miserable. People are miserable because they can't get what they want in life. Some people are miserable because they can't do what they want to do in life. But more often than not, these are also the people who never try enough. They are either blaming fortune or others for their bad luck. Not all of them, but take inventory of such people around you, and you will see what I am saying.

Some people ask the Heavenly Father for a blessing, but they don't want to do what it takes to achieve that blessing. At the first instance of things going bad, they want to give up on the Heavenly

Father. They want to give up on life. They want to blame others or fortune for things not going their way. There is also that group of people who are impatient. They don't want to wait for the right thing. They don't realize that good things take time. But all of that is futile and unintelligent. People do this because it's easier to blame others for their problems.

People should understand that there is no reason to blame others because you didn't get what you wanted when you wanted it. Life is dynamic—always changing, evolving, and if you do it right, always improving. You might get that blessing at the right time or might get something better. We all have a life path to go down. Sometimes you might do something that you think will be better in life, and it falls apart. You might think negatively and start believing that the world is unfair to you. The truth is, sometimes what you are trying to do in life may not be the path for you to achieve at all. It may not be the person for you. It may not be the house, car, job, money, or whatever it may be for you. Maybe God and fate have something better in store for you. Keep working hard and keep looking for the good in the bad. That is the only smart way to move forward in life.

My grandfather used to teach me about asking for the best blessing, not what I like. God will always send you what you need, and if you keep asking Him for what you want, He will give it to you just to show you that you really don't want it. What you want, or what you truly need, is what He has sent you. Another valuable lesson that Grandpa taught me that helped me keep a positive outlook throughout my life is that when it seems like everything is falling apart, in reality, it could all be coming together. That friend, girlfriend, boyfriend, that job, that place you are living in, that car you drive, or whatever it is you thought you needed in your life might not be as useful or beneficial or loyal or honest with you as you think. Maybe because that person or thing, whatever it might be, that you are desiring so bad, may not fit well with the blessing that God has set for you. You think you may be losing, but actually you're winning. You may not see it at first because things or people you have loved or acquired through hard work are being taken away. You just have to remember and convince yourself of this: The things that you had will not fit in the new life that the Heavenly Father has for you. Have faith and patience; they are rewarding virtues. You stay patient, keep your faith firm, and the Heavenly Father will clear out the path for you. Then, it will be up to you to go down that rewarding path or stay on the other one that is only apparently beautiful but dangerous and miserable in the long run.

You are in control of your own life—always have, always will be. It's up to you to wait and work for that blessing or give up on it. The road to that blessing may not be easy, but as long as you keep pushing forward, you will get to where you want to be in life. That is a promise. One thing that might help you stay true to the path is to count all your blessings. Never take any of them for granted. Family, health, religion, community, a free nation—all of them and many more are blessings that are often ignored. Always hold on to your blessings.

And if you are not willing to choose God's path and insist on walking on your own, know this: Eventually, your luck will run out. If you're a thief, or maybe you sell drugs, whatever bad and woeful thing you are doing, karma and justice will catch up with you— sooner or later. You might be getting away with it for now because you are lucky. But luck exhausts. Don't mistake luck with blessings. Luck only lasts for a few beguiling moments. Blessings last for a lifetime.

I know with each passing day, the world is becoming a mess. People are fighting against each other. Countries are waging wrongful and hedonistic wars against each other. And if that is not bad enough, even religions are fighting against each other. Many of us think religions might save the world. We believe that religions are supposed to be about peace and love. But I think we all can look around and see the great mess that is rampant throughout the world in the name of religion. That's why I say that love is losing the battle to hate. If religions can't get along, what makes you think people in the world are going to get along?

The 5Ls

The only reliable and practical way to make this world a better place to live is to start working on ourselves and stop expecting from world leaders, governments, and heroes. We can't fix the world unless we fix ourselves. If you think I'm hard on religion, you're right! I hold a person of God to a higher standard. A person of God should know love. You can be a Christian, Mormon, Muslim, Jewish, Catholic, or whatever religion you choose; no matter what the religion is, love must be the ultimate goal. Love is the ultimate achievement, the ultimate feeling. Without love, you're on the wrong track in life, no matter how correct and rewarding that track might seem. Even if that track might be offering you peace and happiness, I can tell you that it is temporary. True lasting peace can only be achieved with love.

The Heavenly Father is love. If you don't have love, I am sorry, but you don't have the Heavenly Father in your heart and mind. It doesn't matter who you are or what religion you claim. If we are to fix this world, the world we have to share, the world without a substitute, we all need to embrace each other and support each other.

Begin with yourself. Find the greatness within. You are great, but I shouldn't have to be the only one telling you that. You have to look for it, acknowledge it, celebrate it, and let it take control. Ditch your hateful self. Keep hope in your heart. Hope means anything is possible if you believe it can happen. Keep faith in your heart. Faith keeps the flame and energy going. With faith and hope, you can do anything.

And we just don't have to fix "today" only. We have to give our kids a better world to live in. Kids look up to us, and if we can't do better, they will not do better. We need to love our kids enough to give them a better future. The future is in our hands, and when we pass it to our children, we have to ensure that it is in good hands. We have to be better people for our kids. Peace, love, and happiness can go on for generations, but it has to start with us.

Thanks for making it this far in my work. If you are ready to be the change and are looking for a way to start, I've got you. Just hang on to these words of the wisest man I have known:

Right, don't wrong nobody!

The path will show itself! Godspeed!

Closing

LIVE every day being your best. There is only one you. Make sure you give the world a fair show of your greatness. Always focus on your dreams and goals, and never forget how great you are. And yes, they are achievable, no matter how impossible they seem! Read the book again if you still don't believe it. Never take life for granted. Take advantage of life and the beauty of life. Never focus so hard on work that you forget to live. Always love yourself first. People lose sight of that, and that is when life starts to spiral. Also, love yourself so you can love others the way they should be. You can't truly love someone else unless you love yourself first. And do that without being selfish. There is a difference, and we are all capable of knowing that difference. Being selfish only causes self-destruction in the long run. So if you think loving yourself is being selfish, think again. Always try to be the best, no matter what you do. Always love to live and live to love.

LOVE with all your heart, body, mind, and soul. Love others like you want to be loved. Treat people like you want to be treated. Always remember the key to a long-lasting relationship is to not do what you don't want your partner to do to you. Always work together with your partner. Always have their back, and they should always have yours. Be with a person for love and not lust. There are no picture-perfect relationships, but there are great relationships, so a happily-ever-after is a reality, just not how the media tells you. If someone tries to bring any negative energies and intentions between you and your partner, just remember, you and your partner have a bond that can weather all storms if you are willing. Love conquers all—if only you are willing to take the helm.

LAUGH with family and friends always. Life is too short to be boring. Love your kids, and let them be kids. Let kids enjoy their imagination. Tell your kids you love them and hug them every day. Never be your child's friend. Punish your child when they wrong themselves or others. Compliment them when they do good. Always spend family time. Family should always have each other's backs. *NEVER* disrespect your friends and be there when they need you. Never talk bad about your family or friends to anyone.

LET GO of the hate and negativity. Don't let hate camp anywhere in your heart. It will rot your soul and ruin each day of life. Forgive and forget. Never hold a grudge. Never be jealous of someone. Always support the people you love. Don't cling to any negative human being in your life. Let them go, too. Even if you love them dearly right now, cut the chains. You will thank yourself (and maybe me, fingers crossed) later. If you find it difficult to forgive, this might help: Why would you expect God to forgive you if you are not willing to forgive others?

The 5Ls

LET GOD be the first in everything you do. Let the Heavenly Father be there for you always. Love everyone as per His commands. Be willing to help each other the way He taught and showed us. Be willing to help yourself, too. Be pro-life across the board. Every life should matter. Be wary of the evil that lurks around us—the one the Heavenly Father warned us about. Never judge anyone, but be wary of the world around you. Don't listen to what people say, watch what they do.

Money should never come first over people who need help. Money isn't everything.

We have a long way to go. If we work together, there is nothing we can't achieve. Help and support each other. Build strong communities that reach out to anyone and everyone. Fight the evil together.

Always remember: *you are great and you are in control of your own life.* The only person who can stop you from succeeding is you. The only one that can get you in trouble is you, and the only one that can make you happy is you. Believe in yourself and keep moving forward. Stay positive, no matter how bad things might seem. To borrow some wise person's words: The night is darkest before the dawn. Sometimes, when things seem to be falling apart, they could all just be coming together according to some divine plan. Sometimes you will not succeed the first time you try it. Never give up. When you make a mistake, when you fail at something and it seems that you can't get it, ask yourself: ***You breathin', ain't you?!***

Always do the right thing. It is always worth it. Even when someone is trying to hurt you or do you wrong, doing the right thing is always a win.

Always remember the *5 Ls:*

LIVE, LOVE, LAUGH, LET GO, AND LET GO

May you always be blessed.

Thanks for reading!